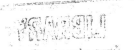

# Teaching Language Arts

## DATE DUE

Demco, Inc. 38-293

D1412220

# Teaching Language Arts

## Learning through Dialogue

Edited by

**Judith Wells Lindfors**
The University of Texas at Austin

**Jane S. Townsend**
University of Florida

National Council of Teachers of English
1111 W. Kenyon Road, Urbana, Illinois 61801-1096

Production Editor: Kurt Austin
Cover Design and Prepress Services: Precision Graphics
Cover Photographs © Elizabeth Crews

NCTE Stock Number: 50357-3050

**Library of Congress Cataloging-in-Publication Data**

Teaching language arts : learning through dialogue / edited by Judith
   Wells Lindfors, Jane S. Townsend.
     p.    cm.
   Includes bibliographical references and index.
   ISBN 0-8141-5035-7 (paper)
   1. Language arts—United States Case studies.   2. English
language—Study and teaching—Activity programs Case studies.
I. Lindfors, Judith Wells.   II. Townsend, Jane S.   III. National
Council of Teachers of English.
LB1576.T378   1999
372.6'044—dc21                     99-35050
                                     CIP

# Contents

# Acknowledgment

We are more deeply grateful to Olivia Becerra than our words can say. Her computer expertise, her attention to detail, her organizational skill, and her unfailing good humor were all essential in making this book a reality.

# Introduction

As students move through their teacher education programs toward K–8 certification, they typically march through one methods text after another: reading, social studies, science, math. And language arts.

We thought it would be helpful to provide a different approach for a language arts methods course.* Why not ask excellent classroom teachers to tell about language arts in their classrooms, thereby inviting readers into a professional dialogue? In contrast to many traditional language arts methods texts, in which a single author speaks, we wanted a collection in which many experienced teachers—all with different perspectives—talk with the reader. And so we asked experienced teachers to write about some aspect of language arts in their own classrooms. This book is their response to our request. Their voices are dialogic: These teacher-authors do not lecture. As you read, you will not hear all-knowing voices of authorities speaking to you from some lofty height; you will hear co-learner voices of experienced teachers dialoguing with you.

And they are honest voices. They write of successes and failures. They tell of ups and downs. They share what is easy for them and also what is difficult. They question; they reflect.

These teachers do not provide sets of "listening activities" or lists of "tips for teaching spelling." Instead, they describe the richly textured fabric of classrooms in which language weaves its way through all the daily experiences of the members of these communities. Yes, the students in these classrooms listen. How else could they enjoy stories read aloud or respond to a peer's proposed solution to a math problem? And yes, the students in these classrooms spell. How else could they write the stories and research reports, the poems and memos they want others to read? But the listening and the spelling do not occur as exercises; they occur within communication events.

We hope you will engage in vigorous dialogue with these teacher-authors. The purpose is not to receive "gems of wisdom" from

---

*As we have worked on this book, we have come to appreciate its value for inservice as well as preservice teachers.

them as you read, but rather to interact with them: to question, to wonder, to reflect, to evaluate, to imagine, and above all, to relate the classrooms you read about to your own current or anticipated one.

How might you modify the classroom experiences these teachers tell of to be effective in *your* classroom with *your* students?

- How might you adapt the Explorers Club Patti Seifert does with her kindergartners for your fifth graders?

- Lynne Strieb sends newsletters home to her first and second graders' parents regularly, thanking them for their participation in classroom activities and informing them of classroom events. How might you write such newsletters so that they would be appropriate for the ESL (English as a second language) children in your sixth-grade classroom?

- How might you incorporate Hispanic/Latino literature (Cecilia Espinosa and Julia Fournier) in your monolingual English third-grade classroom?

- Pat McLure describes Writing Workshop conferences with her first and second graders, and Linda Rief tells about her seventh and eighth graders' writing portfolios. What might writing conferences and writing portfolios look like in your grade 3/4/5 multiage classroom?

- How might you adapt the creative drama experiences Mary Kitagawa describes for your bilingual third graders?

- Would the guided writing Cyndy Hoffman and her grade K/1 children do together, or the regular class newspaper Carol Sharp and her children produce, be appropriate for your fifth graders if you shaped these activities a bit differently? How?

- Mary Krogness describes the lively "burning issues" discussions her (predominantly) African American inner-city seventh and eighth graders engage in. What would "burning issues" discussions sound like in your first-grade classroom? What might your students' "burning issues" be?

- In what ways might your first year of teaching be similar to and different from Abby Foss's first year? And do you think you'll find the surprises Fred Burton, a principal, says may be waiting for you?

This interactive, questioning, flexible kind of reading engagement we are recommending is, as you will see, quite like the lively, ongoing learning orientation of the teachers whose articles you will be reading. And because their own professional reading is an important part of these teachers' continual learning, we have asked them to list a few of the professional books or articles that they have found especially helpful in their own growth as teachers (as well as a few of the fiction and/or nonfiction children's books they enjoy using in their classrooms as read-alouds or for children's independent reading). You'll find these short book lists at the end of each article.

In our own teaching of language arts methods courses, we have often encountered students who hoped our courses would provide them with a supply of activities to use in their own classrooms. Our students are acutely aware that they must provide learning experiences for some twenty-five children every day, five days a week, for seven or eight hours a day—an awesome prospect! Our purpose in this collection has not been to provide a set of prescribed classroom activites. However, as we systematically culled all classroom activities from each of these articles in order to prepare the Activities inventory you'll find in Appendix B, we were amazed at the number and the variety of activities we found. Perhaps it is because these activities were not especially highlighted in these articles—not set off as separate lists or presented as topics—that they had not called attention to themselves when we read these articles initially. This abundant array of activities certainly does not comprise a comprehensive set of children's language experiences in these teachers' classrooms. Such a set would, of course, be impossible, because these teacher-authors are ever responsive to their students' changing interests and concerns; thus the experiences they provide also change. Yet we believe that the activities you'll find in Appendix B comprise a wonderful set of "ideas to get your thinking started" as you reflect on the kinds of language experiences you hope to provide in your own classroom. (In addition to the Activities inventory, you will find a Theme inventory in which the articles of this collection are grouped according to specific topics that may be of special interest to you, e.g., multiage classrooms, diversity, writing, building community).

We have organized this collection into three major sections: Using Language to Create and Imagine, Using Language to Explore the World, Using Language to Connect with Others. You will notice immediately that the focus is language *in use,* language as doing. We believe this language-in-use orientation best captures the descriptions these teacher-authors provide of language as it lives in their classrooms.

These three ways of using language (to create and imagine, to explore, to connect) bring three aspects of language into sharp focus. We can call these the aesthetic, the intellectual, and the social. We make this division somewhat hesitantly, however, for this book is about language in use, and language in use does not live in self-contained boxes. Living language is always multifaceted. However, the articles in the first section (Using Language to Create and Imagine) draw heavily on *aesthetic* aspects of language use. These articles focus especially on students' engagement with literature and their creation of written text for others to read. The second section (Using Language to Explore the World) highlights *intellectual* aspects of language. In the articles of this section, you'll find students using language to learn about the world they live in and to share their knowledge with others. You'll hear them using the language of math and science and social studies. The articles of the third section (Using Language to Connect with Others) bring *social* aspects of language to the fore. These articles focus on the language of teachers and students as they connect both with one another in the social community we call "classroom," and with people beyond the classroom, in the larger social communities to which they also belong.

As diverse as the articles in this collection are, without exception they express two fundamental themes. The first is that "language arts" is not a separate subject. These teacher-authors do not say, "Here is how I teach listening, spelling, speaking, writing, literature." Instead they tell us—or rather, show us—how language lives at the heart of everything that happens in their classrooms. Language arts, for these excellent teachers, is something they and their children *do*—constantly and inevitably—in carrying out their many communication purposes. It is not a subject their students "learn," a set of facts or informational bits that they accumulate—not memorized definitions of "subject" or "predicate," "noun" or "verb," not lists of spelling rules, not "ten characteristics of effective speaking." Language arts in the classrooms described here is the doing of things that are important to the teachers and students in these classroom communities:

- It's second graders mapping their classrooms and bedrooms—and even events from literature and, finally, their personal journeys through second grade (Mary Glover).

- It's fourth graders describing mathematical patterns as metaphors (Phyllis Whitin).

- It's multiage grade K/1/2 children setting up an aquarium, going fishing to bring back inhabitants for their aquarium, and then writing a class book together about this shared experience (Rebecca King).

- It's a fifth grader with a learning disability writing about his trip to the Grand Canyon and reading *Tales of a Fourth Grade Nothing* (Cora Lee Five).

- It's first and second graders participating in literature discussion in read-aloud times (Karen Gallas).

- It's bilingual children in multiage classrooms working out their problems and disagreements in the whole-class forum of Concern Circles (Renée Bachman and Julia Fournier).

- It's literature (Penny Silvers) and CD-ROMs (Bill Bigelow) becoming catalysts for fourth graders' and sixth graders' critical analysis of serious social issues.

- It's children in their grade 1/2/3 multiage classroom making 3-D geometrical shapes out of paper . . . and their teacher observing them closely as they do it (Kathryn Mitchell Pierce).

- And it's teachers like Dorothy Taylor listening to and learning from their ESL students.

It is this language-as-action orientation expressed in all the articles in this collection that led us to group them according to their dominant language purpose (to create and imagine, to explore, to connect).

The second theme shared by all of these articles is one of teaching-as-learning. This theme is so strong (though played out so uniquely in each article) that we have come to wonder: When all is said and done, is this what excellent teaching is—continuing to learn and grow throughout one's teaching life? When we asked these excellent teachers to tell about language arts in their classrooms, not one wrote about teaching as something he or she has mastered. Far from it! Every article shows a teacher who is—indeed, who choses to be—a work in progress. Every piece shows a teaching life that is a learning life.

This, then, is the dialogue that these teachers now invite you to engage in. It is a dialogue about teaching and learning and language all living together in an interdependent and mutually supportive way in classrooms. These excellent teachers invite you into their ongoing learning journey. They tell you about the things they do in their classrooms, and they tell you why. They tell you about the things that challenge them, amuse them, frustrate them, delight them. They tell you about what bothers them, what they wonder about, what they hope to change and do differently in the future. They tell of the celebrations. They tell of the regrets.

Vivian Paley's article opens this collection, ushering you into the teaching/learning/languaging dialogue that is the essence of this book. When you have read this first article, you will have a good sense of the teaching-as-learning journey ahead.

# 1 Walter

**Vivian Gussin Paley**

We hear Reeny running down the corridor on her way back from the library. "Walter! Walter" she calls out as she enters the room, waving a book. "Look here, Walter, it's the same as you. Get your notebook, boy! I got something here to show you!"

A perplexed Walter searches for his notebook while we crowd around Reeny. She has brought us *Pezzettino*, the Leo Lionni book in which all the characters are configurations of colored squares. The reason for Reeny's excitement is clear: The illustrations for *Pezzettino* closely resemble Walter's drawings.

His notebook is filled with the same connected boxes, which up to now have not seemed to him a cause for joy. In fact, he sees them as daily proof that he cannot draw as well as the others, a burden he adds to his general self-doubts as an English speaker.

"I not can it," he tells me when I ask him to dictate a story or paint a picture. Yet he sits with Reeny talking so quietly I cannot hear what they say; he colors in the outlines of the Leo Lionni mice she draws for him and listens intently while she "reads" memorized lines from library books. By contrast, he fends off my suggestions as if I am leading him into a trap.

Walter has recently come from Poland. He is fluent in Polish, reading the little books his grandparents send from Warsaw and writing his own thank-you letters. All of this places him well ahead of most of the children in this kindergarten class, but he does not see it that way. Compared to the confident speakers and mouse painters, he judges himself inadequate.

Pezzettino feels the same way. He is a small orange square in a land of towering creatures named after their special skills: the one-who-runs, the flying-one, the swimming-one, the one-on-the-mountain, and so on. "Am I your little piece?" he inquires of each figure, but their responses are evasive, almost accusatory. ("'Am I your little piece?' he asked the strong-one. 'How could I be strong if I had a piece missing?'

was the answer.") Finally, the wise-one sends Pezzettino to the Island of Wham, where he tumbles down a rocky hill and breaks into pieces. Collecting himself, he realizes that he too is made of diverse parts and is not merely a missing piece of someone else. ("'I am myself!' he shouted full of joy.")

I am more than a bit annoyed by the haughty, insensitive treatment Pezzettino receives. We'll not even try to include the likes of you, his friends seem to say. We have nothing in common with such a no-talent little square. "Aren't they rather unfriendly to Pezzettino?" I ask. "Couldn't they at least try to find out if he belongs to them in some way?"

"He does belong," Anita says. "They're his grown-ups."

"His family?"

"Sure," Jonathan adds. "He can't do all that stuff 'cause he's just a little boy."

Reeny agrees. "The tall one hasta be the dad, and the mom is the swimming one. Those others is relatives of him."

"Then why are they so mean?" I ask, but no one seconds my complaint. The family is not mean, they say, it's that Pezzettino is so little. This is *not* a peer-group story, they are telling me; it is about the weakness of the small child in a world of adults, fully developed grown-ups who are self-sufficient and lack nothing. They do not need little ones to fill in the empty spaces. ("'Do you think I could be wise if I had a little piece missing?' answered the wise-one.")

So then, if Walter is Pezzettino, it must be the teacher who makes him feel inadequate. He plays checkers with Bruce and runs outdoors with Arnie; he allows Reeny to tie a scarf around his head when she needs a prince, and he lets Cory instruct him on how to hold her doll while she's at the sand table. *They* need him. It is with me that he hesitates and falters.

When did I ever properly appreciate Walter's squares? Reeny perceives their artistic integrity, comparing him to Leo Lionni. His "I not can it" is heard when the one-who-teaches comes around. Then he is most like Pezzettino.

Leo Lionni's skill in portraying the feeling of being "less than" is remarkable. Pezzettino is every child who has ever walked into a classroom. "Do I belong here? Does someone care about me?" Perhaps the lonely island Pezzettino is sent to does in fact represent school, where children are broken into pieces in order that adults may observe, label, and classify them. And, having been so dissected, how does the child become whole again?

"Do you suppose Leo Lionni was thinking about real children?" I suggest after reading the book again. "Maybe even his grandchildren, feeling small and lonely in school? I've been wondering if the Island of Wham is something like school."

"It's a rocky place," Kevin reminds me. "How can that be a school because where are the teachers?"

I have known teachers who were like rocks; nothing could move them or alter their ways. Sometimes that teacher has been me. Every path I take these days seems to go inward, to the center of my own memories and regrets. Leo Lionni could have put me in his book as the one-who-remembers, or better yet, the one-with-missing-pieces.

Pezzettino is now "Walter's book." Reeny has willed it so. She and the children draw "Walter's squares" in their notebooks. It is as if he has asked them, "Am I a piece of yours?" and they have replied, "Yes, we need you to make us complete."

––––––––

I stand behind Walter watching him draw in his notebook. He is copying an odd-looking word over and over until it nearly covers the page. It takes me a few moments to realize he is printing his name, his real name, in big letters: WLADYSLAW.

"How do you say your name in Polish?" I ask.

"Vwahdyswahv," he says softly. "Vwahdyswahv," a bit louder the second time. The "l" is pronounced as "wah," and the "w" as "v." Walter has shown the one-who-teaches a piece of himself. No, he has given me a piece I am missing.

## Bibliography

**Vivian Gussin Paley**

*Professional resources that have been especially important to me include:*

Ashton-Warner, S. (1963). *Teacher.* New York: Simon & Schuster.

All books by Robert Coles, especially:

Coles, R. (1967). *Children of crisis: A study of courage and fear.* Boston: Little Brown.

*Children's books that I especially enjoy using with children include:*

Every animal fable written and illustrated by Leo Lionni.

# I Using Language to Create and Imagine

Language to *imagine*. What do you think of first? Possibly the picture that comes to mind is of children in a classroom being read to. What adult does not cherish pleasant childhood memories of sitting on the classroom rug while a favorite teacher read a favorite book aloud!

Language to *create*. What do you think of now? Perhaps you think of children writing in some way—children engaged in *real* writing for *real* people for *real* reasons.

The pieces in this section include both of these and much more. We begin with two conversations in which Cyndy Hoffman and Carol Sharp, and then Pat McLure and Linda Rief talk about the many kinds of writing their students do. These conversations will doubtless engage you in thinking about organizational possibilities for children's writing experiences (e.g., as a separate writing workshop or within the content areas), about writing conferences (what they are like and why they sometimes fail), about the place of spelling in real writing, and so on.

Then Penny Silvers, Karen Gallas, and Cecilia Espinosa and Julia Fournier invite you into various literature events that they provide for their students. Just as important perhaps, they problematize literature engagement: How do we go *beyond* literature response to real social action (Silvers)? What happens to children who do not become engaged in read-aloud events (Gallas)? How do we provide rich literature engagement for bilingual children (Espinosa and Fournier)? There is real probing here as these teachers reflect on and share with you the ways they and their students imagine and create through language.

# 2 Children Become Writers: A Conversation with Two Teachers

**Cyndy Hoffman**
Forest Trail Elementary School, Eanes Independent School District, Austin, Texas

**Carol E. Sharp**
Forest Trail Elementary School, Eanes Independent School District, Austin, Texas

Jane and Judith had the following conversation with Cyndy, who teaches in a multiage K–1 classroom, and Carol, who teaches next door to Cyndy in a multiage 2–3 classroom.

*Cyndy, what kind of writing happens in your kindergarten–first-grade classroom? What do the writers in your room do?*

**Cy:** Well of course, in any given year the kids are on many different levels. And right away I help them realize that there are a number of different ways that are acceptable for them to write. In the language that is most widely used, I introduce stages of writing, from prewriting to conventional.

*You mean, you talk to them about that? You describe this developmental process to them?*

**Cy:** Yes, I talk to them about it. A year-long study is really what it is. It begins with me talking with them about how they are writers and I'll always call them that. I use a trade book as an introduction to that study. It's a rather formal introduction in that it is an intended, planned lesson.

*What kind of book might you use?*

**Cy:** I have used [M. Brown's] *Arthur Writes a Story* (that may get a little too into *story* writing) and then there's *The Day of Ahmed's Secret* [by Heide and Gilliland] about the little boy who's from an Arab family and he learns to write his name. I use that a lot. But I begin that way, by talking to them about how they are *all* writers and they write in different ways and are at different places in this process. I tell them that some of the writing that happens only *they* will understand, and they will need to share it with us. And some of the writing that will happen in our classroom only *some* people can understand, and again they will need to share it. And some of the writing that happens, *everyone* will be able to understand, and that's what they're working toward. So it follows that progression. The children learn, talk about, and accept that they are authors and that what comes from them when they create is something that they have authored. I don't begin by telling them that an author is the person that writes a book. We talk about how writing is a voice, how it's a tool, how it's another way for them to communicate. Every year we do a year-long study about communication. And writing is one of the tools for that. I just move from there. It's just everlasting.

*Do you have some period each day that's designated as a writing time or a workshop time or something of that kind?*

**Cy:** Yes, several. The children come in first thing in the morning and they write in their morning journals. We talk about some possible topics: personal things that happened the night before, thoughts that they have, something that happened at home—I give some suggestions so they have at least some ideas. They sit down and do the journal writing. I read through the entries with each child. I use this writing later for assessment. The children get a new journal each month so that they and I can look at the month before and the month that is present. (Carol, you'll have a first journal, a middle journal, and an ending journal for each child of mine who comes to you as a second grader, so you'll be able to see that span.)

**Ca:** So of the nine months that you've had them, you're giving me the first one and the middle one and the end one, and then there are others in the middle that they've taken home?

**Cy:** Yes. So they come to me individually and read what they've written, and I take notes on the meaning and on the skills the kids have used.

**Ca:** And then do you leave the notes in their journals?

**Cy:** Yes. If the writing isn't in temporary spelling or conventional spelling, then I transcribe it so that I can remember later what the child wrote; but if the writing is in temporary spelling or conventional spelling, then I don't need to transcribe it because I can read it as it is.

*And this journal is a group of pages that you've assembled, or it's a spiral, or . . . ?*

**Cy:** It's paper and wallpaper and I staple it together. Very informal! But that is something they do every morning. In fact, it begins at the door. At the door, there's a clipboard that says, for example, "Good morning! Today is September 16. Don't forget: Put your things away, say good morning to a friend, morning journal entry." So it starts right away. I provide a lot of print in the room, whether or not they can read it. My classroom is multiage so the kids help each other. One will say, "Oh I know what that says." And then that child will help another child.

Then, later in the daily schedule, we have a session of guided writing, a time when we just talk through some of the conventions of writing. I'm not terribly concerned about that, but we do talk about words to describe and action words, punctuation—those kinds of things.

*And what does the child do in "guided writing," and what do you do?*

**Cy:** I work with one group at a time. Sometimes I use the overhead. We might, for example, brainstorm a number of different kinds of ideas that *I* could write about. And then I would ask *them* to brainstorm a number of ideas that *they* could write about. Here's an example. Last year my dog, Jambo, died. And one of our first sessions with guided writing was brainstorming ideas about that. I said, "You know, I really like the idea of writing about my dog because I need to. I don't think I've gotten over my dog dying yet. And I would really like to write about him so that you could get to know him." So we began a story about Jambo. We had only been in school two weeks when that happened, but they contributed so many ideas because some of the older kids had known me the year before. They contributed a great deal to the body of the story. A child who had heard me talk about Jambo last year would say, "Don't forget to tell about the time he did this or that." Guided writing is a cooperative effort in writing. I think that *they* are working as much as *I* am working; I don't think it's something I do that they watch. We're doing it together. And that goes on all year. A guided writing lesson with another group of kids might be much different, but it is still that *kind* of lesson: collaborative and cooperative.

*How do you form these groups for guided writing?*

**Cy:** Oh, through assessment. Since my classroom is multiage, I don't have to spend a great deal of time on classroom procedures and routines at the beginning of the year. So I can spend that time at the beginning assessing kids. When they arrive in my classroom, I want to know what they know. I use Marie Clay's *Stones* and *Sand* and the alphabet (the letter recognition). I also use her sight word lists. I take a first taped reading of every child so that I can see number of words recognized, number of words read in a minute, the sophistication of the words they know. (I continue with this during the year, making a reading tape for each child every month, followed by the assessment.) So I really have a pretty good picture at the beginning of the school year of where the children are in terms of their writing and their understanding of writing. I can form groups and develop appropriate lessons because I know where they are. When I set up the lessons, if I have two groups of kids doing guided writing, I may group them in terms of their level of understanding of print, but both groups will have guided writing lessons, and neither one will seem to be less than or more than the other.

*But these groups don't stay the same the whole year, do they?*

**Cy:** Oh no!

*You just group as it's appropriate for what it is you want to work on at that particular time?*

**Cy:** Yes.

*And you can do that because you've already figured out what each child can do?*

**Cy:** Yes, and the assessment continues; it doesn't just happen at the beginning and at the end of the year. Monthly taped readings are very helpful. I have many books. Many books! I have one group that's a take-home reading collection, another group that's a free collection—different genres for the children to read. I also have a group of "leveled" books, with levels like "emergent reader" or "fluent reader." These are the ones I use in assessing the children.

*So a child will probably write in the journal each day and have a guided writing lesson each day. Anything else?*

**Cy:** Yes. We also read from a chapter book every day, and each child has a log that's separated into three sections. One section is for literature responses, one for math responses, and one for science responses. After I read a chapter in a book, I might raise a question or a child may make a comment that prompts me to ask a question, and the children will write their responses in their logs. After several minutes of writing (maybe five or seven), we share responses and then there's more discussion which leads to more sharing and more discussion. That happens every day. We read several chapter books a year.

*And do you again transcribe for those children who write their entries in a preconventional way?*

**Cy:** Yes.

*Wow! Doesn't it take a long time to get around to everyone?*

**Cy:** Yes, it does!

*And what are the others doing while you're doing that?*

**Cy:** We have a number of different activities from which they can choose. So if I'm working with one child, the other twenty are choosing from a variety of related activities. The children know it's the literacy area they work in during that time. And there are a number of different kinds of activities there, in the literacy center.

*You've organized your day so there's a time for literacy, there's a time for math, there's a time for science . . . ?*

**Cy:** Well, sort of. But it doesn't really happen that way. The content crosses over all the time, every day. But with the "literacy activities" (and we do use the word "literacy" and they know what literacy is), I do have in mind that some of the activities are designed for particular children. So I'll say to a particular child, "Today during literacy activity time, I'd really like you to get the interactive chart with such-and-such a poem, and when you finish that, I'll work with you. Then you may go on to something else."

*How do you help them understand what literacy is?*

**Cy:** We start right at the beginning of the year because one particular area is labelled this way: literacy. We talk about what the children know. "What do you know about reading? What do you know about writing? What do you know about talking?" And we list all that. And those words remain *out.* I tell them that there are some children that *don't* know that; they haven't had the experiences that would let them know that. And we talk about that. We talk about not having those experiences and what that would be like. And we talk about how they have to work to be literate—how it *is* work—and you have to want to be literate. And it's all a matter of knowing, and then knowing more. That's how I explain it. Literacy is a very complicated topic, of course, but I hate when I hear, "Oh, but we wouldn't use terms like 'literacy' with kindergartners." Well, we *would* use those terms with kindergartners! They need to have the opportunity to hear them and use them themselves and know what the terms are *really*.

**Ca:** Can I give you an example?

**Cy:** Sure!

**Ca:** It's an example of a child coming out of your classroom who I had in my classroom. I was being evaluated by the principal, so I was doing a "lesson." And the "lesson" was on similes. When I asked the children if they'd ever heard the word "simile," Beth raised her hand and said, "Yes, that's a figure of speech." Well, the evaluator nearly fell off her chair. You had obviously used these terms with your children: "figure of speech" and "simile." And there're probably twenty other examples I could come up with of your kids using terms like that.

**Cy:** Well, I just don't think real language should be hidden from them.

*Carol, when Cyndy's kids come to you for second/third grade, what sort of writing do they do with you?*

**Ca:** Well, writing in my room is organized more on a weekly basis than a daily basis, because the kids have a weekly contract. And so instead of having "a writing time" every day, we have a contract time every day, when students are working on their assignments. So there's almost always *somebody* working on writing, but they don't necessarily work on the same activity at the same time. The writing is really connected with social studies and science. We might have a specified science or social studies time (officially we do), but we also work on science and social studies during contract time. For instance, last year in science we studied the solar system. And the kids made books— their own books. They chose whatever topic they wanted to write about. We had lots and lots and lots of trade books in the room. Some of the kids worked on their space books for maybe six weeks! At least six weeks! So they were all at various stages of writing their books during the six weeks. They probably worked on those books every single day at some point. But remember, when I get these kids, *they are writers!* And Leann (my co-teacher) and I assume that they're writers, and they assume that they're writers, and they're writing! We do a process approach in that the students get the idea of brainstorming and writing their first draft down, and then we do individual conferences, and they read what they've written, and we talk about it. They also read it to other kids in the room too. And then we talk about what they would like to do—how they could make it better. Lots of times they're still at the editing rather than revision stage. You know, they don't want to add or change, but just "fix it up" so it's ready. So there are kids who are basically editing. Then there are kids who, as they read it to us [and] think about what else they'd like to say, actually do revisions.

*How do you encourage that revision?*

**Ca:** I think it's very much on an individual basis. I team teach (with Leann) so there are two of us for the forty-two children. And Leann and I do *tons* of modeling together. So whenever we talk about revising a piece and making it make better sense, or making it more clear, or adding to it or embellishing it, we do it together. For instance, Leann will write something in front of the class, and then she'll read it to me and I'll ask questions and she'll add some more. We do a lot of modeling of that process. It's wonderful to have a teaching partner in the room that you can do this kind of modeling with.

*You're sort of role-playing back and forth while the kids watch?*

**Ca:** Exactly. In front of the whole class—all forty-two of them. We do a lot of that together. Of course we do other kinds of writing too. The kids have journals. They don't write in them every day, but they write in them a couple times a week. And they have various choices: They know they can write about topics of their own choice in their journals. But then we also offer suggestions 'cause there always are some kids who say, "I don't know what to write" or "I didn't do anything this weekend. It was boring." They could write a story, a poem, answer a question—we've got books full of possible topics. Most of the kids don't use them, but some of them do.

*How do you help them understand about choosing their own topics in their more formal writing?*

**Ca:** We model it; we do it together, we brainstorm as a group (kind of like Cyndy does). We also put out a weekly newspaper (*The Two-Can News*) in our room, so we've constantly got a newspaper going. The children know that their contributions will get published in the newspaper. They know that their pieces have to be edited and turned in so that the mother who types the newspaper can read what they've written. So they have a real reason for making their writing legible and making it make sense.

*Who's the audience for the newspaper?*

**Ca:** The whole class. And their parents.

**Cy:** And our multiage class.

**Ca:** Oh yes. We send copies around the school. But about choosing top-ics, sometimes we just pick a theme. We had a *great* ice newspaper that came out after those ice days! Every kid had a story about what they did with the ice. And some kids wrote stories, some kids wrote ice poems, but we said, "We're going to put out an ice edition." And so they just loved that. We put out a parents' edition, and they all wrote something—poems or stories or letters to their parents. So it's an assignment—it's something they have to do—it's not optional. That is, the *assignments* are not optional—but what they write and how they do it, there's a lot of leeway in there. We try to open it up so that practi-cally anything that they write will be accepted and printed. The kids love to write research articles on topics such as animals and the *Titanic*. So if they turn in a newspaper article, it gets printed.

**Cy:** Once three boys came to interview me for the newspaper.

**Ca:** Yes, they like to do interviews. They go in groups of three. The three who came to interview Cyndy had been in her class. The inter-view was great! It was printed in question–answer form. But they had to write the questions. They went to Cyndy with a set of questions they were going to ask her. Leann and I had told them, "If you get other ideas as she's talking, you can add that in." I don't know whether that happens or not; I think they mostly stay with the questions on the list. Cyndy and I discovered that we both have the same kind of car! When they asked her what kind of car she has, she said, "I have an old car."

*How do you help your kids discover that there are lots of different kinds of writing? It sounds like you give them a choice of genre.*

**Ca:** Oh yes. For instance, we did cinquains. We had a lesson on cin-quains, and then for weeks after that, we got tons and tons of cin-quains. The kids had realized that with eleven words, they could really express themselves! They had a ball with that. Many times it's the assignment that we give out, and the examples—the brainstorm-ing we do, trying to broaden their choices. And then they go from there. They pick it up. For instance, with the space book. Some kids wrote fictional stories—science fiction—but they had to put in some information that they'd learned about space. So a few kids did that. You know, after you've been doing different kinds of writing all year, the possibilities expand. And after they come from Cyndy, where they've been writing for two years, they've got quite a repertoire of kinds of writing that they can do. As I go along, I'm understanding more and more all the time how important sharing their writing is.

One of our goals for next year is to build more sharing into our program. With so many kids—forty-two of them—we've got to come up with smaller groups for them to share their writing with so that they each can have more turns. With that many kids, they have to wait around too long for their turn to come again. This learning how to handle a multiage classroom with double kids and double teachers is taking some time. Leann and I have never done a Writing Workshop approach. We've just used the work time where they have various things they need to accomplish.

*Who comes up with the contract? Do they decide what's on their contract? Do you decide it? Do you decide it together?*

**Ca:** Leann and I decide it together. We decide what's on it, based on what we're teaching and what's going on, but they have choices built in. There are certain assignments they have to complete, but within those assignments they can make choices. And then, when they finish their assignments, they're free to do lots and lots of different activities we have in the room. And that's wonderful. Actually, we're going to try this coming year to do a Writing Workshop. We do a Reading Workshop now—have a time when everyone is just reading. So we want to try it with writing next year—if not every day of the week, at least a couple days a week.

*And why would you want to make this change?*

**Ca:** We think that it would be really interesting and fun to try. Leann and I went to a writers' workshop together this summer. We just loved it! And we thought, "Gosh! You know, we've never really done it quite this way. Wouldn't it be interesting?!"

*When I listen to you talk about the writing in your classroom, I'd say, "Oh, you're doing Writing Workshop." So it surprised me when you said, "We don't do Writing Workshop." You have conferences, kids share their writing; it's like mini-lessons when you do some sort of demonstration, the two of you together.*

**Ca:** Oh sure. We do that. Yes, we do all that. It occurs all week long—all day long, practically. But we never have a time that we're all working on our writing right now. But there *is* a time during the day when *everybody* reads. We *all* read—*every single person:* No matter what they have or haven't done on their contracts, no matter what's going on, everybody reads. Well, we haven't done that with writing, and we kind of would like to see how that would work.

*I was amazed that you say these kids will work for six weeks on their books.*

**Ca:** Oh yes!

*I've heard teachers say, "Oh, my kids will do something and in five minutes they're finished, and I don't know how to get them to keep writing—to keep working on the same project."*

**Ca:** Well, with the space books, it helped that they had written books before. This wasn't their first book. They knew they were going to come out of this with something really neat. And they saw it as something that was going to take awhile to get done. And they knew the process—they knew that they were going to try to first think of as many ideas as they could and then work on getting their thoughts down, and then they'd get to share it with us in a conference. They've just been through the process; they've been there, done that before.

The year before, we'd done dinosaur books. (We try to pick a topic that seems pretty high interest level.) Well, the kids had portfolios, so the kids I had had the year before had their dinosaur books in their portfolios. So we got out the dinosaur books and they looked at those, and they just *laughed* at them. They said, "Oh my gosh. Look at how I wrote back then." And they were great dinosaur books! I think they had a feel for where they were going with the space books. And we talked about it a lot.

One thing that Leann does that I learned from her this year (one of the many things I learned from her) is she makes such a big deal over what the kids are doing. Whatever they're doing that she sees as being wonderful and positive, she lets them all know. So, for instance, right from the very beginning, she would hold up a page that someone had done for their space book and say, "Ah! Wow! Look at this!" And she just managed to get them all excited about this. And she'd use all their words like "awesome" and "cool," and so pretty soon kids would be bringing her—us—what they were doing and sharing it. That's why I think the sharing business makes a huge difference. It's really important.

*You say you had conferences with every child, but how do you organize that when you have so many kids?*

**Ca:** It's hard. It's really hard. We tried various ways. We tried having them write their names on the board when they were ready for us to read what they had written. And then they went on and did something else, maybe something else on their contract, for instance. Or if they'd finished their contract, then they could have a free choice. Then we'd call them.

We might do that for almost an hour one morning, just trying to get around to as many kids as we could and listen to what they'd written. This year, sort of toward the end, we learned how to let the kids help each other. We'd put kids together in pairs so, for example, the one child could figure out how to help the partner spell words that he or she needed or could read the partner's piece and make sure that it made sense. So we really had some peer tutoring going on. That was not the majority of the time, and not all the kids were able to do that, but we tried working on that. What we *didn't* do was take things home and correct them and hand them back. We just felt that we wanted the kids to read their writing to us and talk about it. It's hard. That's probably one of the reasons that the space books took six weeks. *Everybody* wrote a rough draft and *everybody* wrote a final copy, and some kids had some in between. Also, some kids changed their minds totally and started all over again. There are a lot of reasons why it took a long time. Some of the children spent a *lot* of time with their artwork. But every day, we—especially Leann—would find several things that were really neat that were going on and we'd hold them up and the kids would get real excited about it.

*I'm curious. What do you both do about spelling—well, about conventions in general: spelling, punctuation, whatever?*

**Cy:** First of all I had to clearly define what I felt about writing conventions. I happen to be a "perfect speller" and feel secure in writing conventions. But my job is to help the children *want* to write and help them know that they *can*. And the first way, I think, to start chipping away at the children's efforts is to start worrying—or making them worry—about spelling and punctuation. Their feet are not firm yet in the writing itself. And that's all I want them to do: I want them to write; I don't want them to spell words. I want them to use words. Writing needs to be a friend, and it needs to be a tool. And that's what my job is: to help them know this.

We have a bell in our room, and the children know that if they hear it ring, it means that someone important is going to share something important. And somebody might ring the bell and stand up and say, "I'm a temporary speller for the first time today!" And the whole class cheers!

*So what some people call "invented spelling" you call "temporary spelling," right?*

**Cy:** Yes. It's "temporary" because they know that it doesn't last. And if we're reading something, they can talk about, "This word is being spelled conventionally. It's written in conventional spelling." They know we have to go through stages like temporary spelling before we get to conventional spelling. If they're at a stage where they are writing using temporary spelling, I want them to know it's important to go through that. When they come to share their writing (for instance, in a literature response), I don't take it apart letter by letter, sound by sound. Nobody in my room does any grunting!

Sometimes there's a reason why I must have something they write conventionally spelled: for example, if it is going to be put into book form (as we've done), or if it is a parent information note, or if it goes out on the bulletin board in the hallway. If the writing goes anywhere *outside* our classroom, they know that we have to work to make all of the conventions correct.

*And that's so that other people can read it?*

**Cy:** Right.

*If it's going public.*

**Cy:** Right.

*So you talk to them about this whole business of spelling and punctuation.*

**Cy:** Oh yes. I have a big chart that hangs up on the wall, and it says, "Ways Writers Write." And it shows different ways. I'll have a picture I've drawn—perhaps a house and some grass and a tree. And we talk about it. I say to them, "What does that say?" I find it interesting [that] when you say to young children, "What is that? What do you see?" they'll say, "A house. A tree." But when you ask them, "What does that say?" and you point to a picture, they *read* it. Rather than saying "house, tree, grass," they say, "That's a little house and it's sitting next to a tree, and it has lots of grass growing next to it." They read it—as a little story. I've realized over the years of teaching young kids that that's picture writing. There really is something to say, rather than just what it is. But we go through all of those stages that Elizabeth Sulzby mentions, and they're on the poster.

The children have writing dictionaries of their own, and there are dictionaries in the classroom (all different levels), and there's a lot of print everywhere. They know where to access information that they need when they need it. If a child wants to learn how to spell a word conventionally, I ask her, "Where could you go if you wanted to find the word 'rock'? Well, we have all kinds of books having to do with scientific topics. Look in there." They know exactly where they can go.

And they own the classroom, and they can go almost anywhere to do that. So that's how I deal with conventional spelling. My primary responsibility to them in terms of writing is not to teach them to be good spellers or to know where to put the periods and commas. But they learn these conventions because they *see* them and we talk about them and we call these conventions what they are. For instance, in a shared reading, that period at the end of a sentence might just come up in a conversation that we have as part of our discussion about the book.

*It sounds like reading and writing are really tightly together for you.*

**Cy:** Oh yes. Yes. I am always hard-pressed to draw a line between those two because I don't see one very clearly. I hear parents say, "Well, my daughter can write, but she can't read." Yes, she can! "She learned how to write first," a parent will tell me. Well, you know, it's a matter of how you look at it, and maybe reading and writing are two areas of study for some people, but they're not for me. And they just happen to go out into everything else we do.

*Do you think the children's learning to write supports their learning to read?*

**Cy:** Oh, yes! Yes! That's why I provide many opportunities for them to choose writing and also many opportunities for them to choose reading. Both use the same kinds of materials and tools. In fact, last year we had a discussion about this. We were talking about authors and the kinds of things that authors use as their tools. The children started by naming the more obvious tools (like pencils), and I said, "Well, what else do you think they use?" "Oh, they have to use their brains!" "Oh, they have to use their eyes!"

*Carol, what do you do about conventions? Since your kids are second and third graders, maybe your parents are getting a little more nervous.*

**Ca:** They are. They are. When the kids are writing, we have tried to continue this idea that they need to get their ideas—their thoughts—down on paper. So I don't say anything about spelling other than, "Write what you hear." In fact, I've used the term "invented spelling" with them: "If you don't know how to spell it, invent it. Make it up." But I've found that there are kids who really *want* to spell it right. They'll ask you, "Is this right?" or "How do you spell it?" So I read a lot about Regie Routman's "have-a-go" spelling idea. She discusses this in her book *Invitations*. I give the kids little have-a-go books—just a book of blank pages that says "Have-a-Go" on the front. I've kind of modified Routman's idea. First of all I want the children to listen to the word and write it down as best they can. And I tell them, "I'm happy with that. You can stop there. If you really want to know how to spell the word, then bring it to me and ask me and I'll spell it for you. I'll check your spelling." And so they'll write it down the way they think it's spelled—it's just "have a go," try it. Then they'll bring it to me and say, "Is this how you spell such-and-such?" Sometimes it's yes, or, if it's not, then I write the correct spelling. And then they're supposed to copy over the correct spelling and then write it, use it. Mostly I want them to think it through first, and mostly what I find is that they're very close. And, "Oh gosh! You're very, very close!" They look and see.

Let's see. What else for conventions? Well, we have a "Morning Message" every morning that we write out on chart paper. And the "Morning Message" can be news of the day or happy birthday to somebody or what we're planning to do or any special program or whatever's happening or what we learned about. And all of us are there together, and Leann or I will say, "So-and-so, read the first paragraph." So then they have to figure out what a paragraph is and know when to stop. The topic of discussion is really mostly the ideas that are written down there, but then you point these conventions out in a casual way—they just come up in the conversation—and after doing that every single day all year long . . . We had charts and charts and charts! It was like a diary of the whole year! So we dealt with conventions a lot through "Morning Message." Plus we discuss conventions in writing conferences. Conferences are based on where each child is. So if this is a child who is getting commas and can do quotation marks, then they put that in their writing.

*What about grammar?*

**Ca:** You know, we *did* do a little bit of grammar. In the "Morning Message." We would take yesterday's "Morning Message" and say, "All right. Now, this is yesterday's 'Morning Message,'" and they would make it all in the past tense, or something like that. Grammar sneaked in various places, like parts of speech, for instance. I was thinking about the cinquains I told you we did. A cinquain starts out with a topic, and then you get two descriptive words and three action words and four feeling words. So through the action words, we discussed verbs. That's really how they got the idea of what a verb is. And, with the idea of an adjective—well, we would talk about that when we were reading books: "How does this author describe . . . " It just comes in all the time. We never really sat down to teach any of it. It just kind of happens through your discussion.

*You're back to the reading–writing connection, aren't you?*

**Ca:** Yes. Yes.

**Cy:** Carol's kids and mine have some similar experiences. For instance, we both do "Morning Message," and my kids make writing dictionaries that are similar to Carol's "have-a-go" books. But for both of us, it's not through directly-planned lessons that the children get the writing conventions. It's through writing—through *doing* it.

**Ca:** We also did some formal spelling though. We kind of followed what the third-grade teachers were doing. They had a list of words each week that followed a spelling pattern like o-a or silent e or contractions. We took the pattern and we made two lists. One was an easier list and one was a harder list, but both used the same pattern. And we did have a weekly spelling test, and we taught a spelling lesson once a week. The kids had a practice test on Wednesday, and if they spelled the words right, then they were fine for the week. Otherwise they had another test on Friday. So we did "cave in" a little. It was a bit of a compromise. And we did various activities. We made word walls—just a big piece of butcher paper with o-a (or whatever the pattern was). "If you run across words that have o-a, add them to the word wall." So we'd have lots and lots of o-a words. Or when we were reading to them and we'd come across a word that was in the pattern, we'd say, "Oh, who wants to go write this up on the word wall?" and somebody would. Lots of times there were words on the word wall that weren't perfect, and maybe we'd talk about that, maybe we wouldn't. We talked a lot about words that don't follow the pattern. And we gave them challenge words too because we have some incredible spellers in there. We had a really big range. I would say that everybody was at least at the inventive, temporary stage of spelling; we had no kids that were just connecting letters that made no sense. But there really was a big spread. So for a challenge, we'd include words that didn't follow the pattern or more difficult words that did follow the pattern. We didn't do a lot with formal spelling, but sometimes we would have the kids get in small groups and come up with other words that they knew that had a particular sound, and then [we'd] talk about which ones follow the pattern and which ones don't. But we found that parents dwelled on spelling more than we maybe would have liked. And I don't exactly know how to deal with that.

*Do you find standardized testing putting any pressure on you and what you do?*

**Ca:** Oh yes, definitely. Because TAAS [Texas Assessment of Academic Skills] begins in third grade.

*So you miss that pressure, Cyndy.*

**Cy:** Well, sort of. Our kids are screened in kindergarten to see if they'll be put in a structured program we use at our school that's supposed to prevent dyslexia. But this is a real pressure for me because I don't believe that this should be happening to early primary kids. And I always have a very difficult time when a parent gets a letter that says, "Your child qualified" for this structured program for kids at risk in reading. "Qualified!" And then the parent comes to me, because I'm the teacher, and says, "What should I do?" Well, it's then that I feel between a rock and a hard place because most often I can't substantiate what the screener identifies as a potential reading problem for the child. And I just want to burn the place down at that time of year.

**Ca:** But your question about standardized tests . . . I don't know. I feel the pressure at our school because we have to score above 90 on everything: 90 percent of our students have to master the objectives on the TAAS test.

**Cy:** If they don't, then the school is no longer a "school of excellence," a "Texas bluebonnet school."

**Ca:** Yes. The school would lose its exemplary status if we went from 90 to 89, because that's so significant. Officially they're looking at schools so far, not at individual teachers. So if our school is 89, there would not be a teacher singled out.

*Is writing included in this?*

**Ca:** It is in fourth grade, yes.

*In Florida, standardized testing is just having a terrible impact on the instruction that goes on because teachers end up teaching so that students will do well on these tests.*

**Ca:** Exactly! Exactly! I haven't dealt with the writing except for having fourth-grade teachers tell me, "Well, I want you to work on this form of writing (whatever kind the test requires) so the kids will do well in the writing test next year when they're fourth graders." But for math and reading (math in particular), you've got to cover certain skills, and you find yourself—at least I found myself—making sure that I covered things but not going into depth the way I should have or the way the kids need to.

**Cy:** I think part of the problem is that we are working with a multiage philosophy but we're still being asked to implement traditional classroom approaches. Report cards, for instance. We still have to fill out a traditional report card, but if we are really implementing this multiage approach, maybe not all of the children are going to be ready for particular kinds of math problems or have an understanding of a particular kind of writing. It doesn't work that way.

*Talk about a disaster—well, maybe not a disaster, exactly, but something that hasn't gone well for you. When I read education books and articles, the authors usually give the impression that everything always works, nothing ever goes wrong: The teacher does Writing Workshop, and her mini-lessons are wonderful, and her kids are dying to revise, and they all really get into picking their own topics, and they publish these wonderful books, and they all want to share, and nobody's running around the room, and nobody's bothering anybody else. . . . Well, I know* it's not like that! *So talk about something that hasn't always gone well or something that's just hard.*

**Ca:** Sometimes just the sheer management is hard, the sheer number of kids we have: forty-two kids and two teachers. We need four teachers!

I'm thinking about Steven. He's a real, real bright kid! Just . . . what can you say? Just a very, very bright kid. But he did not want to write. He loved to read. I had him just one year (for second grade), and he's now transferred to a different school so we've lost him. But he'd sit and read Louis Sachar, Roald Dahl. A second grader! And he'd chuckle to himself and just have a ball. His independent reading was incredible. He could read anything. Could write anything. Could spell anything. But he did not like to write. He just didn't like to do it. And it was hard for me to look at him and think, "Create something! Elaborate!!" 'Cause I knew all this stuff was going on in his head. With a kid like that, I found I really had to assign writing because he would never choose to write. So that was hard, especially when this kid's potential was so great. It was just hard for me. I felt like I was *dragging* it out of him, *pulling* it out of him. I think modeling helps reluctant writers. I think it really helps for them to see what other people are writing and see other people going through the process and talk about it.

*Cyndy, what do you think is hard about helping your kids develop as writers?*

**Cy:** The parents' lack of understanding about it. They really like a traditional approach. And they go to so much trouble. They make little pin-dots with the pencil, and then the child can trace their pencil dots. You know, it's amazing. But that's an attitude, and parent attitudes are very difficult for us to change. We can educate them, and I try to do that. I conference with each parent four times a year. I also have an evening meeting to discuss writing with whoever comes, and another evening meeting to discuss reading and how we approach both of those. But the parents grew up with phonics. Parents still want to know, "Are the children learning sounds?" I can show them pieces of the child's writing that say, "Yes, they are!" But still . . . But at least I can *try* to give my parents information. I have some books that I bought especially *for* parents so they can read about spelling. There's *Spel . . . Is a Four-Letter Word* [by Gentry]. Also, *I Learn to Read and Write the Way I Learn to Talk* [by Barron]. And I use *Read to Me: Raising Kids Who Love to Read* [by Cullinan], and *Spelling for Parents* [by Phenix and Scott-Dunne] and also *Teachers and Parents Together* [by Botrie and Wenger]. And then there's *Literacy at Home and School: A Guide for Parents* [by Nicoll and Wilkie]—I've used that one too.

*And do the parents read them?*

**Cy:** Those that want to, do. And they are all the better for it, and when they finish, I think they realize that. But it's not the kind of thing you can force-feed.

*Are there other things in your helping kids develop as writers that are particularly difficult or challenging?*

**Ca:** Lots! It takes a long time to develop expertise in this. It's a really growing process! I mean, I'm thinking how I am *no* expert at all on kids' writing. I taught for five years, then went to graduate school full time for a few years, and then returned to the classroom three years ago. And I've spent a lot of time learning all I could about writing and reading and literacy, and I still don't feel like I'm *any* kind of expert on this. Still learning. Still learning a lot. But one thing that's difficult for me is time. You know, we have kids who have difficulty with writing and whose production is just starting to come. And I think that the *time*—the patience and the *time* that's needed for these kids to develop—is sometimes not understood by their parents or even *us*. Even *me*. I think certain kids just need time. They need experience, too, but they really need *time*. And giving them that time—that's hard.

*You mean giving them enough time during the day or over a period of years?*

**Ca:** Both. They need both kinds of time. Just make sure the kids get time to write.

*But how do you do that? Teachers say, "I've got all these different things I'm supposed to be doing. Where do I get this time for writing?"*

**Cy:** Oh, I'm tired of hearing that.

**Ca:** It's a high priority.

**Cy:** Writing is not going to take any time *if* teachers know that it's important.

**Ca:** That's right.

**Cy:** If they let other stuff in, they're not going to be able to fit writing in.

*So it's a matter of priorities? If it means a lot to you, you simply do it. Is that it?*

**Ca:** Yes. And when you can, integrate it. It's easy for us to do because we've got the same kids for language arts and science or social studies. So you kill two birds with one stone as much as you can. We try to do this. We try *not* to chop up the day. We try to incorporate what we're doing in the content areas with writing as much as possible. But writing really does take time. Many, many kids can't be rushed. Oh, you can rush some kids—you can say, "All right, you've got thirty minutes. Fill up your page!" But mostly you can't do that.

*So what do you wish for your student writers as they move on to other teachers? What do you hope those other teachers will do?*

**Ca:** What I would like for my kids would be that they would be with someone who would look at their writing in terms of what they know and what they can do and what they *are* doing so that they feel successful with what they're doing. I was thinking about the two-day workshop I took this summer. We did a lot of writing. And I knew this from before, but it just helped to be refreshed and to have someone look at *my* writing from the standpoint of what I can write and what I can say and do. I would just like for the kids to have that—and for me to continue to work in that direction. To give them the feeling that, "My writing is special and I have important things to say, and people are going to pay attention to it and see what I can do." Because I don't think that happens all the time. I know it doesn't.

It's just so wonderful to get kids coming from Cyndy because they've had so much authentic writing experience. This hasn't always been the case for me. Sometimes I've had kids who thought writing was copying and penmanship. But not Cyndy's kids. They just write! Most of them. I hope the teacher who gets my kids next year will think of writing as communication. I worry about the third graders going on to fourth grade where they do TAAS writing. They start out day one with whatever the kind of writing is they need to do for TAAS. That's a fact of life in Texas schools. And what you wish for them is that there were some other way of assessing in the state of Texas. I have some kids that I think are good readers—[who] understand what they're reading, seem to enjoy reading—but they did not do well on that test. And so it's hard—what do you say to the parents? "Well, you know, don't worry about that test. She really *is* a good reader. She really mostly *does* understand what she's reading, and she enjoys it, and she's motivated." For the parent, the reality is the test score. Also, the test doesn't do justice to the child who has made lots of progress, is doing well, but may still be below grade level. The score doesn't tell you how much they do know, where they've come from, and the story of their lives.

*Having your kids for two years in your multiage classrooms, you must get to know a lot of that "story of their lives." Do all the teachers in your school have multiage classrooms?*

**Cy:** No. Some of them don't want to do it. Some of them are not risk-takers in their own classrooms, so they probably *shouldn't* do it.

*Why? What makes it so risky?*

**Ca:** Shouldn't be. It just is. I don't know why it is. Well, when I think about what Leann and I did last year, we were doing so many new things. We had never team taught. We'd never taught with forty-two kids and two teachers—with the huge range of kids that we'd have. We bit off a huge chunk, and we did a lot of treading. But the reason I decided to do it is just that it is *very* appealing to me as a teacher. It was what I wanted, the direction I wanted to go.

*It seems that teaching—any kind of teaching (multiage or not)—and writing both involve a lot of risk-taking.*

**Cy:** I'm thinking risk-taking always brings that "Oh no!" feeling before you jump. I think some teachers look at writing and think, "Oh noooo. Now I've gotta teach writing." Maybe that attitude could change.

*And are there things that you would wish for your kids, Cyndy, as they move on to the next classroom, as they continue to grow as writers?*

**Cy:** Well, I think I have what I wish for. Years ago, my kids didn't have a place to go. Hoffman's kids—no one wanted them in their classrooms. When they moved on, I was hearing nothing about their having writing experiences like they had in our classroom the year before. But now having my kids go on to Carol and Leann assures me that they'll continue working. But so will I. What we've done together will keep going on.

*So there's continuity?*

**Cy:** Yes, but not only that. Continuity for them, of course, and that's very important. But I sort of go too. What we did together I'll still see continuing, so I will continue as well in that. I guess that's what I would wish. I can see this cycle that is going, and it includes me as well as my kids; I can't take myself out of that picture. It's like there's this flow, this wonderful continuous energy. They're there with Carol, and I am part of that. The kids I had before would run down the hallway to me saying, "Hi, Mrs. Hoffman. Can we share our story about this?"

**Ca:** Did you read Carley's dedication in her book?

**Cy:** Yes. "This is to Mrs. Hoffman."

**Ca:** Two years after she got out of your class!

**Cy:** If you've taught, you know that feeling. And that's what I mean: Two years later we are still going.

**Ca:** It has to do with sharing your writing though, too. It has to do with sharing it and reading it to other people and letting other people see it.

**Cy:** Well, I just know that what I've started wrote the ending. And, Carol, you'll be picked up in that motion and carried on as well. The whole concept is really wonderful. It feels good. It's a feeling of continuing to live.

## References

Barron, M. (1990). *I learn to read and write the way I learn to talk.* Katonah, NY: Richard C. Owen.

Botrie, M., & Wenger, P. (1992). *Teachers and parents together.* Markham, Ontario: Pembroke.

Brown, M. T. (1996). *Arthur writes a story.* Boston: Little, Brown.

Clay, M. M. (1972). *Sand: Concepts about print test.* Portsmouth, NH: Heinemann.

Clay, M. M. (1979) *Stones: Concepts about print test.* Portsmouth, NH: Heinemann.

Cullinan, B. E. (1992). *Read to me: Raising kids who love to read.* New York: Scholastic.

Gentry, J. R. (1987). *Spel—Is a four-letter word.* Portsmouth, NH: Heinemann.

Heide, F. P., & Gilliland, J. H. (1990). *The day of Ahmed's secret.* New York: Lothrop, Lee & Shepard.

Nicoll, V., & Wilkie, L. (1991). *Literacy at home and school: A guide for parents.* Rozelle, N.S.W., Australia: Primary English Teaching Association.

Phenix, J., & Scott-Dunne, D. (1994). *Spelling for parents.* Markham, Ontario: Pembroke.

Routman, R. (1994). *Invitations: Changing as teachers and learners K–12.* Portsmouth, NH: Heinemann.

Sulzby, E. (1990). *Emergent literacy: Kindergartners write and read.* (Video recording). Bloomington, IN: Agency for Instructional Technology.

## Bibliography

### Cyndy Hoffman

*Professional resources that have been especially important to me include:*

Calkins, L. M. (1983). *Lessons from a child: On the teaching and learning of writing.* Portsmouth, NH: Heinemann.

Calkins, L. M. (1986). *The art of teaching writing.* Portsmouth, NH: Heinemann.

Clay, M. M. (1985). *The early detection of reading difficulties: A diagnostic survey with recovery procedures* (3rd ed.). Auckland, New Zealand: Heinemann.

Cullinan, B. E. (1993). *Pen in hand: Children become writers.* Newark, DE: International Reading Association.

Graves, D. H. (1983). *Writing: Teachers and children at work.* Portsmouth, NH: Heinemann.

Paley, V. G. (1981). *Wally's stories: Conversations in the kindergarten.* Cambridge, MA: Harvard University Press.

Paley, V. G. (1986). *Mollie is three: Growing up in school.* Chicago: The University of Chicago Press.

Paley, V. G. (1990). *The boy who would be a helicopter: The uses of storytelling in the classroom.* Cambridge, MA: Harvard University Press.

*Children's books that I especially enjoy using with children include:*

Balian, L. (1972). *Aminal.* Nashville: Abingdon.

Brett, I. (1989). *The mitten: A Ukrainian folktale.* New York: Putnam.

Ets, M. H. (1955). *Play with me.* New York: Viking Press.

Fox, M. (1989). *Koala Lou.* San Diego, CA: Harcourt Brace Jovanovich.

Hoffman, M. (1991). *Amazing grace.* New York: Dial Books for Young Readers.

Keats, E. J. (1962). *The snowy day.* New York: Viking Press.

Rawlins, D. (1988). *Digging to China.* New York: Orchard Books.

Wood, A. (1990). *Quick as a cricket.* New York: Child's Play (International).

## Carol Sharp

*Professional resources that have been especially important to me include:*

Calkins, L. M. (1983). *Lessons from a child: On the teaching and learning of writing.* Portsmouth, NH: Heinemann.

Cullinan, B. E. (Ed.). (1987). *Children's literature in the reading program.* Newark, DE: International Reading Association.

Graves, D. H. (1983). *Writing: Teachers and children at work.* Portsmouth, NH: Heinemann.

Routman, R. (1994). *Invitations: Changing as teachers and learners K–12.* Portsmouth, NH: Heinemann.

*Children's books that I especially enjoy using with children include:*

Brown, M. W. (1949). *The important book.* New York: Harper.

Berger, M. (1995). *A whale is not a fish and other animal mix-ups.* New York: Scholastic.

Cherry, L. (1990). *The great kapok tree: A tale of the Amazon rain forest.* San Diego: Harcourt Brace Jovanovich.

Gleeson, L. (1993). *Where's mum?* Norwood, S. Aust.: Omnibus Books.

Parsons, A. (1990). *Amazing snakes.* New York: Alfred A. Knopf.

Schecter, E. (1995). *Real live monsters* New York: Bantam Books.

Schwartz, D. M. (1985). *How much is a million?* New York: Lothrop, Lee & Shepard.

*The Incredible Snapshot Series.* New York: Covent Garden Books.

# 3 Putting Ourselves on the Line

**Pat McLure**
Mast Way School, Lee, New Hampshire

**Linda Rief**
Oyster River Middle School, Durham, New Hampshire

This is a conversation that Pat and Linda tape-recorded in response to some questions Jane and Judith sent them. Pat teaches first and second graders, and Linda teaches seventh and eighth graders.

*Let's think back to your beginnings as teachers of writing. What do you wish someone had told you about teaching writing before you began? What advice would have been helpful for you?*

**P:** I wish someone had told me about the important role that illustrations play for young children in their writing. Lots of times, in talking with teachers who are just starting to work on writing with their students, I find they almost devalue the illustrating part of it. Or they think of the illustrating as just a rehearsal for the writing. But really for young children, it's so integrated—their illustrations and their print are so integrated in terms of the way they're trying to tell their story on paper. Ruth Hubbard's [1989] research really helped me see the role that illustrations play. But I think that's really important. I guess I always liked the illustrations that children did, but I didn't realize the importance of them in the beginning. I think there is great value in having children do the illustrations and giving them the time and materials and space to do that, as well as to put print down on paper.

**L:** It's interesting that you say that, Pat, because in seventh and eighth grade I think we devalue illustrations even more. It never occurs to teachers who work with older kids that those illustrations could be very important in telling the story. I'm thinking about Adam, who I had last year. Adam truly is a cartoonist. His journal is filled with cartoons and he hates to write, but he's got incredible stories in his comic strips that he draws. He really *is* a cartoonist . . . an artist. And I have to look at kids like Adam as artists when I look in their journals. It's not that they just use drawing to illustrate a story: Their art work *is* writing to those kids, so that it does play a major role.

You know, when I think about getting started as a writing teacher, I feel pretty lucky because of all the wonderful mentors that I had who helped me understand writing in a different way. When I was in school, I *never* had anybody talk to me about my writing. We were told to write an essay, [and] it got handed in, graded, and handed back.

**P:** And it might have some marks over it, and it might have a few comments in the margins (like a one- or two-word response), but that was it.

**L:** Right. But it wouldn't give you enough information to know how to make that writing an awful lot better. Actually, it never occurred to me that they *wanted* me to make the writing better.

**P:** No, it was a one-time assignment. I don't remember ever going back and working on a piece anymore after it was once handed in.

**L:** I guess I wish also that someone had told me how hard teaching writing is. Today even, I had two kids crying after I talked to them about their writing, because they handed it in as finished drafts, and I had never talked to them about it. They thought these were A pieces of writing and they liked the writing just fine the way it was, and for me—even gently—to say to those kids, "You know, I just think there are things that you could do to make this better writing," it just really hurt them. I think I have to tell myself *every single time* I talk to these children, one-on-one, or even when I talk to them on paper, that each child's whole being is so tied to that piece of writing that that conference is probably the most important thing. And when you get with older kids and the writing gets longer and longer, a lot of times I can't manage one-on-one conferences all the time in forty-five-minute periods. And so I end up writing things on the writing, I forget the child, and it doesn't work as well as it should.

**P:** That whole time factor—I guess that's one of the things, too, in the beginning: to understand that it's going to take a lot of time if you're going to try to get to everybody. And it takes a lot of time to bring pieces through a process. You can't rush it. You can't just speed it up. It's going to take time.

**L:** I also think something that I didn't really realize was how connected reading is to writing and how much kids need to use professional writers as mentors. That was pretty clear to me this year when my seventh graders were writing what they said were poems. I said to them, "How many poets have you read?" And they said, "*What*?" And I said, "Well, who's your favorite poet?" "Well, Shel Silverstein." Or a few kids knew Robert Frost. But to actually know poets, or to write fiction and to know fiction writers—I don't think they really make the connections until we make the connections more explicit for them.

**P:** Well, it is so intertwined, what they're reading and what they're writing. I've noticed that. You know, we've been doing interviews to get ready for these parent conferences that we're doing tonight. And so one of the questions I've been asking them is, "What will help you to become a better writer?" And several of them have said, "To read more."

**L:** Wow! See, that's great, for first and second grade, that they can say that.

**P:** Yes. They'll say, "The more I read, then the more I'm gonna be able to write, because I get ideas from lots of different writers to put in stories." It always impresses me. But I think that sometimes they lose some of this understanding as they move through the grades.

**L:** I think they do too, Pat. And I can't figure out when that happens. I know what *you* do with kids, and I know what other teachers do with the kids. And yet they will come to me in seventh grade and say, "No, I've never written anything before." They've written! I know they've written! And I know they've read too. I know they've got many authors at their fingertips. I don't know why this happens.

**P:** Is it just the age—the growing stages they go through? They get more self-conscious about it, and they don't want to admit to having written before?

**L:** I think that's part of it. They truly forget! There is something about seventh grade—many are not real committed to making something. I think it's hormones kicking in. What's most important to many of these kids is who they're sitting with at the table, who's looking at them, and who might have bumped them in the hallway. And truly, everything else seems to go right out of their heads.

**P:** Eighth graders do some wonderful things.

**L:** Well, I think there's a big difference between seventh grade and eighth grade. I think we work hard at getting the seventh graders to try to remember all the things they did in elementary school, because I really do know they did wonderful things.

But in a more positive light, I wish someone had told me what incredible fun it is and how it takes just one child's discovery in a piece of writing; that can keep me teaching for months and months.

**P:** It's so exciting! I mean, there really *is* excitement to it, and *they* feel so pleased. One of my children, Mary, shared with the class a book she'd written about the guinea pig. And one of the children, in responding to her, said that she thought Mary had done a very good job on it, and she wondered if she was thinking about publishing that. And Mary said that well, she didn't know. And so the other little girl said, "Well I really think you ought to. It's a very good book." And Mary just *beamed.* She just *beamed.* It was so pleasing to her to think that someone else in the class recognized her work as being good. I think that's something that we forget. And I forget that too. It's that one thing that you say that can keep a child writing.

**L:** And it's also the one thing you say that can *stop* them from writing. And it's that fine balance all the time—that in the rush . . . that's the hardest part for me. It's having twenty-seven kids for forty-five or fifty minutes and trying to conference with that many kids in each class in a week. And it's in the *rush*—it was in the rush that I probably made this little boy cry today. He thoroughly believed that he had done the best piece of writing he could do, and he felt an A was what he deserved; and when he ended up with a B on it, the tears just flooded. And it was so honest that I thought, "Wow, I really missed the boat." I think of Tom Romano's [1987] comment about evaluation. He says that evaluation should keep the writer writing. So if what I'm saying is stopping them . . . every time before I try to give feedback to them, I have to ask myself, "Am I going to stop them, or am I going to keep them moving forward?" And that is so hard!

**P:** Oh, it's terribly hard! And with the little children it's hard too. You have to *really* be careful because they're just trying things for the very first time. You need to keep giving some positive feedback, but also keep talking to them so that they will take a few more risks and try something different and experiment a little with their writing.

**L:** It's tricky at all stages. It seems like a balancing act.

**P:** Even with adults. We're vulnerable when we're talking about our writing. But in a classroom, we tend to forget that. It may not look like the kids are emotionally tied to the pieces they write, but many of them are.

*What about as your students proceed through school from the first graders you teach, Pat, to the seventh and eighth graders you deal with, Linda? What kinds of teachers would you want them to have over the years to help them develop as writers?*

**P:** I guess I would hope that it's teachers who can appreciate the work they're doing and can respond to them as individuals.

**L:** Yes. When I think about older kids, I hope it's teachers who see they're teaching children, not a subject. I mean, I certainly want the kids to get the content of what makes a good piece of writing, and I want them to know authors and do a lot of various kinds of reading. But I think I've learned over the years that those kids know if you don't like them as human beings, and if you don't, you'll never teach them anything.

**P:** Yes, it really comes down to knowing each one as an individual, and I think one of the pluses of teaching writing is that through their writing, you get to know them in a way that you wouldn't normally get to know students if you weren't doing something like this. They share so much of themselves, and you're sitting down one-on-one and talking with them, and I think you have an opportunity to know each of them as individuals.

**L:** Absolutely. You know, when I'm working with teachers in other schools, I find that a lot of times they're afraid to do some things with kids because of the parents. I just worked with some teachers in another state, and they said, "How can you let kids keep journals? We've got parents who are afraid kids are going to say things in the journals that they don't want teachers to know."

**P:** Oh really?

**L:** And so they don't want their students keeping journals. And that was a really legitimate, serious question that I had to think about. You and I have a lot of autonomy here. We've been in the district a long time, and it's a very liberal district. We're trusted as teachers, and I think you and I can do a lot with kids that a first-year teacher may not be able to do. Things that I couldn't do when I first started teaching either. I knew in my gut what made sense to me, but I wasn't prepared to defend a book if it was controversial. I wasn't prepared to explain to a parent why it was OK for kids to be truthful in their journals or why I think it's important they're truthful now. But I feel more experienced at that now. I was pretty stunned when some beginning teachers I was working with said, "This list of books that you've given us—the books that your kids most highly recommend—more than half of them on here are incredibly controversial, and we would never be able to have them in our classrooms." And so I think sometimes, until you've got enough experience to understand how you're using something and why you're using it and why you feel perfectly comfortable doing something, you do kind of hesitate a little bit. I also think there are teachers who deal with things that we don't have to deal with here.

**P:** So maybe some of the advice to people starting out is to be cautious and to really think through everything that they're doing, being sure that they can justify or they can give reasons for what they're doing—really understanding what they're doing.

**L:** Right. I think it's *knowing why* you're doing *what you're doing.* I think what it boils down to is you know yourself. You know where you're coming from in your own experience, you know your children, and you know the district in which you teach. And if you know the district and you know your kids and you know your community, then you know what you can do. I just worry sometimes that beginning teachers are dealing with some really difficult issues, and we have no idea how hard it can be for some of them. It surprised me that those teachers I worked with said they were no longer allowed to have their kids keep journals. Although what I *did* say to them was that these were academic journals. I really make that a point with seventh and eighth graders—that they're not diaries. And I think that's something that we really need to clarify with teachers as well as with the kids. This is not a confessional, it's *not* a diary. And if you've got something really difficult going on in your life, certainly I would help you in any way I could if you needed to talk to somebody about it. But I think we have to use the journals as academic journals. This journal is who you are as a reader and a writer. But if it's honest, it's who you are as a thinking, feeling human being.

**P:** And it's also a journal that they know is being read by someone else.

**L:** Absolutely.

**P:** It's not just for personal reflection, just for yourself, so that's known right up front—that there is an audience.

**L:** And that knowledge changes what's written in the journal. Definitely.

*Could you talk a little bit about what you see as the easiest aspects of teaching writing?*

**P:** Well you know, with the little ones—and I know this sounds funny—but we just put out blank books and paper and they write. I mean, it sounds too simple, but they do it. They really do. You know, from the first day of school, they start with—some start with pictures, some start with words, some—you know, it's back and forth. It's not always the same thing they do. It depends on what they're writing. But they just write.

**L:** OK. So what happens between first grade and seventh grade? They come into seventh grade, and they often don't want to write.

**P:** There is something, though, about a six-year-old or a seven-year-old: They're really quite uninhibited. And they're very giving and open about what they're going to do. And so they enjoy putting their ideas down on paper. They love to show their writing to other people—or most of them do. Not everyone. I mean there's always some child that's a little hesitant, somebody that waits before sharing with the class. But a lot of them are quite open about it and want to show their work and want to do their pictures and put words with them, and they really seem to move through it so easily. Now, I know there's effort on their part; it's not so easy, but at the same time, it's not a big struggle for them or for me. Of course there are some that you have to work with a little more, but a lot of them just—you have the paper, you have the markers, you have the pencils—and they come in and they write.

**L:** And actually, I have to say that most seventh and eighth graders—the majority—want to write. They have things to say. Some even come in with journals already. They know they're going to be reading and writing so they're prepared to do that. But I wonder what happens to those few kids who are hesitant. I wonder if what's happened for five or six years is that it's been so painful for them to get words down on paper, that they'd rather do nothing than have to go through what they've gone through. Maybe they expect negative comments. And maybe they really feel they're not as good a writer as somebody next to them. I don't know.

**P:** I do think it's true that some students judge themselves in ways that we would never judge them. I mean, there are some that just are overly harsh on themselves. And that's all tied in, I guess, with self-image and other things that are happening for them. But I think that probably gets in the way of their writing.

**L:** Oh yes. I think another thing that gets in the way, too, is that now these kids have five major teachers, and so they're trying to figure out what does this one want, and this one, and this one. And that's very hard! I can't imagine going from classroom to classroom to classroom and having to figure out what does *she* want, what does *he* want. Every forty-five minutes, going to another class. It's *very* hard.

**P:** And yet, that's the way middle schools are set up.

**L:** I don't know why! We keep talking about getting to block scheduling, but we can't quite seem to make it work—at least in *our* middle school—because there are so many places these kids have to be.

**P:** But that comes back to that time thing that we talked about before— how if you've got them all day, even though we have one segment of the day that we call Writing Time, still we are writing all through the day. They're writing about their reading, and they're writing about the guinea pig and they're keeping journals for that, and—during Free Choice Time—some are choosing to do writing then. Writing's not really a compartmentalized subject for them.

**L:** So they can see writing in all the different areas of the classroom because you're in a self-contained classroom. For me, it's a lot harder, and it takes a lot more encouragement for me to say to those kids, "Look, you told me that you feel very comfortable when you're writing a science lab report. That lab report that you love should be in your portfolio." And the kids'll go, "But I didn't write it in here." So it's very hard for me to convince them that that social studies current event piece that they absolutely loved, or the fabulous comparison–contrast piece they did (a wonderful persuasive piece)—that these belong in their portfolio too, even though they didn't write these pieces in my classroom.

**P:** Well, I'm sure there are probably other writing teachers that wouldn't recognize these pieces as valuable writing that should be in the students' portfolios.

**L:** That's true. They would separate those.

**P:** So I think it's not only the students that maybe separate those topics or those subjects. Some teachers would separate those subjects too.

**L:** Probably. But you can't separate subjects, despite the fact that you're in walled rooms and you're divided by forty-five-minute segments. You would hope that writing teachers would value the kinds of literacies that kids can bring from all the other disciplines that they're in, whether it's art, or social studies writing, or science writing, or pictures, or photography—all kinds of things.

**P:** So whether it's called an integrated program or not, in fact, writing *is* an integrated medium: It's something that you're using through every subject.

**L:** I'm lucky to be on a team of teachers that really understands that, because in every single one of the disciplines—whether it's math or social studies or science—the teachers on our team write really positive comments back to the kids and ask really good questions and give suggestions like, "This lab report could be a lot better if you did this or this," or "Would you consider giving an opposing side for this current event, and you're more than welcome to turn this back in as a second draft." I don't see that happening in an awful lot of classrooms.

**P:** True. But the teachers on your team really are responding to the writing as well as to the content of the piece.

**L:** Absolutely. Definitely. And so the kids begin to see that writing matters in all their classes. And I think that's helped them see that the writing they do in other subjects should be part of their portfolios also, to really show who they are and what they can do. You know, Carl (who doesn't have any writing in his portfolio) was telling me last week, "I only work well when somebody tells me what I need to write." And I said, "Well, why don't you have your social studies or science in here?" And he said, "I didn't know I could put them in here." And I've *said* it again and again, but they don't *hear* it. So he felt an awful lot better when he knew his social studies and science writing could be part of what I'm looking at to see what he can do as a writer. So it does matter.

Well, I'm not sure I just answered what's the easiest part of teaching writing, but I know that the most engaging thing for me is to see kids draft a wonderful piece of writing and feel that they've really worked hard at it, and then kids burst into applause when they read it out loud. That is *so* exciting! I don't know if I could teach if language arts was not writing and reading.

*You've talked a bit already about some of the challenges of teaching writing: the time pressures, the special emotional and social pressures of adolescence. Is there anything else you find particularly difficult or challenging as you work with student writers?*

**P:** Certainly, the conferences. Conferences can be wonderful, but they can be hard too.

**L:** Absolutely.

**P:** Because there's no way to really prepare for them. The university interns in my classroom always have questions about how you do conferences, but you can't really set them up for it because it's such a responsive way of teaching. It's not until that student shares the writing with you that you can respond to it. You can't prepare that ahead of time; you can't know what you're going to say ahead of time. You just have to be there with the student.

**L:** And I don't know if you do it the same way I do, but I do ask the kids to read their writing to me so that I can really focus on the content. But by the time kids get to eighth grade, there are some kids who've written ten, fifteen, twenty pages. And so I find that sometimes I have to say to the kids, "I'd like you to read the part that you're having the most difficulty with" so that I can at least hear the voice and maybe focus on that one thing. Often they have to give me the pieces of writing to read for myself, but that's where I run into trouble. If I don't hear the voice of the writer, I may make faulty assumptions, and then when I hand that back to kids, sometimes the tears just flow, and I know I've missed something that I wouldn't have missed in a one-on-one conference.

**P:** If he had read it to you and you had talked to him about it, you would have understood him better.

**L:** Absolutely. And so I realize every time I take a piece of writing home, and I don't have the writer read it to me, it's very different. And I think I need to try and make those conferences happen more.

**P:** There is an advantage to working with the younger children because their pieces are shorter. I notice by second grade, and certainly by the second half of second grade, some of them are starting to write longer and longer pieces, and then we will sometimes just choose a part of it that the child wants to focus on right now for this conference. But up until then, often they can just read the whole thing to you—six, seven, eight sentences. Each sentence is another page of the book, but they can read till they get through the whole piece of writing. So it's usually not until [they get] into second grade that we're choosing a part to focus on for a conference.

**L:** I think that's the hardest part for me. I've got twenty-five kids in a class (and now we've got twenty-seven, twenty-eight kids), I aim for one conference a week with each one. And it still doesn't happen. I can't quite get it in. But I noticed something last year. I had a doctoral student in my classroom, and he was trying to pay attention to how I listen to kids, so he recorded many, many conferences I had. And what was so ironic was that sometimes the conference would go on for twenty minutes, but after I'd listen to the tape of it, I felt I could have done the same thing in twenty seconds because the kids can only take in so much information. And if I had just shut my mouth and stopped asking all of these questions, I think I could have targeted right in. It was very helpful for me to see that.

**P:** Well, that's probably another important thing to say about conferences, that conferences can be very short. In my room they can be. You know, sometimes one or two comments is all it takes, and you move on to somebody else. Conferences aren't always very detailed sorts of meetings. And not formal meetings, either.

**L:** By seventh and eighth grade, though, there's so much that you're focusing on. Sometimes, with the kids who really want to make their piece the best they can, I'm going through three and four conferences over the same piece of writing before we even get to editing. So it takes a couple of weeks for them to really construct a thorough piece of writing.

**P:** Oh, I would think so.

**L:** Then there's that time thing again too. You've got to have plenty of time to do it. Sometimes people think you need to get students to keep finishing pieces, and yes, it's important to bring pieces to conclusion. But you need time to keep working on a piece too.

**P:** Well, I want the children to bring their pieces to conclusion, but I also want them to begin to realize all the hard work that goes into making a piece of writing the best that it can be. And I just have to know the stopping point. I mean, kids look at me and go, "This *is* my final draft!" and I go, "OK. We've done enough for today!"

**L:** I know what you mean. Sometimes I just push it too hard, and I make them go back too often.

**P:** That reminds me of something Tom Romano [1987] wrote. He says if you know that the students are going to be doing several pieces of writing—it's not just a one-assignment kind of writing—then one piece might have really good dialogue in it, maybe the rest of the piece doesn't hold together real well, but that's OK because you know there's going to be another piece coming along, and you can work on something else with the next piece. You don't have to get everything just right in every piece of writing. There are going to be other opportunities.

**L:** Yes. And what I do now, too, is I just tell the kids I really want to see three to five rough draft pages a week so that they can't ever say to me, "I'm really done. What do I do now?" We're *never* done! (Which probably aggravates the heck out of them.) But I just want them to start to be able to evaluate for themselves: With all these pages of writing in front of me, it's pretty obvious that in this piece the dialogue's working really well, but this other piece holds together better because it's got some other characteristics that make it a better piece of writing. I just want them to do volumes of writing so that they can begin to identify what makes a better piece.

**P:** Yes, and unless you do a lot of writing, you just can't develop that.

**L:** Maybe we should talk a little more about how we set up conferences.

**P:** Well, I tend to roam for conferences. The students come in each morning, and they get their writing folders, and they get started with writing right away. As soon as the first people are here, I start roaming and settle down beside somebody and talk with them about their piece. I keep lists for myself or use a name list so I know who I've talked to already this week and who I haven't, and so I know who else to get to. And then, once we get into publishing pieces, I keep a whole stack of notes on the table that say, "I would like a conference for publishing." And the children sign up for that and leave the note there for me.

**L:** Oh, that's a good idea.

**P:** And so I pick up that note and know that that's somebody I need to get to that day. And then we continue to use the notes, so that if I sit down and I'm having a conference with a child and we decide on one thing she's going to do for that piece of writing, I'll make a note about it on the back of this little slip of paper and I give it back to her. Then when she thinks she's done that, she just puts the note back on my table and that's kind of a signal to me that she wants another conference to go over that. But mostly I'm just roaming unless somebody has told me they want a conference.

**L:** That's fairly similar to what I do. All of the kids have conference sheets in their working folders. They sign up for conferences, and I tell them my goal is to have one good conference with each of them during the week. But I keep a list too, and if they don't sign up after a couple of weeks, then either they have to give me the piece of writing they're working on or they need to talk to me about it. But that conference sheet that they have is kind of a record of how I responded to their piece, and it's in their working folder so that they can see—and I can see—if it's blank; then I need to talk to those kids I haven't talked to. Our class periods are about fifty-two minutes now, and I tend to do something at the beginning of the class to get them started. Maybe it's a quote I'm asking the kids to respond to, or I might put up a piece of poetry and ask them to do a one-to-two-minute quick-write about it, just to kind of get some juices flowing. And then I say, "Whatever you need to get, you know you've got so many pages of writing due this week," or "Now we're at the deadline, so you need two finished pieces." And then they work on those things they need to work on. I go to the kids who've signed up first, or I might put kids' names up on the board to go to them because they haven't seen me for a week or two. It seems to work pretty well.

**P:** I would think that if writing is coming, say, in the middle of the day or they're coming from something else to writing (like they do in middle school), you would need a mini-lesson or something to get started with, to kind of move them into it. But I've found now, by being able to do it just first thing in the morning, they often are thinking about their writing on the way to school. They come in with ideas; they know what they're doing. And some need that time to kind of roam the room a bit before they settle into it. But that's OK. That's part of coming into school.

*And where do your kids get their ideas for their writing?*

**P:** Well, you certainly can't minimize the importance of sharing writing. I notice that *so* much. You have whole class sharing times for them to share their writing with the group, and you start to notice some ideas that spread from one to another. This little boy's got a space story going and in the space adventure story he's taking other classmates, and so then you start to notice somebody else doing that too. "Oh, I could have my friend in my story." So they start to include classmates in their stories, and you start to notice these conventions that sort of spread throughout the room. Or somebody realizes that someone else wrote about his cat. "Well, I need something to write about. I can write about my cat." I think having lots of opportunities to share their writing is really important, whether it's informally because there happen to be four people sitting at this table and they're gonna say, "Hey, look what I just wrote!" or whether we set up the time for the whole class, and a couple of people share their writing with everyone.

**L:** In my classes, it's with those four or five kids sitting at a table—that's where the most sharing happens. *Very* informally. And I see more teaching going on—those kids teaching each other in an informal situation—than when I try to set up response groups when they have a formal sharing. That does *not* work really well with my kids. And I do a *terrible* job (I admit it and I feel guilty about it), but with 50 minutes, I'll look up and there're three minutes left, and nobody has read what they've been working on. Plus the fact that with adolescents, trying to get them to share in whole class is like pulling teeth. No matter how safe it is, it takes *months*. I was just noticing today there were some kids who, for the first time, began talking to the kids at their table. And this is the end of October. It has taken eight weeks for those kids to feel comfortable enough to even share with three other kids. They're *so* self-conscious.

**P:** And see, that's the difference in ages too, I think. Although I've had some young children who took awhile. I can think of some through the years. With one little boy, I remember it was February before he would share with the whole class. But that's more the exception than the rule with younger kids.

**L:** Well, you know what I've also been thinking, Pat? For years I've said, "The sharing has to be done by the writer." But a year ago I started to wonder about this. I try to write when I'm asking kids to write. I don't mean that they're writing a particular thing, but I'm usually writing something too. When we were writing a musical last year, I was trying to write song lyrics. Now, I didn't get up on stage to sing what I had written, but the kids who sang that song that I contributed lines to—I was so excited! I felt like one of the kids! It was so exciting to hear somebody sing words that I wrote. "Oh! That's the line that I thought of!" And I thought, "This is really stupid. What on earth made me truly believe that other kids can't present a finished piece of writing someone else has done?" When you go public with a piece of writing, I think it *should* be almost a performance, if the writer chooses it to be, and maybe somebody else could read that poetry, say, far better than the writer could. Writers don't come with their books; poets don't come with their poetry. I think that writers don't have to be the only ones who present a finished writing.

**P:** Yes, I think most of us have that mind-set to it.

**L:** Well, I really have been thinking about that, and thinking we just really need to teach the other kids how to take another child's piece of writing and consider, "How would you present that to us? Would it be in a performance? Would it be in some different kind of reading? Would you have multiple voices presenting this?"

**P:** There really is a performance aspect with *any* kind of sharing with the group. It is an element of the sharing.

**L:** Oh, I believe it is. Yes.

**P:** In the last few years I've had some students that have gotten into writing poems for two voices. They really like the books by [Paul] Fleischman [1988]. Well, that's performance to read those poems for two voices. But then they started writing their own and then performing their own. And it sort of made me step back and think about how much performance is part of any of the sharing that they do.

**L:** Definitely.

**P:** When they take that space in front of the group, that's a performance.

**L:** It's taken me twenty years to learn that before I read something out loud to those kids, I'd better know it really well. In a sense, I'm performing it too, because if I'm reading poetry to them, I really want to read it in a voice that I think the poet would be pleased with. So even when we're reading books out loud—if we're reading a novel together—I want the kids to know we need to practice ahead of time and really take the parts, so that we're listening to each other, and it's not just some deadly boring reading like I did when I was in high school. You know—don't look at the teacher because she'll call on you.

**P:** And then you'll have to read!

**L:** Yes, you'll have to read, so don't make eye contact! Oh, weren't we talking about where the kids find writing, and you were saying how the kids kind of find writing from each other?

**P:** Also from books that they're reading. And one of the children said to me the other day that he just looks around the room at the pictures, and he sees a picture, and then that gives him an idea for something to write about.

**L:** I have to almost point all those things out to my kids! I'll point out that I've got quotes hanging all around the room. And I do a lot of quick-writes with the kids—I might put a piece of poetry up on the overhead and just ask them to do a one-to-two-minute write from it. I read a piece from Cynthia Rylant, "My Grandmother's Hair" (I love that piece!), and I asked them to respond to that for one to two minutes. And they've got a lot of writing in their journal that they know they can go back to again and again. What else do I do? I might read the lead of something to them. They construct a positive–negative chart so that they might aim towards the good and the bad things that have happened in their lives. Then a couple years ago kids said, "Could we just do dislikes and likes?" And they did. They actually did a great job on those. Just to be able to say to Jan, "Tell me more about these things that you really hate," or "Friends are at the top of your list. Tell me more about friends," or "Tell me about the beach. What do you love about the sound of the ocean? What happens here?" So when they're stuck for writing, they have another source to draw on.

**P:** Well, you know, Linda, you mentioned the difference between first graders who are clamoring for their turn to share, and middle school students who are reluctant to share with the whole class. We do try to build in two times right at the end of writing time for children to share their writing, and then later in the day there's always a time for somebody to share some reading with the class. Then we end the day with another sharing time, and that can be either writing or reading or something from their portfolio or any kind of work that they want to share. So there's at least four students who are sharing with the whole class just about every day.

**L:** That's great. That's really great. But you've also got them in that self-contained classroom. I'm fighting that fifty minutes all the time. There are some other ways that I get the kids to think about finding ideas for writing. I do set up a whole bunch of things at the beginning of the year where I'm doing a lot of quick-writes with them, I'm reading some professional writing to them—short pieces or pieces from previous years—and asking the kids to respond with whatever comes to mind. Or I ask them sometimes to borrow a line and write off that line for a minute or two. So they've got their journals *filled* with possibilities. I've got quotes hanging all over the room; there are pictures hanging all over. I also share a whole bunch of writing contests with them and say, "Here's a possibility, here's a possibility, here's a possibility." I suggest they write book reviews for *Voices from the Middle*, because we try to publish twelve book reviews in each issue. But I know how hard it is for teachers to get kids to send their writing out at middle school level, and so I'm always pushing our kids to do that. But most of them have ideas. It's the kids who don't feel good about their writing or have never felt good about it who have a hard time. It's trying to convince those kids that they have something to say so that they will write.

**P:** Part of it, too, is creating those opportunities for lots of different kinds of writing.

**L:** Definitely.

**P:** Or if there is a student who's really reluctant to share a personal narrative writing, she has the opportunity to try a book review. There's something else that she can write and still be part of the writing community.

**L:** I think that's tied to reading too, Pat. For a long time I just had novels in my classroom and I was having the kids read novels, yet I couldn't figure out why they were all writing fiction! Well, that's what they were reading. You have to start to kind of put two and two together and say, "I need to get a lot more nonfiction in this classroom. I need to show them that it's perfectly OK for them to be reading some skateboarding articles because that's what they want to be writing." So let them look at how somebody else constructs something like that. So it *is* important to surround them with a variety of kinds of reading. And with the middle schoolers, they're writing in every single genre or discipline: They're writing in science, they're writing in social studies, they're writing in geography. But our kids don't seem to see the connections unless I make them explicit, saying, " *Please* make your portfolio as full as it can be with these wonderful pieces of writing you're constructing in other classes. They matter to me too because they show me what you can do as a writer."

**P:** So for a middle school teacher, it's really important to invite that writing into the writing classroom.

**L:** Definitely. To see their language arts classroom as a laboratory for the language arts. And it may not all happen in that room during that fifty minutes, but you certainly hope that those kids show you what they are capable of doing as writers.

*Some teachers say that revision can be a problem—that their kids just don't want to revise their writing. What's your experience with this?*

**P:** Well, for young children revision tends to be just adding some information. Maybe we can work on sequence sometimes, but rarely is anything ever taken out of a piece of writing. That's very difficult for young children to deal with. More often than not, revision is just adding information—trying to make something clearer so that everybody can understand what the writer means. But that's the bulk of our revision, and most of our revision conferences are just about adding information.

**L:** I think for us, especially at eighth grade, it's quite a bit more sophisticated. Kids are actually looking at what makes a good lead: What should a good lead do (and let's practice a few )? How should that lead look different depending on the kind of writing that you're doing? What is it that makes this such a good piece of writing? How does the ending work?

**P:** Now that comes up sometimes with first graders too. That's an issue that all writers deal with: How do I bring this to an end? But for the little children, sometimes it's just 'cause they come to the last page in their book. And that's the end.

**L:** You know, Pat, when I think about it, I'm not sure there are so many real differences between your kids and mine. It may be a little more complicated at seventh and eighth grade levels, but truly the characteristics or elements of a good piece of writing that six-year-olds are looking at are very much the same. They're talking the same elements, but the older kids just have more information. But they're reluctant to take away, too, when they revise. But then, so am I. I'm reluctant to take away.

**P:** Oh yes! What writer isn't?!

**L:** I've spent hours writing this twenty-page article, and then somebody tells me it doesn't start till page eleven—well, it's pretty hard to take out the first ten pages.

When I'm thinking about teachers that I've worked with who have never done much writing themselves, I realize it's awfully hard to have conferences with kids and help them revise their writing if *you* don't know how *you* have been affected by this experience as a writer.

**P:** I think what's really important is just writing *yourself.* Whether it's having a conference or sharing a piece of writing, if you haven't done it yourself, you really don't understand it in the same way.

**L:** No. No. And I believe that even if you're working with 125–150 kids, every teacher at least has time to keep a journal and can do a one-to-two-minute quick-write, when you're asking kids to do that. That you *can* get that seed of an idea, just so you're getting the feel of what it's like to capture a moment even in one wonderful sentence. It *is* important—really vital—to teachers of writing that they're doing some kind of writing themselves.

**P:** Whether you're writing at the same moment the students are, or whether you're putting yourself in another writing group at some point in time, it's just that you get that experience of being a writer.

**L:** You know, there have been years when I haven't done much writing or shared it. I'm always writing in a journal, but there have been a couple of years when I wasn't writing for myself (either a memoir that I wanted to write or a fiction piece that I wanted to try). But this year I'm working on a piece of young adult fiction, and I'm also trying to write the text for a children's picture book. Well, when I shared this writing with the kids, their comments were *so* helpful because they knew these weren't fake pieces of writing that I was working on. I really want to send these out: I really hoped that this could be a picture book someday, and I really hoped that this could be a young adult novel. I used the kids' interaction with me as a model for how I wanted them to be responding to each other. I showed them how helpful their responses were to me and how their comments helped me change my writing. It made such a difference when I responded to them in conference: They were much more receptive to the kinds of comments I was making to them because they saw me as a writer more than a teacher. I don't know how we define ourselves. I hope they see me as both writer and teacher. But I hope they never see that one is off balance from the other. I hope they see that I can't separate teacher from writer and writer from teacher. I hope my writing is teaching them as much as what I'm *saying* to them is teaching them. And *they* are teaching *me*. They truly have helped me revise those pieces.

**P:** I think our students need to know that there are things that we can learn from each other and that it's not just a one-way street. We do value the help and the comments that they make to us.

**L:** Well, I'm thinking something else, too, Pat. When we put ourselves on the line—if I'm writing about my mother's death, say—then the kids know that that's a serious piece of writing to me. And they don't laugh at it, and they don't make fun of it. So the kids see that I put myself at risk in front of them, and then they're much more able to write honestly and take some risks themselves. It may not be an emotionally-charged piece that they're writing, but it may be something that they really care about, and they're able to risk the writing of that if they know that other kids have not made fun of me. Then they know the kids are probably not going to make fun of them.

**P:** I think the important point is that, even if you don't have the chance to write all the time, you still build in some ways for you to be a writer. Whether you're going to have your own drafts of a children's book this year, that doesn't matter. But the fact that you, the teacher, do have some ongoing experience of writing and sharing within the community of writers—that *does* matter.

## References

Fleischman, P. (1988). *Joyful noise: Poems for two voices.* NY: Harper & Row.

Hubbard, R. (1989). *Authors of pictures, draughtsmen of words.* Portsmouth, NH: Heinemann.

Romano, T. (1987). *Clearing the way.* Portsmouth, NH: Heinemann.

Rylant, C. (1991). My grandmother's hair. In N. Larrick & W. Lamb (Eds.), *To ride a butterfly: New picture stories, folktales, fables, nonfiction, poems, and songs for young children.* (p. 85). New York: Bantam Doubleday Dell.

## Bibliography

### Pat McLure

*Professional resources that have been especially important to me include:*

Graves, D. (1994). *A fresh look at writing.* Portsmouth, NH: Heinemann.

Hansen, J. (1987). *When writers read.* Portsmouth, NH: Heinemann.

Hubbard, R. (1989). *Authors of pictures, draughtsmen of words.* Portsmouth, NH: Heinemann.

Murray, D. M. (1989). *Expecting the unexpected: Teaching myself—and others—to read and write.* Portsmouh, NH: Heinemann.

Power, B. M., & Hubbard, R. (eds.) (1991). *Literacy in process: The Heinemann reader.* Portsmouth, NH: Heinemann.

Romano, T. (1986). Something afoul. From the video series *The writing and reading process: A new approach to literacy* developed by J. Hansen and D. Graves. Portsmouth, NH: Heinemann.

Wells, G. (1986). *The meaning makers: Children learning language and using language to learn.* Portsmouth, NH: Heinemann.

*Children's books that I especially enjoy using with children include:*

Fleischman, P. (1988). *Joyful noise: Poems for two voices.* New York: Harper & Row.

James, S. (1991). *Dear Mr. Blueberry.* New York: McElderry.

Jarrell, R. (1964). *The bat-poet*. New York: Macmillan.

Krupinski, L. (1992). *Celia's island journal*. Boston, MA: Little, Brown and Company.

Munsch, R. (1985). *Thomas' snowsuit*. Toronto, Canada: Annick Press.

Yolen, J. (1987). *Owl moon*. New York, NY: Philomel.

**Linda Rief**

*Professional resources that have been especially important to me include:*

Atwell, N. (1987). *In the middle: Writing, reading, and learning with adolescents*. Upper Montclair, NJ: Boynton/Cook.

Carnegie Council on Adolescent Development. (1989). *Turning points: Preparing American youth for the 21st century*. Washington, DC: Carnegie Council on Adolescent Development.

Dillard, A. (1989). *The writing life*. New York: Harper & Row.

Fox, M. (1993). *Radical reflections*. Fort Worth, TX: Harcourt Brace.

Tobin, L. (1993). *Writing relationships: What really happens in the composition class*. Portsmouth, NH: Boynton/Cook Heinemann.

Wolf, D. (1988). *Reading reconsidered: Literature and literacy in high school*. New York: College Entrance Examination Board.

*Children's books that I especially enjoy using with children include:*

Cisneros, S. (1991). *House on Mango Street*. New York: Vintage Books.

Cisneros, S. (1996). Eleven. In *Woman hollering creek* (pp. 6–9). New York: Vintage Books.

Fox, M. (1984). *Wilfred Gordon McDonald Partridge*. Brooklyn, NY: Kane/Miller.

Hesse, K. (1997). *Out of the dust*. New York: Scholastic.

Hinton, S. E. (1967). *The outsiders*. New York: Viking Press.

Janeczko, P. (Ed.) (1983). *Poetspeak*. Scarsdale, NY: Bradbury Press.

Lowry, L. (1993). *The giver*. New York: Houghton Mifflin.

Paulsen, G. (1993). *Nightjohn*. New York: Delacorte.

Philbrick, R. (1993). *Freak the mighty*. New York: Blue Sky.

Rylant, C. (1989). *But I'll be back again: An album*. New York: Orchard Books.

Rylant, C. (1990). *A couple of kooks and other stories about love*. New York: Orchard Books.

Soto, G. (1990). *A fire in my hands*. New York: Scholastic.

# 4 Rethinking Literature Discussions

**Penny Silvers**
Reading Coordinator, Aptakisic School District 102, Buffalo Grove, Illinois


Reading has always been one of my passions. Talking about books and sharing interpretations with friends has significantly enhanced my understanding and enjoyment of stories and has expanded my appreciation of literature. However, as much as I crave these conversations for myself, my language arts instruction has only recently begun to provide an opportunity for my students to engage in meaningful discussions about what they are reading. In the past, I followed the teacher's guide and controlled the students' conversations, led the questioning, did most of the talking—and probably, most of the thinking. Now, however, I know that collaboration and talk are necessary for creating a learning community in which the participants can generate meaningful dialogue, take risks in their reading interpretations, and expand their comprehension.

Research has shown that reading is an active process of meaning making and that, through talk, we can expand our thinking and move toward greater understanding (Barnes, 1993; Britton, 1970; Wells, 1986). We know that our prior knowledge (personal knowing) is shaped by our interactions with others and that this social learning is the means through which we learn more about our world (Vygotsky, 1986). Although we grasp this intellectually, we may find it difficult to apply the theory in our classroom practice. My experience with literature discussions has helped me rethink what I believe about teaching and learning.

## Literacy within a Learning Community

As a language arts resource teacher, I spend most of my time working in classrooms with students and their teachers. However, I was given an opportunity to conduct a literature study with my own group of fourth-grade students when I was invited to participate in a video teleconference, sponsored by NCTE (National Council of Teachers of

English), that focused on student learning through talk. My fourth graders were a volunteer group from three different classrooms who agreed to give up their forty-minute lunch recess once a week in order to meet with me in the reading resource room to talk about books. With this group of students, I learned to listen to what they were really saying and to contribute genuine questions and comments—or remain quiet—as a member of the group. Together, the children and I learned to trust each other with personal issues, and we became comfortable taking learning risks through our exploration of the tensions and ambiguities offered by wonderful pieces of literature.

Our dependence upon each other in exploring our reading was reinforced by our need to better understand the story chosen for us by NCTE. *The Giver,* written by Lois Lowry, was selected because of its complex content and because it provides a challenge to all readers, children and adults alike. *The Giver* is a science fiction story of a futuristic community in which many rules and regulations control the thinking and lives of the members. Focusing on twelve-year-old Jonas, the story seduces the reader into believing that community members are happy with their assigned jobs, their contrived family units, and the predictability and orderliness of their daily lives. When Jonas is selected to be the next Receiver of Memory under the mentoring of the Giver, he begins to understand feelings, memories, choices, and relationships he has been deprived of by the mind control of the Elders. The reader gradually realizes, along with Jonas, that this community is not a good place and that the lack of freedom and enforced sameness are dangerous. As Jonas learns more about the community, contradictions and conflicts increase until Jonas has to make a choice about what he must do to survive. The ending is ambiguous and compelling, leading the reader to make an interpretive choice and to reflect on the values in our society that contrast with those in Jonas's world.

Initially, I had great concern about using this book with fourth graders because it is considered to be a junior high school book. I worried about the fourth graders' ability to comprehend, to grasp the significance of the story, and to deal with its potentially disturbing and controversial content. I wanted to ensure that our time together would be pleasant and productive. I felt the need to protect my students from being exposed to a story that might upset them or that might prove too challenging and ultimately, frustrating. I see now that I underestimated both their ability to deal with the complex issues that the book raised, and also their interest in exploring the questions about their own lives that emerged through our reading. The book was an intellectual stretch, and the students met the challenge confidently and competently.

Imagine a group of eight fourth-grade students deeply engaged in an intense literature discussion of *The Giver.* Listen to the comments of students relating the text to their own personal lives—families, relationships, memories, feelings, choices, careers, religion, democracy. Observe their attention to each other's points of view and their willingness to think together to generate new ideas beyond their immediate frames of reference. Notice their respect for each other's ideas, their eagerness to discuss an issue in depth, to share their thinking as they use exploratory talk (Barnes, 1993), to give substance to dense concepts. Recognize that the teacher is only one of the players in this discussion—a participant in the group, occasionally asking for clarification, restating a key comment, or contributing her own newly discovered idea as it seems appropriate.

This was the nature of our discussions. An observer of these literature discussion groups would see knowledge being constructed collaboratively as individuals advance various interpretations of the text from diverse perspectives, and deepen their understanding as they share personal experiences. As Stuart pointed out when we began to really get into *The Giver,* "The book has many layers. You think you have it figured out, and then something happens to change your mind. You think about what it would be like to live in their community, with all their rules and jobs that are already picked out for you. It sounds nice at first, but then you begin to see how wrong it is and how there really are no choices at all." Or, as Alice commented, "We take so much for granted in our own lives. We can wear anything we want, say anything we feel, do whatever we are interested in, and have whatever we can afford. We have choices, opportunities, our own families, homes, and friends. Nobody watches us to keep us from feeling happy or sad, from being friendly or staying by ourselves. We don't even think about how good we have it."

The students were making connections to their own personal lives, relating this book to others they had read, and generating new ideas as they expanded their understanding of the story. They were not searching for one best interpretation of the story. Instead, they were supporting each other in the construction of meaning.

## Starting Out

Because of some explicit descriptions and potentially controversial content of *The Giver,* I was concerned about parents' approval of this book for their children. I asked them to read the book at home, and I invited them to an evening adult literature discussion at school, where they would have an opportunity to talk with each other about *The Giver,* to ask questions, and to express any personal issues they had about the book. As I suspected, a few parents were worried about some of the story events. Of particular concern was the subject of "stirrings" (sexual feelings of the twelve-year-olds that were repressed by a pill administered daily), and the idea of "releasing" (killing by lethal injection) people who didn't measure up, were too old, or were no longer useful to the community. Andrea had come to this meeting with her parents and assured the adults that while killing was "gross and awful," they saw "worse stuff" all the time on the news, so she felt they could "handle it." In this group discussion process, the parents worked through their issues and agreed to allow their children to continue with the literature study of this book.

I also knew that the students needed some experience in talking about books before taking on such a complex novel. They needed to become comfortable with each other, to have some experience in sharing ideas, to learn to trust the group to support their thinking. With the help of the school and local librarians, I pulled together an extended text set of thematically linked books for them to read (see the bibliography of children's books at the end of this chapter). These books addressed issues of families, relationships, feelings, acceptance of diversity, choices, and freedom—topics I could foresee being discussed when we got into the novel.

I decided to use picture books to help students talk about stories that were easy to read but which have deep meaning that would relate to the themes embedded in *The Giver.* The students read each picture book individually or with a partner first, and then came together as a group to discuss the stories and the issues that they believed provided a connecting link between the books. Favorite picture books that provided the best transition to *The Giver* were *The Big Orange Splot* by Pinkwater, and *The Araboolies of Liberty Street* by Swope. These books helped the students gain confidence in talking about stories, and they really got conversations going about expressing individuality, appreciating differences, and accepting diversity.

As the students became comfortable talking with each other about ideas in the picture books, I brought in short stories such as "Slower Than the Rest," by Cynthia Rylant in her book, *Every Living Thing.* In this story, a child with special learning needs experiences success when he writes about his pet turtle and wins a school contest. Discussion about this story focused on people with differences and how diversity (rather than the "sameness" in Jonas's community) enriches all our lives. This led to conversation about our "inclusion" children and how terrible it would be to exclude them from our classrooms because of their disabilities.

We then read *The Children's Story,* a complex short story by James Clavell, which was easy to read but very difficult to comprehend. This was the group's first exposure to the concept of mind control, and how a seemingly pleasant person could turn everything that we value upside down, making what we believe is wrong, seem right. By the time the students finished discussing all these stories, they were accomplished at talking about diversity, choices, individuality, and freedom. It was the perfect time to begin *The Giver.*

I had no idea how the students would handle the book. I was nervous for the students and for myself. I felt that my main goal was to help the students respect each other's ideas, listen and respond thoughtfully, and expand their understanding of the book by sharing ideas about the issues in the story. To organize the reading of the book, we divided it up into several chapters per session. The students agreed on how many chapters they thought they could read on their own before coming to the next meeting. The students kept response journals (Figure 4.1) to help them remember ideas they wanted to discuss or questions they wanted to bring to the group. The journals were also used to record their predictions, their reflections about the characters, the author's intent, and any other ideas that were of importance to them that they might want to share with the group as a way of generating conversation.

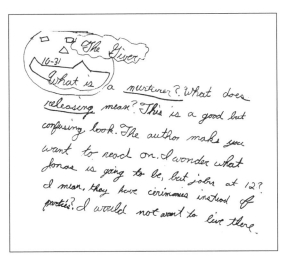

**Figure 4.1** Response Journal Entry

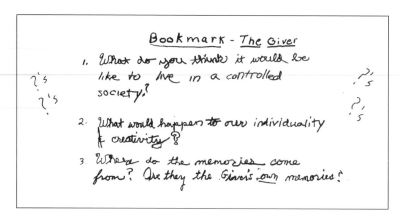

**Figure 4.2**   Student Bookmark

**Figure 4.3**   Student's Journal Illustration

**Figure 4.4** Student's Journal Illustration

I never told the students what to write, but as they shared some of their written comments, they learned from each other about the range of responses and kinds of connections and questions that would lead to good conversation and deeper thinking. They also used "Bookmarks" (Crafton, 1991; Figure 4.2) to record anomalies, unfamiliar vocabulary, and predictions; they drew illustrations in their journals to enhance their comprehension (Short, Harste, & Burke, 1995; Figure 4.3 and Figure 4.4); and they wrote reflections and personal connections in their journals. These all helped generate a wealth of ideas to talk about when the group came together.

Each time we met, the students set a discussion agenda, writing down what they wanted to talk about from the reading (Figure 4.5). Along with "stirrings" and "releasing," agenda items included a range

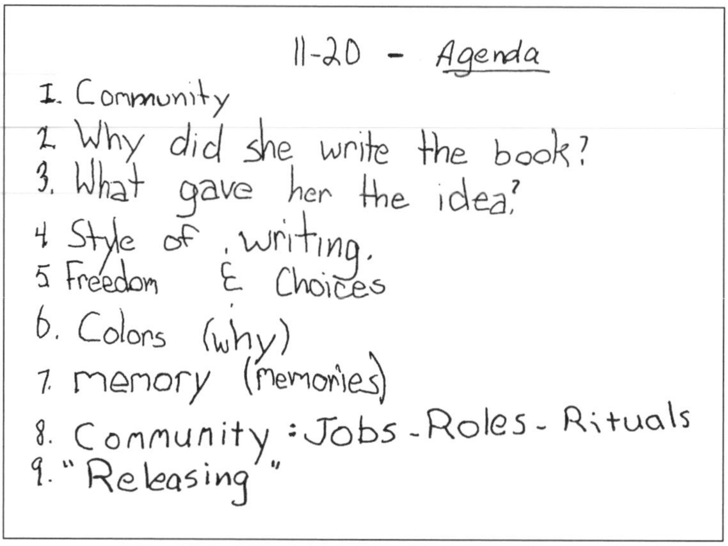
11-20 - Agenda

1. Community
2. Why did she write the book?
3. What gave her the idea?
4 Style of writing.
5 Freedom & Choices
6. Colors (why)
7. memory (memories)
8. Community: Jobs - Roles - Rituals
9. "Releasing"

**Figure 4.5** Agenda for Literature Discussion

of topics such as receiving assigned jobs for the rest of your life, birth mothers and adoptive families, comparative governments (Stuart was an "expert" on socialism, communism, and democracy), relationships (love, feelings, and memories), and having choices in your life. Ideally, the agenda was supposed to focus the discussion and keep the conversation moving along. In reality, though, we usually started with the last item on the agenda, which—as we gained momentum—generally proved so interesting that we rarely got to most of the other issues listed. We were never at a loss for discussion topics and usually ran out of time before we exhausted what seemed important to talk about.

Our initial discussions were somewhat chaotic and disjointed. The students kept interrupting each other in their eagerness to contribute to the conversation. Topics kept changing before they were fully explored, and we spent most of our time retelling what had happened in the story rather than discussing issues in depth. I videotaped each session. When we viewed the videotapes in order to reflect on how the discussion had gone, the students could see how much they interrupted each other.

An ingenious idea emerged as a solution to this problem. The students decided to role-play their interrupting the way the children did in *The Giver.* Each time someone was interrupted, an apology had to be offered and the person who was interrupted had to say, "I accept

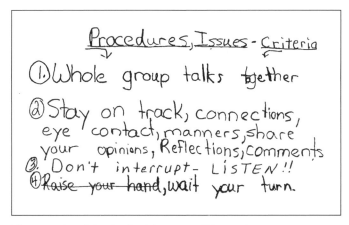

**Figure 4.6** Criteria for Literature Discussion

your apology." The children loved doing this, but it slowed down their sharing of ideas, and after two sessions it was abandoned. However, the role playing served as a subtle reminder to listen until someone was completely finished talking and then to comment specifically about what was said before starting on a new subject.

To help establish rules for the group, we developed a list of criteria for meaningful literature discussions. We revisited our list from time to time and revised what wasn't working. For example, after two weeks of discussing the book, we decided to eliminate "raise your hand when you want to say something" (Figure 4.6). The students could see that although this was what they usually did in class, our group dialogue allowed them to enter and exit the conversation as their comments connected to the topic being discussed. All that was required was to listen carefully and respond thoughtfully to the subject being addressed. Anyone could have the floor when it made sense to do so.

Some sessions were very exciting, generating ideas and interpretations we had not thought about before. Other times, we got sidetracked by making personal connections and sharing individual experiences that were interesting but that didn't add to our understanding of the story. The group viewed my videotapes of the sessions and we all became co-researchers, reflecting on our discussions and adjusting our interactions as we came to understand what behaviors and responses supported our thinking and which ones only maintained the status quo or were counterproductive. Together, we analyzed what worked and what didn't, and then we tried to improve the discussion the next time.

The fourth-grade students were serious and sincere in their efforts to interpret the books we read, from picture books to novels. They were actively engaged in comprehending *The Giver*, supporting each other when their reading fell behind, or helping each other with difficult vocabulary or complex ideas. When the content got too dense or the action too painful, the group talked each other through it, using their own life experiences to rationalize, explore, or interpret the meaning.

More than working together cooperatively, the students thought together, exploring new perspectives and growing beyond themselves. Aaron noted during one of our discussions, "Our room is like the Giver's room. We have lots of books of all kinds in here, but we can also make our own rules. We don't have to raise our hand when we have something to say. We can agree or disagree with each other, and nobody's feelings are hurt. We can feel things, be angry, be sad, or have fun. This is like our secret."

Together, the students wondered about Lois Lowry's purpose for writing the book, relating her theme of sameness to the Holocaust in her book, *Number the Stars.* They discussed everything from reproduction and death to career choices, families, adopted children and birth mothers, and the moral dilemma of lying in order to do a job or to conceal knowledge from others.

These literature discussions reveal a literate learning community in which everyone was able to take learning risks and participate as a co-collaborator in the development of shared understanding over an extended period of time. The discussions enabled the students to move beyond simply comprehending the story toward reflecting critically on themselves and their world. The discussions gave these students an opportunity to explore significant issues in their lives.

As Alice said in her final reflections about the book, "*The Giver* changed my life. I will never take my friends, my life, my things, my clothes, and my family for granted again. I never thought about a world without color or choices before, and now I think about it all the time. Whenever I have to make a decision about something, I think about how lucky I am. I also like to read more now, especially when I know I will be sharing my ideas with the group. It makes me want to read more."

## Rethinking Literature Discussions: The Next Step

In the literature discussions of *The Giver*, my students were using reading and writing to think, relate, respond, and learn. We worked hard to get to the high level of interaction that was achieved. I was proud of their understanding of such a complex story and of their eagerness to share their ideas and support each other. When I reviewed the videotapes with colleagues, we agreed that the depth of the children's comments was exceptional and that the discussions were an outstanding example of what we could expect of a successful literature group. Yet, as rich as these literature discussions were, I realized that I had missed many subtle social, cultural, and political issues that were embedded in our talk.

While the literature discussions provided an excellent example of talk about books, they could have done more. They could have pushed us toward understanding our own personal beliefs and attitudes more clearly, toward exploring how our thinking is socially constructed, and toward taking some kind of socially responsible action in the community. We could have asked, "Why are things the way they are?" We could have sought opportunities for change toward more just and equitable relationships. I needed to help the students see that they can have an impact on their world—that reading and writing can become vehicles for personal inquiry and for critiquing the world (Altwerger, 1996).

Questions could have been raised in our discussions that challenged us to think about injustices in our own lives. For example, I could have asked if the "releasing" of people in Jonas's community was any worse (or, perhaps, more merciful) than people choosing to kill their newborn babies, shooting each other in a quarrel, or bombing a subway in our society. I could have moved beneath the surface layers of all our interactions and questioned our unexamined beliefs, assumptions, and understanding of issues like gender, diversity, and social expectations. During one of the discussions, Christine raised the issue of gender roles and expressed surprise that the chief elder was a woman and that Jonas's father was the nurturer of the family unit. That would have been a perfect opportunity to raise the issue of gender stereotypes and invite interested students to pursue the question as an inquiry to further inform the group.

When the children discussed the idea of "releasing" with such a passion, I could have brought up other issues such as what role the "inclusion" kids play in our schools, diversity contrasted with sameness, grades and competition, status, rank, making choices, or politics. I could have helped the students put their own personal lives into a broader social perspective.

## Becoming Aware of Gender Inequities

The students and I had thought we were being critical in discussing some of the political issues that were a part of the story. We had thought we were being activists by considering what our lives would be like without the freedom and choices inherent in our democracy. We had thought we were socially aware because we discussed issues related to homelessness, child abuse, and caring for the elderly. But when I reviewed the videotapes of our discussions again, I realized it was only talk. None of us had really believed that we could work strategically to make change happen. Even though we had recognized a range of injustices in the story as well as in our own lives, none of us had questioned our own actions. We had challenged the behaviors of others but had seen nothing wrong with our own. Although we had reflected on injustices, we had not believed ourselves to be in a position to make a difference. And while the children and I had considered gender injustices, I had failed to see these within our own discussion group. Awareness of this aspect of our own group might have helped us all become more conscious of the need for social changes within our own lives, right within our own school. Reviewing the videotapes with my colleagues gave me the opportunity to examine the students' discussions more closely, to rethink the dynamics of the group's interactions and explore the potential for even more significant learning for the students and for me. Colleagues gently pointed out examples of my own sexist behavior in the way that I responded to the three boys more than the five girls. They showed me where the students also engaged in stereotypical sexist interactions and made comments reflecting unconscious gender biases (e.g., "The girl who was supposed to become the new Giver must not have been strong enough to receive all the memories. She probably couldn't stand the pain as much as Jonas could.")

My colleagues also questioned my extensive support for Stuart, whose oral language impairment made me hover unduly to ensure that his voice would be heard. They wondered about Katy, silent throughout the twenty-minute tape except for one very cogent comment in which she connected the exodus of the main character (Jonas) with the exodus of the pilgrims from Europe to America to live where they could honor their beliefs. My colleagues noticed the life-connections that the girls made, focusing on issues of families, feelings, adoption, clothes, school, and dreams. They observed that, although the boys were respectful of these topics, they were more invested in topics they could relate to logically or rationally, such as comparing forms of government or considering the mechanics of transmitting the Giver's memories and feelings.

I reviewed the videotapes of our literature discussions again, examining the interactions and conversations much more closely than I had before. I recognized some of the subtle interpersonal dynamics related to gender issues that had eluded me even when I had reviewed the tapes with my colleagues. I could see how the boys and girls had different issues and inquiries they would have liked to pursue. Stuart was fascinated by different kinds of governments. The other boys had an interest in dreams and memories, predetermined jobs and careers. The girls were interested in relationships and extended families, as well as in the plight of individuals categorized as "different." Alice was very interested in specific gender issues, and then wanted to research societies and civilizations that revered women as their leaders.

I hadn't realized how much the three boys and Alice had dominated the discussions. The other girls' contributions were few—comments about family, relationships, or daily living issues. In addition, by continually deferring to Stuart, I had unintentionally excluded some of the girls by ignoring their comments in preference to his issues. At first, I denied to myself that I had behaved in such a sexist way. Concerned, however, that I had in fact silenced some of the girls and treated them unfairly, I later confessed to the group that I was worried about any discomfort my behavior might have caused them. I asked for their comments and help in correcting the situation.

Alice immediately came to my defense, commenting that she felt she had as much opportunity as the boys to express herself. However, when we all reviewed the final videotape together, we saw that some of the girls seemed to be overpowered by the more vocal members of the group. We discussed who talked more, wondered why, and analyzed some of the more visible group dynamics.

The boys, predictably, didn't feel they had dominated the discussions at all. The girls, equally predictably, agreed with them. I have come to understand, from my subsequent gender research, that the girls' passivity in permitting the boys to dominate the conversation (except for Alice), is characteristic of female behavior such that they actually become invisible within the group. The girls typically allow the boys' assertive behavior to continue, thus encouraging it by not stopping it or becoming more assertive themselves (Sadker & Sadker, 1994).

It was Alice who pointed out that she had tried to bring the other girls into the conversation by sharing her own personal examples as a way of inviting others to take a risk and share their stories, too. Tannen (1990) has written that females' interaction is oriented toward connecting and establishing closeness. For women, "life is a community, a struggle to preserve intimacy and avoid isolation" (p. 25). The focus is more on friendship than on power or negotiations between winning and losing. Alice's behavior seems to fit this description.

Although the boys in the group were sensitive and respectful, their comments were objective, action-oriented, rational, and informational—descriptions so often applied to masculine thinking. They were more logical and analytical than the girls, emphasizing what the characters *did*—not what they *felt*. Stuart paid attention to objective information, discussing the overt behaviors of the members of the Giver's community and comparing their society to socialism and communism. Aaron and Dino described characters but did not relate to them personally.

The girls' orientation, on the other hand, was more personal. They engaged in a "discourse of feeling" (Cherland, 1992), focusing on emotions, human relationships, loving-kindness, and caring. They responded with "I liked," "I wanted," and "I hated," as well as with embarrassment, shyness, fear, and disgust. They were interested in social relationships; they focused on characters' lack of choices in the story (about clothes, toys, jobs), the assigned family units, and the role reversals. It was Alice who pointed out that the chief elder was a woman and that the mother of Jonas had an important official position, while the father was the nurturer of the family unit.

Through Alice's use of affective dialogue in our discussions, the group grew closer. When I asked Christine if she had felt uncomfortable entering the discussion, she said, "I just kept waiting for the discussion to move to a topic I was interested in. I didn't want to jump in and say something if it didn't fit what was being talked about. So I kept quiet." It didn't occur to her that she could take control of the conversation like the boys and Alice did and make it go in the direction that she wanted to discuss. Alice jumped in and said, "I knew Christine would feel comfortable discussing the different roles of the family members. That's why I brought up the idea of Jonas's mother being an important government official, and about the chief elder being a woman, too." She was the one who sensed Christine's discomfort and reached out to include her in the conversation.

Alice was also the cheerleader for expanding our awareness of gender biases. Picking up on my "confession" about not recognizing the girls as much as the boys, Alice asked if most teachers usually called more on boys than girls. I told the group about the Sadkers' research (Sadker & Sadker, 1994) and cited examples of this happening in classrooms all over the country. Alice was fascinated with this, and during recess the next few days, she convinced her fellow classmates to develop a survey with her for tallying the numbers of times their teachers called on boys and girls. According to the results of Alice's survey (which she presented to our group), several of the teachers did call on the boys much more than on the girls.

Soon, Alice started to notice other gender biases in our school. She tried to educate her friends to be more aware, commenting about sexist behavior she had observed and remarks she had overheard throughout the school day. Our literature group discussions expanded her knowledge of gender issues, and Alice began to act on this new information in a variety of ways, such as keeping a journal in which she recorded a list of gender-biased situations she had observed in school. A partial list included the following:

1. Boys were calling each other "girls" when they wanted to be mean. (Being told, "You're a girl!" was a fate worse than death for the boys.)

2. Boys didn't want to sit with certain girls in the lunchroom.

3. Girls were saying "stupid" (Alice's word) things to get the boys to notice them. Boys were showing off for the girls on the playground to get girls to notice them and "because they think they're better than we are. I told them, you guys get with it."

4. In gym, "we were doing this fitness thing where you have to do curls. The girls were only required to do seven sit-up curls. The boys had a higher number to do—maybe fifteen or twenty curls." Alice pointed out this discrepancy to the gym teacher. "I said, 'Mrs. K, that's really sexist.' She said, 'I know. If it was up to me, it would all be the same.'"

5. Alice seemed to feel that her teacher was still calling more on boys than girls. Alice also resented being asked to work with one of the slower children when none of the boys were ever asked to do this.

Alice has remained interested in gender issues and continues to talk with me about her observations. She has expanded her awareness of social issues and has begun to consider ways she can make a difference. I hope that over time Alice will come to better understand that "life could be different and that she has the right and responsibility to act. That is [to be] . . . critically literate—perhaps for life" (Shannon, 1995, p. 89).

The after-the-fact reviews of the videotaped discussions allowed us to recapture our missed opportunities for genuine inquiry. They provided a way to increase the students' social consciousness as well as their literacy involvement. Analyzing the tapes gave us the chance to examine our personal beliefs and our interactions with each other. We took a huge risk in moving beyond the boundaries of conventional literature discussions, venturing beyond school and out into the world. It was the perfect time to begin to explore our individual and collective biases about gender and to take some small, tentative steps toward action. However tiny these steps were in the scheme of things, they were giant steps for us, as we tiptoed gingerly away from our old selves, toward a new vision of who we wanted to be and what we hoped we—and others—would become.

## Lessons Learned

When our literature group began, my goal was for students to enjoy *The Giver*, interpret it at their own level of understanding, and take from their dialogues whatever was important and meaningful to them. I knew the content of the book was difficult: The ideas were complex, and there were many levels of interpretation. I was concerned that the vocabulary would be too difficult for some of the students, that their interest would not be sustained, that they would not have enough to talk about, or that they would not finish the book in time for the video-taping. I was worried that some of the content was too brutal and there would be parent objections.

I wanted the students to reflect—about their learning, about their reading strategies and accomplishments, about their group inter-actions. I hoped that my regular videotaping and our discussion of each session would encourage thoughtful reflection about what had been said. I wanted this taping strategy to enhance the students' inter-personal communication and their reactions to the story. I hoped for a lot and worried about the students' ability to succeed.

In retrospect, I should have had more confidence in the students and their ability to make meaning out of texts. I should have under-stood that quality literature, a trusting learning community, opportu-nities for genuine inquiry, and knowledgeable facilitation could lead to meaningful conversation and genuine learning, no matter what the age or grade of the participants. These students' collective comprehending of a story was so much greater than any individual interpretation. Had I known what to listen for and how to move the students' thinking beyond analysis and interpretation of the story, there would have been great potential for deeper personal understanding and social aware-ness. Our literature discussions could have been—and ultimately became—the catalyst for delving more deeply into our personal beliefs and values, and finding ways to rethink—even change—our previ-ously unexamined behaviors and attitudes. I could have also supported the students' personal interests that emerged as we read and discussed books, involving them in focused inquiries in which they researched issues that were important to them.

Literature study has the potential to open a new kind of dialogue in which social issues such as gender can be confronted, explored, and acted upon within the supportive, connected learning community. The group's interactions invite students to become critical, active learners who make a difference in their own and each other's lives.

## References

Altwerger, B. (1996). *Teaching for social justice in a whole language classroom.* Paper presented at the Whole Language Umbrella Conference, St. Paul, MN, August.

Barnes, D. (1993). Supporting exploratory talk for learning. In K. M. Pierce & C. Gilles (eds.), *Cycles of meaning: Exploring the potential of talk in learning communities* (pp. 17–34). Portsmouth, NH: Heinemann.

Britton, J. (1970). *Language and learning.* London: Allen Lane.

Cherland, M. (1992). Gendered readings: Cultural restraints upon response to literature. *The New Advocate, 5,* 187–198.

Clavell, J. (1981). *The children's story.* New York: Delacorte.

Crafton, L. (1991). *Whole language: Getting started . . . moving forward.* Katonah, NY: Richard C. Owen.

Lowry, L. (1989). *Number the stars.* Boston: Houghton Mifflin.

Lowry, L. (1993). *The giver.* Boston: Houghton Mifflin.

Pinkwater, D. (1977). *The big orange splot.* New York: Hastings House.

Rylant, C. (1985). Slower than the rest. In *Every living thing.* New York: Aladdin Books.

Sadker, M. & Sadker, D. (1994). *Failing at fairness: How America's schools cheat girls.* New York: Charles Scribner's Sons.

Shannon, P. (1995). *text, lies, & videotape.* Portsmouth, NH: Heinemann.

Short, K., Harste, J., & Burke, C. (1995). *Creating classrooms for authors: The reading–writing connection,* 2nd ed. Portsmouth, NH: Heinemann.

Swope, S. (1995). *The araboolies of Liberty Street.* New York: Crown.

Tannen, D. (1990). *You just don't understand: Women and men in conversation.* New York: Ballantine Books.

Vygotsky, L. (1986). *Thought and language.* Cambridge, MA: The MIT Press.

Wells, G. (1986). *The meaning makers: Children learning language and using language to learn.* Portsmouth, NH: Heinemann.

**Bibliography of Related Children's Books**

Bunting, E. (1994). *Smoky night.* San Diego: Harcourt Brace.

Burningham, J. (1985). *Granpa.* New York: Crown.

Clifford, E. (1985). *The remembering box.* Boston: Houghton Mifflin.

dePaola, T. (1989). *The art lesson.* New York: G. P. Putnam's Sons.

Haseley, D. (1991). *Ghost catcher.* New York: HarperCollins.

MacLachlan, P. (1991). *Journey.* New York: Delacorte Press.

Polacco, P. (1988). *The keeping quilt.* New York: Simon & Schuster.

Rylant, C. (1987). *Birthday presents.* New York: Orchard Books.

Van Allsburg, C. (1979). *The garden of Abdul Gazazi.* Boston: Houghton Mifflin.

Van Allsburg, C. (1982). *Ben's dream.* Boston: Houghton Mifflin.

Walsh, E. (1989). *Mouse paint.* New York: Harcourt Brace Jovanovich.

**Penny Silvers**

*Professional resources that have been especially important to me include:*

All books by Nancie Atwell, Lucy Calkins, and Donald Graves.

Bigelow, B. et al., eds. Rethinking our classrooms: Teaching for equity and justice. (1994). A special issue of *Rethinking Schools* (Milwaukee, WI).

Crafton, L. (1996). *Standards in practice grades 1–2.* Urbana, IL: NCTE.

Hill, B., Johnson, N., & Noe, K. (1995). *Literature circles and response.* Norwood, MA: Christopher-Gordon.

Sadker, D., & Sadker, M. (1994). *Failing at fairness: How America's schools cheat girls.* New York: Charles Scribner's Sons.

Short, K., Harste, J., & Burke, C. (1996). *Creating classrooms for authors and inquirers.* 2nd ed. Portsmouth, NH: Heinemann.

Short, K., & Pierce, K. (1990). *Talking about books: Creating literature communities.* Portsmouth, NH: Heinemann.

*Children's books that I especially enjoy using with children include:*

Bunting, E. (1994). *Smoky night.* San Diego, CA: Harcourt Brace.

Buss, F. L. (1991). *Journey of the sparrows.* New York: Lodestar Books.

Byars, B. C. (1977). *The pinballs.* New York: Harper & Row.

Creech, S. (1994). *Walk two moons.* New York: HarperCollins.

Dorris, M. (1992). *Morning girl.* New York: Hyperion Books for Children.

Dorris, M. (1994). *Guests.* New York: Hyperion Books for Children.

Filipovic, Z. (1994). *Zlata's diary.* New York: Viking Press.

Fox, M. (1994). *Tough Boris.* San Diego, CA: Harcourt Brace Jovanovich.

Lowry, L. (1989). *Number the stars.* Boston: Houghton Mifflin.

Lowry, L. (1993). *The giver.* Boston: Houghton Mifflin.

Paterson, K. (1978). *The great Gilly Hopkins.* New York: Crowell.

Paterson, K. (1987). *The bridge to Terabithia.* Newark: HarperCollins.

Pinkwater, D. (1993). *The big orange splot.* New York: Scholastic.

Spinelli, J. (1991). *There's a girl in my hammerlock.* New York: Simon & Schuster Books for Young Readers.

Swope, S. (1995). *The Araboolies of Liberty Street.* New York: Crown.

# 5 Story Time as a Magical Act Open Only to the Initiated: What Some Children Don't Know about Power and May Not Find Out

**Karen Gallas**
Brookline Public Schools, Brookline, Massachusetts

As a first- and second-grade teacher and the parent of two grown children, I know the importance of reading to preschool children to prepare them for formal reading instruction in school. In my classroom, story time has always been a habitual practice, a routine that is a central part of the literacy program. Over the years, however, I have had many students who were not read to at home. At first, they usually struggled with reading and, as a result, with other subjects. Often, the students were poor, their home life unstable, or both. I attributed their difficulties with school to some nebulous combination of circumstances resulting from poverty and believed that their socioeconomic legacies exerted a tremendous, perhaps insurmountable, obstacle to success in school. In my mind, their lack of exposure to storybooks loomed large as a seminal literacy gap, that is until I met Denzel, a 7-year-old African American boy. Until then, I had never examined the deep, symbolic meaning of storybook reading as a critical literacy event.

Reprinted from *Language Arts* 74 (April 1997): 248–254. Used by permission.

## Denzel

Although I normally have students for first and second grades, Denzel came to my class as a second grader. He was nearly 7 and was one of the healthiest students I have ever taught. He was not sick, hungry, tired, or hurt. He had no learning disabilities or handicapping conditions. He came to school well-dressed, well-fed, and well-rested, and was much loved by his working-class family. In fact, ten family members, including his mother, father, brothers, sisters, cousins, and nephews, lived in a four-bedroom apartment. Denzel knew more about the intricacies of his family tree than I knew about mine.

Denzel was also serious about school and worked hard to please his teachers. Therefore, I was surprised early in the school year when he would not listen to stories during our daily read-aloud time. It was a problem that began in September and lasted until June, and it perplexed me for three years. This article describes my year-long effort to help Denzel understand the purpose of storybook reading, and it also relates my efforts as a teacher-researcher to understand both his and my beliefs about reading. The article examines story time or the read-aloud experience, an implicit part of early education, for what it says about educational equity, for who has access to this equity, and for what our assumptions about the transparency of classroom rituals may deny some students. My interaction with Denzel and my ruminations about how better to serve him helped me to peel back the layers of story time, asking what it means to listen to a story being read aloud and to look at the pictures in the book, what are the intrinsic implications for reading and receiving other kinds of texts that are embedded in this activity, and what assumptions have we made about the "naturalness" of this activity for children.

## Research Perspective

It is common for teachers' questions to be borne of the prosaics of everyday classroom observations. The contextual nature of such observations are often presented as anecdotes that are embodied with the observer's assumptions about the event. For example, I made the following observation in September:

> Denzel and I have a problem: He won't listen to story. Won't look at the pictures either. This just makes me crazy. He's a good little kid, and I can't for the life of me engage him in story time no matter what book we use or what devices I muster.

To someone unfamiliar with the context of the event in this anecdote, this entry in my field notes might suggest that something is wrong with the student or with my teaching. The anecdote isn't complete, but it does raise some questions.

Yet, before considering any questions, I must consider the origin of the observation. As Bakhtin pointed out, the unfolding of the ordinary events of daily life, of life's prosaics, has much to offer our understanding of a language, a culture, a social milieu (Morson & Emerson, 1990). Observations that describe points of rupture in the life of the classroom, points of confusion, missteps, or even chaos give access to the moments when teacher intention, as it is embodied in a method, encounters the prosaic world of the students' daily life. What Bakhtin called the "unfinalizability" of human discourse—the understanding that each new human encounter cannot rely on past scripts but rather must be freshly and mutually constructed in the moment—is captured in such moments.

My inquiry into storybook reading began with this perspective, but it is important to note that my efforts to understand why Denzel didn't like story time did not result in a clear solution or resolution. He never fully participated in story time as a whole-class activity. However, my lack of success in trying to get him to participate is instructive. It magnifies the value of classroom inquiry as it examines the meanings of habitual practices, and it helps us to consider pathways to equity for all students.

## The Setting

I teach in an urban school that has a multiracial, multiethnic, and multilingual student population. There are approximately thirty-two different languages—and hence nationalities—represented in the K–8 population of about five hundred students. In my class of twenty-two students, four of them were non-English speakers. I had East Asian, African American, and Hispanic/Latino students. The Asian and Caucasian students were primarily from professional, middle, and upper middle-class families, while the African American and Latino students were from working-class families.

The classroom mix makes for a diverse site of inquiry. I have students who have had enriched home lives in terms of literacy preparation: They have been read two and three books daily since early childhood and have regular exposure to museums, the arts, and cultural events. I also have students who speak little or no English and have just emigrated from foreign countries. Some of these students are true immigrants, settling permanently in the United States, and others are here for only a few years while their parents pursue university degrees. I also have what I term less-privileged students whose families are on public assistance or live in homeless shelters or whose families struggle but remain on the edges of poverty. Some of these students have also been exposed to reading at an early age. However, others, like Denzel, have no preschool reading experience and may not have attended kindergarten.

## Denzel in Second Grade

From the start, Denzel and I agreed that he needed to learn to read. He did not go to kindergarten, but he did learn some prereading skills in first grade, where he received Chapter I reading services as well as individualized instruction. Those interventions continued in second grade. When I met Denzel, he knew the letters of the alphabet, how to count, and some basic phonics skills. He set out with a vengeance to learn to read. All year, Denzel read and reread texts, constantly applying newly acquired phonetic and print understandings to the process.

Most teachers agree that reading is more than saying the words in a story. Reading includes understanding word meanings, and, as children get older, understanding the nuances of a story. Although he made it his goal to learn to read, there were times when not knowing the meaning of words frustrated Denzel's efforts. For example, he loved fairy tales such as *Little Red Riding Hood, The Three Bears, The Ugly Duckling, Thumbelina,* and *The Princess and the Pea,* but he was not familiar with them until I introduced them to him. There were many words of importance that he tried to read but could not—words such as *cupboard, shawl, porridge, swan,* for example—and, therefore, he stumbled over them. However, not knowing word meanings is a common problem for many new readers, especially those who do not have strong literacy backgrounds. I knew strategies that would help Denzel learn new words, and he willingly participated. In fact, he began to use his mastery of the books to acquire new vocabulary.

## Denzel and Story Time

From the day Denzel walked into my classroom, he purposefully set out to learn to read. In contrast, however, he did not see a purpose for story time and listening during read-aloud. If he was not coaxed through a story in either a one-on-one or small group situation, with the context for all events in the text made apparent and the reading made a social event,

Denzel would not participate. Variations in subject matter, narrative style, illustrations, main characters, or any other alterations we made in reading strategies and selections of texts had no affect on his participation. Denzel simply was not interested in hearing stories read aloud.

If the book read aloud was not familiar to Denzel or was one he had not heard before in a more intimate setting, he would not listen to the story or look at the pictures. He would sit doubled over with his head tucked between his knees or would gradually move beyond the group and direct attention elsewhere. Although he was not disrespectful or disruptive, he was clearly impatient with story time and often told us so before or after a reading. If we tried to engage him in conversation about the book to see if he had been listening, his remarks usually indicated that he was not paying attention.

Denzel's behavior is something that teachers might expect from a kindergartner or possibly a first grader. With a second grader who was already at a disadvantage academically, but who clearly worked hard, this behavior is a great concern. I knew Denzel took reading, books, and his teachers' efforts seriously, but he did not see the relationship between our whole-class practice of storybook reading and his own goals as a reader.

My earliest reactions to Denzel's behavior ranged from irritation to bewilderment. Because I couldn't characterize his resistance as a challenge to my authority, I examined his ability to listen and attend in other areas. He seemed to have no problems beyond his inability to listen during read-alouds. Thus, I began to question my own reaction to his inattention. I began to question the deeper implications of story reading and think about its purpose within the framework of school. I asked myself why it was important for Denzel to listen to stories and to look at pictures and what did I think was happening when students listened intently to a story.

My first strategy was to talk to Denzel to find out what he understood about books, asking him whether he was read to at home (he wasn't) and if he understood what books were for. The following excerpt is from our discussions of what books are for.

> *Denzel:* (Thinks a long time.) Books make you read more.
>
> *Gallas:* Books make you read more. But what do you do with them? Why do we even have them?
>
> *Denzel:* So you can learn how to read. You look at the books, and so that you know the words. And for little kids to look at the pages.

> *Gallas:* Do grown-ups ever use books? Do you ever see grown-ups using books?
>
> *Denzel:* To practice reading. In case they forget some words.

I realized during this conversation that he did not understand the purpose of storybook reading beyond an instrumental word mastery function. The stories, or the real, imaginative fictions, that he thought *were* worth listening to were part of sharing time when he and other students told "fake" stories. Denzel actively and skillfully participated in the sharing of personal stories. Storybooks, however, were not associated with "reading" as he understood it. Reading was where you would "look at the books, and so that you know the words." During read-aloud time, he could only see the book's pictures; he could not follow along with the words on the page, which seemed to be necessary for reading to be worthwhile to him. Denzel's response to my questions about books made complete sense within the context of his experience with books, which he saw as utilitarian, or a means to an end. In this sense, his not participating in read-alouds was understandable. Knowing this, I asked: "How could I add to his understanding of storybook reading?" and "What was missing from his interpretation of what storybook reading means?"

## Storybook Reading as Ritual

A few weeks after Denzel and I discussed what books are for, a colleague who had been reading with him once a week on a regular basis said that Denzel had told her that he thought every book in the classroom was handmade. It occurred to me that for students like Denzel, who have not been exposed to books and intimate readings with family, books and events associated with them must seem mysterious. Indeed, the whole event of hearing a story read aloud must seem magical. Imagine being in kindergarten or first grade for the first time, and a woman whom you probably only recently met makes everyone sit down on the floor in a group or in a circle while she sits in a tall chair. Everyone looks up at her and is quiet. She picks up this object, which you know is called a book but which no one has ever explained what it is for or does, and she opens it, holds it up in the air, and begins speaking. Some of the words you have never heard before. As she speaks, she points to the pictures and turns the pages Then she closes the book and puts it back, and the next day, at the same time, she does the same thing again, but probably with a different book.

If you're an uninitiated participant in this ritual, you may think it is magical. How does she know the words? Where do the words come from? Where do the pictures come from? In fact, where does the book come from? As the questions multiply, it is easy to realize how precarious the assumptions that I made about students' understandings of books and the event of story time were. I assumed that all students were like my children, were like me, were like my friends and their children, and that they understood everything about books and their purpose as cultural objects when they entered school.

## "The Look"

Realizing that Denzel may have a different perspective on story time than my other students, I examined what the other students in my class—the already-initiated students—did to listen to stories. First, I noticed they became still, then their eyes glazed over, their mouths dropped open, and they took on what I call "the look." "The look" struck me as being slightly zombie-like or being mesmerized by the story and the pictures. As I read, the students examined pictures carefully. For example, if I turned the page too fast, they protested, often requesting a second look at the page. As I read, the students did not move for almost the entire story, unless there was an exciting or disturbing transition that took place in the plot. Then they gasped, moaned, or squealed. Their hands covered their eyes and mouths in fear or suspense.

All of these gestures were reactions to being inside of the story. Chapter books without pictures had the same effect, only students looked directly at me as I read, their faces reflecting "the look." If the books were nonfiction texts, "the look" was slightly different: brows furrowed in concentration, questions silently but sometimes audibly mouthed, but bodies still and mouths opened. I asked myself, "What does 'the look' mask?" and "What's happening in their heads?" I responded from my own experience as a reader and listener: The students were allowing themselves to be transported to another time and place; they were engaged in an imaginative exercise. In fact, the books *were* magical, producing an altered state of being.

I began to understand my motives for wanting Denzel to participate in story time. I also began to clarify what was not happening for him and tried to talk to him about some of those things, but we made little progress.

In late January, as she gathered the class for story, Denzel asked my intern, "Why do I have to listen to story? Couldn't I just read a book by myself?" She, as frustrated as I was by that time, asked the other students the same questions. Their comments implied that story time offered a window into this magical activity, into a different place and time. The following excerpt presents some of the students' responses to why we listen to stories. Although Denzel did not say anything during this discussion, he listened.

*Mia:* Because, so you can calm down a little after you've been running around, like at recess.

*Donna:* It makes, like, your, some of the teachers want your imagination to, like, let go, because sometimes . . .

*Latia:* To learn things.

*Kelly:* To read much better and listen.

*Nate:* To help you concentrate.

*Latia:* If you listen, you'll know how to read the words better because stories have been told to people for centuries and centuries, and the people pass them on, and it calms them down.

*Charles:* It gets them still and interested in what you're reading. Well, I think that when you listen to a story you can learn new words, and like, you can learn a lot from stories, and people that don't understand things, they can learn words.

*Mia:* By reading stories you can also tell it to other people, and you can pass it on, and it becomes a big story.

*Matt:* One story has probably been passed on for centuries and centuries and they change them.

*Charles:* Can you explain that a little more?

*Matt:* Like, somebody thought of a story, and they passed it on to somebody and each person changed it a little.

*Yuan:* I think we read stories because we have to pass things on. It' not like we're immortals or anything, we have to pass it on. Just think about how bad the world would be without language, and then just flip it back to stories. 'Cause stories would just die out.

*Eli:* But you don't have to pass them on.

*Yuan:* But if we forget about stories and how to make them?

*Eli:* But we could just make new ones.

*Matt:* But Eli, if we don't know the old ones, how can we make the new ones?

The excerpt suggests the nature of the other students' understanding of story and what the purpose of story time was to them. Stories transport them, presenting cultural, perhaps even archetypal, knowledge and memory. At the least, stories teach them things. This is what "the look" embodies.

## Reading a Text

I began to think again about what it means to "read" a text. And what, in fact, is a text. Bakhtin (1986) defines text as "any coherent complex of signs . . . even the study of art deals with texts" (p. 103). Thus, words in a children's book are only one part of the text to be read. The pictures also tell the story. All the students in the class except Denzel habitually scrutinized every picture in a book and had long discussions about the implication of the pictures.

As I thought more about "the look," and talked at length with Denzel about why I wanted him to look at the pictures in books, I realized that the practice of carefully "reading" pictures is essential for mastering many subjects. For example, when we look at a painting, we are "reading" a text; when we study biology, we "read" the slides under the microscope; we learn to "read" maps, graphs, music, and equations. Each of these readings gives us a different kind of knowledge. There are probably many more examples of texts that could be mentioned, but the point is that in all of these "readings" we must learn to use "the look" to penetrate the meaning of a text. And further, in many of these readings what we are doing is using our imagination to place us in another space, another time, another framework. To really read a text, read it with understanding and insight, we must move inside of the text, pulling our lives along with us and incorporating the text and our lives into a new understanding of the world. Anything less is not a complete and informed reading. Anything less is only peeking, or browsing, or dallying with a text. I wanted Denzel to get "the look," because the look meant he might use his imagination and the text to move to places he had not been, to read himself into worlds and discourses he would need to master.

My efforts to bring Denzel into story time as an active participant continued all year. For example, when we studied Native Americans, Denzel never fully embraced and involved himself in the study. He remained cooperative but detached from the activities. As with story time, he was physically present and well-behaved, but he was unable to take advantage of the many reference books and artifacts we gathered as resources for learning. In math, when presented with materials such as Cuisenaire rods whose specific application to mathematics was not obvious, Denzel remained distant and skeptical, voicing his opinion that they were not "real math." At different times in the year, when presented with an unfamiliar organism or event in science, Denzel could not see the phenomenon. This kind of separation occurred in virtually every subject, and we labored together, with inconsistent results, to help him understand my intentions as teacher and the uses that other kinds of "texts" might have for him as learner.

## Analysis

Children bring different social and cultural understandings of print to school (Cochran-Smith, 1984; Heath, 1982, 1983, 1986; Heath & Thomas, 1984; Ninio & Bruner, 1976; Scollon & Scollon, 1981; Taylor, 1983; Teale, 1986; Wolf & Heath, 1992). Introductions to literature and story are social processes, framed, orchestrated, and scaffolded by the parent and the family in ways that reflect not one pervasive cultural understanding of story but specific cultural orientations that may or may not resonate with that of the school. Some of those understandings can be characterized as being either embedded in the events of everyday life, as contextualized, or disembedded and separate from the events of daily life, or decontextualized. Signs, shopping lists, notes, letters, and directions are examples of contextualized print that children use every day in their lives. Storybooks, however, are decontextualized because not only do they present imaginary worlds, but for some children like Denzel, they are not used outside of school.

Heath (1983) suggests that the stories told in the African American community of Trackton were embedded in the close social networks of family and friends, and reading was used to further the day-to-day functioning of home, neighborhood, and work. Reading, for the Trackton children, was instrumental and contextualized, and the transition to school presented them with different "notions of truth, style, and language appropriate to a 'story'" (p. 294). Denzel's understanding of reading and story time reflects a similar dichotomy: Books are for learning how to read, but stories are dramatic events that further social interactions. Story time in my classroom fell into the category of reading and books, while personal stories were exchanged in sharing time or among friends.

Rosenblatt (1978), in describing how readers approach texts, contrasts "efferent" and "aesthetic" readings. These categories add further distinctions to the notion of contextualized and decontextualized texts. The efferent reader "concentrates on what the symbols designate, what they may be contributing to the end result that he seeks," while the aesthetic reader's "primary purpose is fulfilled during the reading event, as he fixes his attention on the actual experience he is living through" (p. 27). These contrasts remind me of the contrasting images of Denzel and the other students in my class. Denzel was disengaged, looking to master both the mechanics of reading ("what the symbols designate") and listening for practical information. The other students, however, caught within the grasp of "the look," were "living through" the events of the text. Their engagement was, I believe, evocative of Coleridge's (1907) "willing suspension of disbelief" (p. 6), a position that places trust in the ability of texts to expand our experience of the world from the utilitarian to the transcendent. That position was not one that Denzel could take.

## Conclusion

My questions and reflections about the nature and purposes of storybook reading have not changed my belief that such activities as story time and read-aloud are critical to achieving full literacy across a wide variety of disciplines. Full literacy means a deep, decontextualized, and aesthetic appreciation and understanding of texts, including those that seem odd or unfamiliar. Every student should be offered the opportunity to engage in the subject matter of every discipline. In other words, every student should have the opportunity to acquire the many different discourses that will make him or her successful in school and in life. Such a multiple literacy approach to schooling proposes that each subject or discipline studied requires different kinds of expressive and receptive language functions. Within this framework, the process of education, from kindergarten through graduate school, is one of mastering different discourses at increasing levels of complexity.

For me, then, discourse acquisition is the lynchpin of schooling; it is the point at which real educational equity occurs. It is more than, for example, learning the names and dates of events in history or regurgitating the main themes in a short story. It is learning to walk, talk, write, think, and perhaps even dress like a historian, a writer, a mathematician, or a scientist. It is more than memorizing facts on a test. It is more than sitting through a fifty-minute class three times a week and taking notes. It is a way of being in the world. The more ways of being you acquire, the more discourses you master, the more easily you move through the different strata of society and the world. The process of discourse acquisition is something that I see myself initiating for some students, but, quite frankly, it is something that some middle and many upper middle-class children come to school already having experienced. They have a head start in learning new discourses. Their home life has already started them on the road of potentially mastering *many* different discourses. It is not that these children are more capable than other children; it is simply that they have more access to educational achievement because of personal resources and preschool experiences.

Thus, from the time children enter the classroom, there is a basic inequity in schooling that goes beyond readiness to read or developmental issues. This inequity cannot necessarily be neatly addressed by special intervention programs such as Reading Recovery or Chapter I reading programs because these programs address more narrow, competency-based goals that toe at the edges of literacy. Remedial programs can fill in the gaps in the skill areas of language arts or mathematics by striving to bring the achievement of disadvantaged students up to grade level, and they are clearly helpful for some students. But reading or math skills are only the skin of the literacy process. The process of real literacy acquisition is a much more complex and intricately constructed corpus. An understanding of the nuances of this process may prove to be critical to the achievement of real literacy for all children.

With consistent drill and practice, Denzel mastered the basic skills of reading and writing, but I knew that he was an intelligent, serious student for whom I was not building a bridge between skill and depth of understanding; I was not moving him from dabbling in a discourse to fully engaging in it. My failing in Denzel's case was a failing of purpose, a contextual failing around a decontextualized activity. In other words, in our time together Denzel never understood the purpose of storybook reading in the larger framework of his possible life history. I was not able to persuade him to enter the worlds created by good literature or to engage him in other texts that would open other worlds of experience and understanding.

When the year ended, I understood, in part, why I could not help Denzel. The basis of our failure was my inability to comprehend the nature of Denzel's imaginal world and to enter it and find ways to bring him into the world of the storybook. Although that realization came too late for me and Denzel, it forced me to reconfigure my classroom approach to storybook reading, and it also set me on another path of investigation that will enable me to better serve students like

Denzel, some of whom I have in first grade. I must now consider how to gain access to their imaginal worlds, how to help bridge the gap between their "now," or the prosaics of their lives, and the new worlds of the texts I want them to enter.

This year, I have Tommy, a Caucasian child from a working-class family who also has not been read to at home and does not listen during story time. I noticed this during the first day of school. He is eager, healthy, and respectful but has difficulty understanding the purpose or intention of a lesson in any new area. For example, in math, Tommy, like Denzel, does not easily master new strategies for computation in addition, such as counting up or using Cuisenaire rods. After thinking so long about Denzel and considering how I might have taught him better, I have changed several aspects of how I structure my classroom and my teaching to target Tommy's needs as I perceive them. For example, I offer many more opportunities for retelling of stories using drama, art, and storyboards. I have allotted more time to basic expressive opportunities like building with blocks, painting, clay work, and especially creative dramatics to help all the students develop personal narratives about new topics or texts that we are studying in all subjects.

I am using these structures in the hope that they will help Tommy and other "at-risk" students find different ways to understand new subject matter and to engage in experiences that seem disconnected from their lives. In essence, as a teacher-researcher, although I initially focused on a specific problem because of my inability to reach and understand one student, that focus has changed the way I teach all students.

## References

Bakhtin, M. M. (1986). *Speech genres and other late essays.* Austin, TX: The University of Texas Press.

Cochran-Smith, M. (1984). *The making of a reader.* Norwood, NJ: Ablex.

Coleridge, S. T. (1907). *Biographia literaria.* London: Oxford University Press.

Heath, S. B. (1982). What no bedtime story means: Narrative skills at home and school. *Language in Society, 11,* 49–76.

Heath, S. B. (1983). *Ways with words: Language, life, and work in communities and classrooms.* New York: Cambridge University Press.

Heath, S. B. (1986). Separating "things of the imagination" from life: Learning to read and write. In W. H. Teale & E. Sulzby (eds.), *Emergent literacy: Writing and reading* (pp. 156–172). Norwood, NJ: Ablex.

Heath, S. B., & Thomas, C. (1984). The achievement of preschool literacy for mother and child. In H. Goelman, A. Oberg, & F. Smith (eds.), *Awakening to literacy* (pp. 51–72). Exeter, NH: Heinemann.

Morson, G. S., & Emerson, C. (1990). *Mikhail Bakhtin: Creation of a prosaics.* Stanford, CA: Stanford University Press.

Ninio, A., & Bruner, J. S. (1976). The achievement and antecedents of labeling. *Journal of Child Language, 5,* 1–15.

Rosenblatt, L. (1978). *The reader, the text, the poem: The transactional theory of literary work.* Carbondale, IL: Southern Illinois University Press.

Scollon, R., & Scollon, B. K. (1981). *Narrative, literacy and face in inter-ethnic communication.* Norwood, NJ: Ablex.

Taylor, D. (1983). *Family literacy: Young children learning to read and write.* Portsmouth, NH: Heinemann.

Teale, W. H. (1986). Home background and young children's literacy development. In W. H. Teale & E. Sulzby (eds.), *Emergent literacy: Writing and reading* (pp. 173–204). Norwood, NJ: Ablex.

Wolf, S. A., & Heath, S. B. (1992). *The braid of literature: Children's worlds of reading.* Cambridge, MA: Harvard University Press.

## Bibliography

**Karen Gallas**

*Professional resources that have been especially important to me include:*

Ashton-Warner, S. (1963). *Teacher.* New York: Simon & Schuster.

Cazden, C. B. (1988). *Classroom discourse: The language of teaching and learning.* Portsmouth, NH: Heinemann.

Heath, S. B. (1983). *Ways with words: Language, life, and work in communities and classrooms.* New York: Cambridge University Press.

*Children's books that I especially enjoy using with children include:*

Wood, A. (1987). *Heckedy Peg.* San Diego, CA: Harcourt Brace Jovanovich.

# 6 Stepping Stones: Literature in the Classroom

**Cecilia Espinosa**
Machan Elementary School, Phoenix, Arizona

**Julia Fournier**
Machan Elementary School, Phoenix, Arizona

In this chapter, Cecilia and Julia, both bilingual teachers, respond to Jane and Judith's questions about children's literature in their classrooms.

*There's so much children's literature out there nowadays. How do you choose books for your classroom?*

**J:** I think when we look for books for our classrooms, we're thinking about helping children develop an understanding of literature. We want the books to be really strong aesthetically, but along with the books being beautiful—gorgeous to look at and engaging to hear—we want them also to raise questions in the children's minds. We want the children to feel they're included in the story, that this book is not about issues that are not connected to them. It's not about people that are not connected to them. It's important that the literature that we use has some kind of opening for our children to enter, that it offers the possibility of being a stepping stone to larger ideas and to the world outside and around them.

*How do you get started with the children—I mean, at the beginning of the year?*

**J:** To begin with, you need to have some really, really, really good chapter books I think. Because for me, the chapter books become like an anchor in the room where we can refer back to them all throughout the year, because it's an experience we're all sharing together at the same time.

**C:** In our class, we start the year with lots of picture books—things about community and taking care of each other. The whole idea at the beginning of the year is to start building a history together, both for Spanish speakers and English speakers, to learn about each other's language and also about each other's literature (insofar as they can have access to each other's literature). But the whole idea is building a solid foundation together, so we spend a lot of time doing that at the beginning.

**J:** Starting the first or second week, every day we read aloud. In my class, we have an ongoing chapter book, and it's a challenge—not just with the chapter books, it's also a challenge with the picture books you select for the first couple of weeks of school—because you want the kids to know that when they sit down to listen to a story, it's going to be really good and that they're going to do a lot of thinking because the book is going to bring up a lot of thoughts that they're going to want to talk about. Sometimes I start the book by saying, "Can I tell you why I really love this book?" I guess this puts a little bias on it by telling them that, but I want them to be really hooked into wanting to read the book and hear the book from the very beginning.

*Some of the teachers I know are rather casual about reading aloud to their kids. It becomes a kind of filler—"Let's see. I've got ten minutes before lunch," or "I'd better read a little to settle the kids down after recess so we can get on with our work"—that sort of thing. But as I listen to you two, I get the feeling that you take reading aloud pretty seriously, that sharing children's literature occupies a prominent place in the life of your classrooms. You seem to see literature as contributing in a major way to building classroom community, but also as contributing significantly to individuals' learning.*

**J:** You're right. We really do feel this way. But you can't just grab a book, start reading to the kids, and watch wonderful things happen. There's no magic about this. I learned the hard way that you can't just read books and expect that kids are going to talk about them in meaningful ways just because you're reading a good book. That's what we were told when we started a literature-based focus at our school. You know, we had the experts telling us, "Oh, just read really good books and the kids will just say great things." Well, it wasn't happening. It takes a lot of work to help the kids develop what they know about literature into ways of talking about it interestingly and productively in the classroom. Even after years of teaching, it still takes a lot of thought and mental preparation to know exactly why you're reading this book or why this book is going to fit. You could buy me ten really good books and I could never read them to myself before I read them to the class. So when I read them to the class, they'd just be nothing because I hadn't prepared like, "What questions am I going to ask, what questions does this raise?" Knowing my class ahead of time—what questions they've asked about other books, and what kinds of discussions we've had—helps me know ahead of time what connections they're going to make.

Let me tell you about a terrible experience I had when I didn't read the book myself first before reading it to the kids. One day we came back from the nursing home, and we had not had a very good experience there. The kids had been really disengaged from the people there and they said that. I was saying, "Why weren't you talking to them? Why aren't you engaging with the residents?" The children said, "Well, I just don't have anything to talk to them about." So some other children suggested that we read some biographies that would put us in touch with the lives of those people when they were younger, like when they were young adults or when they were teenagers. The children thought that by reading about people, they would find something in common with the residents. Some of the suggestions were for Amelia Earhart, Babe Ruth, Shirley Temple. Well, Babe Ruth was the easiest one to find. There were several Babe Ruth books at the bookstore, and of course I didn't have time to read all of them. I had seen one of them before, so I picked that one up and I took it to school. I didn't read it ahead of time. It was horrible. It was completely reconstructed conversations—very unreal, perfect situations—and the kids saw right through it, and it was not engaging at all. It was just not interesting, and you know, it was totally my fault. I hadn't read the book beforehand, and I guess that is the perfect way to have a terrible experience. So many teachers do that, and I just don't understand how they can do it. I mean, there is nothing worse than reading a book out loud and all of a sudden realizing there's something very controversial, and you're in the middle of the book. I mean, what do you do? You really need to read the book beforehand. The next book we read was Amelia Earhart, and it was a wonderful biography of her life, and so that had the opposite effect. That biography engaged the children, and they were excited to go and talk to the residents about that.

**C:** Of course the literature that we use in our classroom affects the rest of our lives at school, and that makes the literature important. But I think that it also affects our everyday lives and the way we lead our lives. It affects the way we relate to each other. I think that it's the same way with adults: When you read a good book, the book changes you and affects you in many ways, and you understand many more things; so after reading the book, you're a changed person. I think that it's the same way with the children. The whole idea is for literature to change us, to affect us, to touch us.

**J:** Yes. We were reading the autobiography of Helen Keller. We got to the place where it talks about the first time she made a connection between the word that was being spelled into her hand and the abstract concept. It was love. And all of a sudden, she knew what it was, and it was just this weird connection, and the kids—that was such a wild idea for them to understand, what the difference between something concrete and something abstract was and how difficult it would be to learn something like love if you couldn't see and you couldn't hear. It was really interesting because it's like what you said: The literature we use in our classroom changes the way they see things forever.

**C:** When discussing literature with the whole group, I think it's really important to be sure that everybody has a voice. Every child needs to feel validated, and every child needs to know that everybody has something to share and that what is important is listening to each other—listening to what other people have to say, but also knowing that *you* have something to say. Sometimes it's really hard to validate every child's contribution. I'm thinking of one time, in my classroom, when a student in the class brought a coloring book of *The Three Little Pigs* and he wanted me to read it to the class. I was so hesitant to read it because it wasn't what I would think of as a great book to read to the whole group. But the student kept insisting that I read it to the class. He said that he had brought his book and that I should read it to the class. So I ended up reading it, and while I was reading it, I realized how important it was to read this book that the child had brought from home. It was probably the only one or else one of just a few books that the child had. So the whole idea is accepting what the children bring and building from there.

*Does all your literature sharing and discussion take place as a whole group? Do the kids ever interact in smaller literature discussion groups?*

**C:** Well, at the beginning of my teaching career, I tried doing literature studies the way we had been taught to, and soon I realized that my children hadn't read as many books as one person needs to have read to have a discussion like that. For some of the children, our read-alouds are the very first experiences they've had with books. It takes a lot of reading experiences to develop a knowledge of literature. I think about how many books it took me to read or how many movies it took me to watch to start recognizing certain literary elements. So I think that what we're doing in our classes is trying to build a history of books that we have read together, an abundance of books. And we're modeling for the children how to talk about books. And of course we're also learning from how the children respond to the books. So there's a lot of read-aloud in the class.

**J:** The people who were the experts in literature study, who were sort of modeling for us what literature studies were supposed to look like, were people who had been working with teachers in real middle-class environments or teachers working with older children. Those children already have thousands of experiences with print behind them. But we've got kids coming every single day, new from Mexico, that have never ever held a bound book in their hands.

**C:** Or even kids who live here but whose families don't use a lot of books.

**J:** Right. So we're continually having to consider those children who are building their knowledge base. I mean, you can't compare one book to another book if you haven't read another book. So we spend a lot of time just reading and sharing and reading and sharing books, but not necessarily doing literature study groups.

**C:** What I notice this year is that the children enjoy reading books together in small groups, but I don't dare to call that literature studies. But they like to get some books that I have several copies of and read the book together and talk about the book, and they can spend five to six days on the same book—taking turns reading it, teaching each other to read the book. I'm not always sitting there with them. I come in and out of the groups, acting as a facilitator, checking with the children. That seems to be working really well in my classroom this year. The whole idea is just people coming together to enjoy reading a book and talking about it, but it's not led by a teacher or someone else. As the year progresses, we "study" different books or themes—like civil rights or empowering children, something like that. We'll spend days and weeks really thinking about the ideas a book presents, and then we'll find other books with similar themes. So the books are stepping stones to new ideas, and then the child refers back to those ideas in discussing new literature.

**J:** Over the years, my ideas about literature study have changed. I feel that children who are six, seven, eight years old are capable of intense intellectual discussions. But in the ten years I have been teaching at Machan and have been doing literature discussions, I have found that these intellectual exchanges usually occur during other times of the day, not necessarily during literature study time—sometimes [they occur] during problem solving time, or meeting time when we're talking about social and political events. It seems that children are most involved and engaged intellectually at this age when the ideas are directly related to their lives. So what students will do during literature discussions is share a parallel personal experience or their favorite part of the story. Those seem to be the most common. They'll just give general responses to the literature. In the past, that's how my literature studies would go. Sometimes the discussions would become more intense, where the kids were actually exchanging ideas and listening to each other, but all the students weren't being involved in this way and the involvement wasn't with every book. So now I try to lay down a bit more expectation ahead of time. I'd say the groups would ideally be seven or eight (but usually they're more), and the expectation is that everyone will share his or her general impression. We just go around the circle and everybody talks about his or her general impression of the book and then, after that, a favorite part. I know that that's what they want to share, and so I just do it up front and get it out of the way first so that it's not the only thing that the discussions can center around. Then, once the students have shared and have had a voice in a circular way, I give them a question (or several) to think about. Depending on the group, we may read the book over again with the questions in mind. I like the questions to come from the general impressions or favorite parts that the students have shared. And I would say that the group dynamics are just as important as the piece of literature you choose. You want those kinds of kids in your group that always draw ideas together, but you don't want them to overpower the more reserved children. So I like the practice of all sharing in the beginning, and at the same time that they're sharing, I'm writing down (next to their names) what they're saying. That just sends a message to the kids that I want to hear everyone, that we all want to hear everyone because everyone's voice is valuable to us. That practice, I think, is very powerful and carries over for the less structured discussion times too—sort of sets up an expectation. I would also say that the better prepared I am and the more focused I am on the words the kids are using, the better the discussion goes.

*So far we've mostly talked about using picture books, chapter books, and biographies with your children. Are there other types of literature you use also?*

**C:** Oh yes. We also have poetry from the very beginning of the school year. We read poetry out loud and discuss it and act it out. And poetry is also in the homework we give. Poetry is really a powerful way to include the parents. It's a very good way to include them, and I find that they respond in a very positive and active way to the poetry that we send home. We send a poem home in English and in Spanish. We try to find parallel poems, but if we can't find this, it's okay. And the children are supposed to read the poem a few times and have somebody read the poem to them, because you hear poetry differently when somebody reads it to you. Then they can talk about the poem and they can write about the poem, they can illustrate the poem, they can copy the poem, they can do a project around the poem, but by having to share it with somebody else at home, it gets another person involved in poetry, so it's a great thing.

One of the most powerful experiences that I've had was with the poetry homework. The grandmother of one of my English-speaking students came to my class and she said, "Do you have another copy of that poem you sent home?' I can't find it. Fernando must have taken it back, and I don't have it. I've been saving all the poems that you send home, and I want you to know that I just love the poems that come from homework. I never heard that kind of Spanish before in my life, and I am reading them to Fernando in Spanish even though he doesn't speak my Spanish, and he's enjoying them and learning Spanish through that. So I want a copy of the poem." That was quite an amazing story for me, because I thought of how she had never heard the poetry of her native language. She was going through life without having access to that.

The great thing about poetry is that it's so easy to make it accessible in the homes of the students. You know, you can type poems, the children can cut the poems out, the children can copy the poems, they can have a poetry notebook at home with the homework. The parents know a lot of the poems, so it's a great way for connecting home and school.

**J:** Poetry is always a part of the classroom, but during certain times of the year there's just a special focus on poetry. Usually this intense focus doesn't happen until we're back from the winter break, but this year the kids in my room are already making their own poetry books [in November], so I know that I'm going to have to start focusing on it and working with reading the poetry of the masters of Spanish language poetry and talking about their lives and their thoughts much earlier than I usually do, just because the kids are already into it. They're already teaching each other, and so I need to be involved in that learning process too.

*One theme that weaves its way through your conversation about literature in your classrooms is your use of Spanish literature with the children. I know you both teach Spanish-speaking children. Can you talk a little more about this part of your literature program?*

**C:** I think it's really important to make Spanish literature come alive in the classroom. Spanish has a really strong and rich tradition in literature, and it didn't just happen when people started translating English children's books into Spanish! Spanish had its own tradition way before.

**J:** I look for Spanish literature for the children in which the language is beautiful, the characters are interesting, the use of time is compelling, the setting is beautiful or interesting or something that the children can relate to, the plot makes the kids think, or the situation that the characters find themselves in is something the kids can relate to or there are some parallels to other books they've read before or to things that have happened in their own lives. I mean, all those are just regular components of literature that, we would just say, make a good book. But when we talk about "good books" as bilingual teachers, our position is more political than another teacher's might be— say someone who teaches in a situation where all the children in the school speak only English and work toward literacy only in English and are from homes where English is the only language spoken. For us, there are other factors in our idea of what makes a book "good" for our classrooms. For us, ethnicity is important. We want books that include the children we teach. There are questions of power here. The power structures and social classes portrayed in many children's books exclude our children. They have no place in those books. So we think about social classes within the book and whether we can see our students as being included.

There's something else we think about, too, in relation to Spanish literature. You know, for a children's book to be marketable in the United States, it has to have a beginning, middle, and end and a definite plot, and everybody has to end up happy with everything resolved and tied up neatly at the end. Well, that just doesn't happen all the time in Spanish language literature, and we need to accept that things like unhappiness and death and tragedy are really powerful and prevalent in Spanish language literature and in the lives of our children as well. If we exclude that literature from our room, we're really taking away part of the Spanish language aesthetic, I think.

**C:** Also, there are different Spanish books that you like for different reasons: because of the complexity of the ideas or the descriptions of the characters or the strong presence of dreams or of fantasy or of magic. In my selection of books, I work really hard at seeing the Spanish-speaking world as much bigger than Mexico or Spain, and including other Latin American countries as well. I am so glad I can provide opportunities for my children to experience literature in two languages. Throughout the day, there are times when we just sit and listen to a Spanish book or an English book as a whole class, and the whole idea is to continue to educate ourselves about each other's language and culture. I want the children—the Spanish-speaking children and the English-speaking children—to get the best possible literature in their native language, but I also want them to learn about each other's literature and to learn to respect it and celebrate it and understand it. And so there are times during the day when I read to the whole class a book in Spanish or a book in English or a poem in Spanish and a poem in English, and the children choose the language that they respond to the reading in. That may be in their native language, even though they have heard the book in their second language.

**J:** Another thing I was thinking of is that at our school, instead of traditional report cards, at the beginning of the year we have goal-setting conferences, and the teacher and the child and the parents sit down together and talk about what things they're going to work on together at school and at home to make happen for the child. We have a lot of English-speaking children who choose to work toward Spanish literacy, saying that they want to learn Spanish. Then one of the ways that they choose to make that happen, is to pick a Spanish-dominant "buddy reader" in the older grades for "buddy reading," and those children then work together. The older one helps the younger one learn Spanish, but many times it works the other way too: The English-dominant younger child helps the Spanish-dominant older child learn English. As far as second language development goes, it seems to me that it happens best and most easily in the least structured times. I see kids learning each other's language a lot during science and during science projects, and a lot during problem-solving times. Of course, on the playground when I'm not seeing it, I know that it's going on. In the morning before school and during playtime in the classroom, I see it happening.

*But you both are bilingual. What if you're a teacher who only speaks English, but you have kids in your classroom who have Spanish (or some other language) as their dominant or only language? You may genuinely*

*value the child's home language and culture and want to (as you say)*
*"include" the child in the literature you choose, but you just don't know*
*the child's language or culture. What can you do?*

**C:** You look for ways to bring people in that can help you strengthen the children's culture and literacy—the literature part, the tradition, all that. This has a lot to do with just not seeing language as a barrier and not seeing people from other cultures as being people that you need to study about.

**J:** Or work around.

**C:** Right. But you need to believe that by working with them, you'll learn about them, if you're really open.

**J:** We have a friend who is a monolingual person, but everybody thinks she's bilingual because she just—she doesn't see language as a barrier. When she's a substitute teacher at our school and a child comes up to her, she doesn't stop and say, "Get a translator" or "Here, let me have someone help." She just lets the child talk. Now, as a teacher, you know it's not like this child is coming up to tell you something that you've never heard before. Chances are it's one of about five things. The child is probably coming up to ask for help, and you know through the child's body language what he or she wants help with. So she can usually figure out the message the child is trying to get across and respond appropriately, like, "Oh here, let this person help you" or "Here, let me get you this pencil." She's so open to the Spanish language, even though she's not anywhere near proficient.

**C:** But if you keep an open mind, there're always people around to help you and to help you learn, and there are resources available. It's just a matter of looking around and talking to a lot of people and making the decision to become informed.

You know, we have to do this, too, because we also include, in our collection of books, books from different places or about different people in different parts of the world. As much as we want to give the children the richness of their own cultures and literature and traditions, we also want them to become aware of and learn about the traditions and literature of other places. When we use the literature of other places, we probably don't have the richness of firsthand experts that we have among the staff, or among the parents at our school who can share their knowledge with us. So if we're reading a Japanese story, our resources are probably going to be limited to a smaller group of people who know about the culture of the book. So the experiences we can provide, even though they'll be there, won't be as rich.

**J:** Both of us have become really careful about doing culture studies that we don't have firsthand knowledge or experience of. We started seeing culture studies like, "Oh, we're going to study Japan" or "Oh, we're going to study China" or whatever, as being really reductionist. You tend to reduce Japanese culture to a few stories and a few little bits of information about clothing and food and celebrations. So we've really gotten away from that. But we have a lot of books in our collection that are about African American children and that are about Native American children, and written by people from those groups.

**C:** And we try to find people who attend conferences where they hear presentations by people who have a firsthand experience about those books or the cultures they present. They can give us information. But you know, you just have to be careful not to present other cultural groups simplistically because you don't know much about them.

*Well, we know that we have an increasing number of Hispanic/Latino children in our classrooms. So suppose you have a (probably monolingual English-speaking) teacher just starting out, and he or she wants to include some excellent Spanish children's literature in his or her classroom library. Where does the teacher begin? What are the "musts"?*

**J:** I guess if you had an amount of money and you were starting from scratch, one of the first things you'd want is poetry. You need to have a lot of poetry, and you need to immerse yourself in reading the poetry so that you start to get a sense of what it is. That means you need to get poetry that's written by the masters—Pablo Neruda, Gabriela Mistral, . . .

**C:** Rubén Darío, Rafael Alberti, Octavio Paz, Federico García Lorca, Juan Ramón Jiménez.

**J:** You need to have a sense of how they wrote, these people who are considered the best of the best in Spanish language poetry. Then, at the same time, you need to have a lot of really fun poetry that's writtten specifically for children, like by María de la Luz Uribe, María Elena Walsh, Gabriela Mistral, Jairo Aníbal Niño, Rafael Pombo, Nicolás Guillén. And then I think it's absolutely necessary to have really, really funny books in the classroom, and serious books, too, that have real life situations, and also books that reflect and honor the oral tradition of Mexico.

*What are some of your own favorites—books you love to share with the children?*

**J:** There are the rabbit stories. Tio Conejo stories exist in all cultures. In Native American cultures in the United States, they're called coyote stories. In the south, they're Brer Rabbit stories. And there're the Jack stories from Appalachia. These are really fun to use with kids, especially when you demonstrate through examples that the stories are the direct ancestors of the cartoons that are on television. I mean, all the plots are exactly the plots that are in Bugs Bunny or Sylvester and Tweety, and that's just so motivating for the kids. They love them, and they ask for these stories over and over again. These stories help them see character development in a very simple way. The rabbit is always up against, for instance, the wolf. If a rabbit and a wolf are up against each other, who's going to end up winning? Well, the answer is, the rabbit is always going to end up using his brain over the wolf's sharp teeth, and he'll outwit the stronger animal, in this example, the wolf. If the rabbit is up against the turtle, who's going to win? Well, the kids know the turtle is going to win because the rabbit is quicker, and somehow the turtle is going to use his perseverance to outsmart the rabbit or just to "outendure" the rabbit. So the children can see that these traditional paradigms of literature are used again and again.

We both really enjoy using nontraditional fairy tales in our class. The first one I really remember being just a total favorite in our classes was the English *True Story of the Three Little Pigs.* I remember, when it came out, everybody thinking it was so funny, and since that time, we have found so many in Spanish—some that were even on our shelves and that we never even realized were there. There's one called *El asunto de mis papás.* It's Red Riding Hood's side of the story. She is upset that out of all the things she has done in her life, she is only known for going to her grandmother's one day and meeting up with the wolf. And then there's *La bruja hermosa,* a book about a smart woman who was beautiful. Because she was smart and beautiful, people said she was a witch, so she went to a place and turned herself ugly so that people would stop bothering her.

And there's another one called *La princesa y el pirata* [by Gómez Cerda] where this princess is singing from a tower—a beautiful song— and she attracts all kinds of famous princes to her tower. Each one is on some sort of quest but is willing to give it up if she'll only agree to be with him. It's just very funny the way it's told, and the kids love to figure out which prince each one is. For example, the princess will say,

"What are you doing here?" The prince will answer, "Well, I'm on my way to kiss a girl who swallowed a poison apple, but you know, if you'll agree to marry me, I'll forget about her." So the kids know that that's Sleeping Beauty's prince. So all these famous princes pass by her tower, and she doesn't want to be tied down by any of them, and she ends up falling in love with a pirate who is free and travels the seas and doesn't offer her a castle.

Another one is *La niña de los tres maridos,* where a princess is told that she has to choose between three suitors, and she asks her dad, "Why do I have to choose just one? I like all three." And the father puts them through some trials. They have to bring back something new and interesting, and the one with the most interesting thing will get to marry his daughter. What happens is that they each end up finding something interesting, and through a set of circumstances, the girl dies and they bring her back to life by putting all three of their powers together. So the girl wakes up and says, "See, Dad? I told you I needed all three of them." We both really like these nontraditional fairy tales where the woman is not powerless, where she makes decisions for herself. We like to tear apart those traditional stereotypes and get the kids to question them. And it's really a very different level of thinking it takes for the child to appreciate a nontraditional fairy tale. They have to have in place an understanding of what constitutes a traditional fairy tale to understand what is nontraditional about the nontraditional fairy tale. What makes it funny? You have to have a very sophisticated understanding of the traditional fairy tale in order to appreciate the humor in a nontraditional fairy tale. One of the most interesting writers in this genre is Adela Turin. Her books have all the traditional elements of a fairy tale. But the women in her stories are in charge of their own destinies. They're not waiting around for a man to show up and awaken them from a hundred years of sleep.

*Wow. There's obviously just so much out there. It feels kind of overwhelming. Obviously what's most important is to love literature yourself, to believe in the importance of children's literature in your classroom, and then to provide plenty of good books and opportunities for reading them. But that's easier said than done. How do you go about building your own classroom collection so that kids have an abundance of good books right there all the time?*

**J:** In our district, the monies are decentralized, so every year we get an amount of money to spend in our classroom. One year it was $1200, another year it was $900. Everything that we're supposed to cover curriculum-wise is supposed to be covered with that money (math,

handwriting). So, since most of us in the past were just buying literature, there are some pretty large collections of books at our school. We
know that it's always going to be easier and cheaper to get books in
English (than Spanish) because of the availability of book clubs and
book sales and book stores and discounts available on English books.
As bilingual teachers, we need to be more creative and resourceful to
get really great book collections. For example, in our school, for years,
whenever anybody's going to visit another country where Spanish is
[spoken as] the first language, people will just give you $100 and say,
"I trust you. Buy $100 worth of books for me."

C: I think the powerful thing has been working together at it—like
keeping an eye on each other's collection, bringing books for each other,
reading the books together, talking about the books.

J: Yeah. When I select new books, I look for something that really draws
me: if the format is interesting, or if the illustrations are beautiful or
thought provoking. I look for the use of language, the use of time, is the
setting interesting, is there a hero or heroine in the book, do they follow
the classic description of a true hero or heroine? And I guess one of the
most important aspects is if the text is inclusive rather than exclusive.

C: Yes. There are books that exclude children just by the nature of the
characters and situations. The situations aren't large enough to include
them, so there's no entry point in that book for some children.

J: Also I ask, "Does the book make you think?"

C: That doesn't mean to say that every book has to be really deep. It
can also be a really stupid and funny book where the children just
relate to it because it's just so stupid and funny. It still stimulates thinking and discussion, and that's what we're looking for. We want books
that really motivate kids to read them again.

J: There are some books that you're going to elevate to special status.
You'll read them in front of the kids or do a literature study with those.
In my class and Cecilia's class, we have maybe (just guessing, and it's
a pretty moderate guess) two thousand books each in English and
Spanish, so of course there are some books in there that are not as good
as other books. But that doesn't mean that some child won't like them
or some child won't identify with them.

C: As a teacher, you have to read as many books as possible and ask
yourself about each book: What is good or not so good about this
book? Other people can't tell you that.

## References

Goytisolo, J. A. (1992). *La bruja hermosa.* Barcelona: Edebé.

Piérola, M. (1991). *El asunto de mis papás.* Barcelona: Ediciones Destino.

Scieszka, J. (1989). *True story of the three little pigs.* NY: Viking.

## Bibliography

### Cecilia M. Espinosa

*Professional resources that have been especially important to me include:*

Carini, P. (1986). *Building from children's strengths.* VT: Prospect Archives and Center for Education and Research.

Edelsky, C. (1991). *With literacy and justice for all: Rethinking the social in language and education.* Bristol, PA: Taylor and Francis.

Edwards, C. P. (1993). *100 languages of children.* Norwood, NJ: Ablex.

Freire, P. (1972). *Pedagogy of the oppressed.* New York: Herder and Herder.

Kohl, H. (1994). *I won't learn from you: And other thoughts on creative maladjustment.* New York: New Press.

Neruda, P. (1977). *Memoirs.* New York: Farrar, Strauss & Giroux.

Wells, G. (1986). *The meaning makers: Children learning language and using language to learn.* Portsmouth, NH: Heinemann.

*Children's books that I especially enjoy using with children include:*

Farías, J. (1994). *El hombre, el árbol y el camino.* Madrid: Ediciones SM.

Gómez Cerda, A. (1991). *La princesa y el pirata.* México, DF: Fondo de Cultura Económica.

Innocenti, R. (1987). *Rosa Blanca.* Salamanca, España: Editorial Lóguez.

Neruda, P. (1994). *Odes to common things.* Boston: Little, Brown.

Snunit, M. (1993). *El pájaro del alma.* México, DF, México: Fondo de Cultura Económica.

## Bibliography

### Julia M. Fournier

*Professional resources that have been especially important to me include:*

Carini, P. (1993). *Images and immeasurables.* North Bennington, VT: Prospect Center.

Freire, P. (1972). *Pedagogy of the oppressed.* New York: Herder and Herder.

Green, M. (1978). *Landscapes of learning.* New York: Teachers College Press.

Kohl, H. (1994). *I won't learn from you: And other thoughts on creative maladjustments.* New York: New Press.

Smith, F. (1986). *Insult to intelligence: The bureaucratic invasion of our classrooms.* New York: Arbor House.

Wells, G. (1986). *The meaning makers: Children learning language and using language to learn.* Portsmouth, NH: Heinemann.

### *Children's books that I especially enjoy using with children include:*

Berenguer, C. (1992). *El rey mocho.* Caracas: Ediciones Ekare.

Farías, J. (1988). *El hijo del jardinero.* Madrid: Ediciones Anaya.

López, C. (1984). *Julieta y su caja de colores.* México: Fondo de Cultura Económica.

Vasconcelos, J. (1971). *Mi planta de naranja-lima.* Buenos Aires: Editorial El Ateneo.

Velthuijs, M. (1991). *Sapo enamorado.* Caracas: Ediciones Ekare.

# II Using Language to Explore the World

You have already been reading about children exploring their world as they read and wrote and talked together. In the articles of the first section, you read about students interviewing (Hoffman and Sharp), students including history research reports in their writing portfolios (McLure and Rief), students observing instances of gender bias in their own school (Silvers). Surely these students were exploring their world through language. And just as surely, the students you'll read about in this section are creating and imagining as they explore their world. Real language—language in use—is always multifaceted. But it is the exploring aspect we draw special attention to in the six articles that comprise this section.

The six are remarkably diverse. You'll find kindergartners carrying out individual research projects (Seifert), sixth graders engaging in an extended creative drama experience of survival simulation (Kitagawa), and all kinds of things in between. Yet this diversity seems appropriate given that the focus is "Using Language to Explore the World," for you just never know where exploration may take you. As you will see, it takes these teachers and students in many directions.

We know that we don't all have the same questions about the world we live in, nor do we pursue our questions in the same ways. The remarkable teachers of this section respond to their students' individuality in quite wonderful ways. Notice how these teachers balance their complementary roles of guiding students and of responding to students. These teachers lead. They also follow. They provide a range of experiences and they plan them carefully. But deliberately built into these teachers' plans is provision for students' shaping of their own learning experiences:

- Patti Seifert provides Explorers Club for her kindergartners. This is a structure designed to help children choose topics they individually wish to study and to help them pursue their research.

- Mary Glover introduces mapping at the beginning of the year by reading *My Map Book* to her second graders. Then, throughout the rest of the year, she picks up on and supports her children's ideas for all sorts of mapping.

- Phyllis Whitin writes of her "intentional plans to include surprise in [her] day-to-day teaching." That is, she deliberately provides interactions within which her students can—and do—surprise her, letting her know "where they are coming from" so that she can come to that place—their place—and respond to them there.

- Mary Kitagawa intentionally poses the question, "What makes a poem a poem?" in order to focus her sixth graders' attention on this particular literary genre. But her students "own" the exploration as they generate and finally compile their ideas.

- Kathryn Pierce consciously fosters children's "exploratory talk" in a host of small-group activities, not only because this kind of talk supports the children's learning, but also because it supports her own: It enables her to identify areas of confusion or areas of interest among the children, both of which she can then respond to in supportive ways.

- And as you read Rebecca King's weekly letters home for the first five weeks of the school year, you'll see and hear her leading *and* following her grade K/1/2 children as they write Big Books, addition equations, and graphs; read counting books, *Clifford* books, and poetry; plan a fishing trip, a pet show, and a garden. None of these activities would happen without Becky's careful planning; neither would they happen without her students' active input.

How skillfully these teachers maintain that delicate balance between teacher-as-guide and teacher-as-supportive responder.

These six articles may show quite clearly why it is that "language arts" is not a separate subject. Children are using (and thereby honing) the arts of language as they write and read and talk their way into a deeper understanding of the world. It's learning; it's language; and it's *language learning* in the process.

# 7 Inquiry in the Kindergarten

**Patti Seifert**
Aspen Elementary Schools, Aspen, Colorado

A university researcher was working on a project in Chris Boyd's kindergarten classroom (Boyd, 1993). The children were asked, "What do we study in this class?" They answered, "Bones, temperature, space, water, animals . . ." They were then asked why they didn't study the ABC's. The children just stared! They answered, "Letters are something you use to study, not something you study about." This revelation coming from the mouths of babes truly applies to all of our teaching. In our classrooms, are we using the tools to uncover something that we're curious about, or are we just studying the tools?

Children are meaning makers; they begin trying to make sense of their world from birth. As infants, they use their mouths as sensory organs to explore objects within their grasp. As they begin to crawl and walk, their world expands, as does their understanding of it. By the time they come to kindergarten, they are not only interested in their own immediate backyard, but they are curious about the whole world and are continually trying to make sense of it. Surely it is our responsibility to foster the child's continuing natural desire to make sense of the world. It is our job to provide a safe place for experimenting and for approximating, a place where we invite children to continue their search for meaning by allowing them to pursue their passions, just as they have been doing at home. Inquiry has been going on from birth for each child. Learning is not an occasional event to be stimulated, provoked, or reinforced; it is what the brain does naturally, continually, inevitably (Smith, 1988a).

This chapter is about children using writing and reading and other sign systems (e.g., drawing) to explore their own personal questions so they can get to the real business of bones, temperature, space, water, animals. It's about my kindergartners' inquiry through Explorers Club (Copenhaver, 1993).

## Getting Ready for Explorers Club

What was to become Explorers Club in my classroom probably had its real beginnings several years ago when I became interested in the work of Harste, Burke, and Short focusing on Inquiry Curriculum (Short & Burke, 1991; Harste, 1993). I began thinking about my own classroom. "If it's February, it must be dinosaurs." Every February I launched a unit study on dinosaurs. It was a time in the school year when I felt five-year-olds were ready to sink their teeth into a topic (no pun intended). We learned about meat eaters and plant eaters. We talked about how the land at that time was different from the way it is today, we read books, and I pulled out an impressive collection of puzzles, stuffed dinosaurs, dot-to-dots, film strips, and so on. We made clay dinosaurs, created big murals, produced books, and finally brought the study to an end. The outcome was predictable, the children learned factual information, and occasionally I found some carryover into conversations, writing, and drawings. Although some of the children were very interested in dinosaurs, most did not share that passion. I realized it was time to put theory into practice. In February, I would launch individual research projects with my five- and six-year-olds.

Though the children's research *formally* began in February, it *actually* began the first day of school and continued throughout the year, as we wrote and read and inquired together.

*We wrote.*   Every day we wrote for one hour in Writing Workshop. Every year I am reminded that the first day of Writing Workshop is not easy. The children want to share their work with me all at once. Some children can only stay at the task for a very short time. On the first day, I not only talk about drawing and writing, but I also talk about the procedure of the Writing Workshop. We act out, or "fishbowl," a scenario of my conferencing with one child. Another child approaches and we demonstrate how a child can sit and join us quietly while we finish our conversation. We also act out how not to interrupt. This mini-demonstration is referred to throughout the school year. It takes patience and demonstration to get five-year-olds to understand the importance of finding help from other sources in the classroom, to work independently of the teacher, and to be brave and take chances with the work they are doing. But it is well worth the effort, so we wrote in Writing Workshop from the beginning of the year. I asked the children to draw about anything that they were interested in, wondering about, or thinking about. I then asked them to write as best they could, using invented spellings, to continue making sense of their world. At the beginning, writing looked like Figures 7.1 and 7.2.

**Figure 7.1**   Early Writing: "Rainbow"

**Figure 7.2**   Early Writing: "Bear"

During the Writing Workshop, I would conference with children individually, and periodically I would make anecdotal entries in the children's writing folders. During the daily Authors' Circle, I would take notes on adhesive labels that I eventually put into each child's portfolio. Each year I become more committed to the value and importance of the Authors' Circle. It not only allows two children to share their work with their classmates each day, but it also helps the other children understand that ours is a safe place to stand and be heard. When a child shares a book that contains all pictures and no words, it tells those other children who have similar work that their efforts are valued and honored. Those children who are reluctant to share learn that it is safe and that they can do what others have done. They, too, can enter the literacy club (Smith, 1988b).[1]

So we wrote and conferenced and shared our writing in our hour-long Writing Workshop every day, but as the children began to view themselves as writers, they found reasons to write all day long.

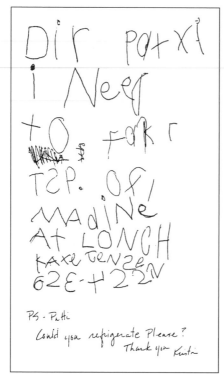

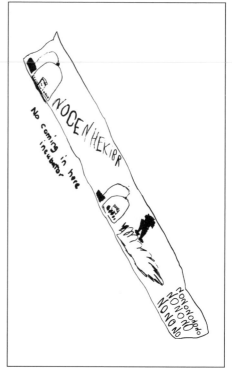

**Figure 7.3** A Reminder: "Dear Patti, I need to take 1 teaspoon of medicine at lunch."

**Figure 7.4** Directive: "No coming in here. Incubator."

They wrote reminders (Figure 7.3).

They wrote directives (Figures 7.4 and 7.5).

They wrote complaints (Figure 7.6).

And in his journal, Sam noted the daily changes in the chicks we hatched in the spring (Figure 7.7).

***We read.*** Writing is never done in isolation. We did author studies, marveling over the works of poets, young and old, and seeking out beautiful language long before we actually wrote our own free verse poetry. We read, read, read—shared chapter books and picture books. We engaged in book talk that would be the envy of any adult book club. The children noticed, compared, and contrasted the work of one author to that of another, and made connections between the text and their own lives. And we read to learn more about our world.

**Figure 7.5**   Directive: "Please knock before you come in."

**Figure 7.6**   Complaint: "Remy put a pencil point close to my eye."

***We inquired.***   Our inquiry began even before the first day of kindergarten when I sent a handwritten letter to each child, welcoming him or her to our class and informing each one that—in addition to having a great time—he or she would find a reptile in our room. I assured the children that it would not harm them but that it was big and moved slowly. I asked them to guess what the reptile was and then, when they arrived at school on that first day, to see if they could find it. The reptile had gotten out of the box (as it does every year, for some mysterious reason!). We searched the building, looking for the

**Figure 7.7**   Journal Entry: "The chicks are bigger and Blackie has been laying down."

mysterious creature and asking everybody we saw if they had seen the missing reptile. Our search, of course, had the dual purpose of familiarizing the children with the building and the other teachers, as well as finding the missing reptile. We found the reptile—a desert tortoise—in the school office and promptly returned it to the classroom. The children suggested that it needed a better home, one that it couldn't get out of. And so began our first inquiry study, the building of a habitat for the desert tortoise, Gus. Our study involved gathering information from experts at our Environmental Studies Center, reading books and viewing videos, and, most importantly, observing Gus. We compared domestic animals to wild animals. We learned that many desert tortoises are taken from the desert and can never be returned to their natural habitat. Although the outcome of this study was fixed, in that I knew we would build a suitable, temporary home for Gus, the children learned important things, such as why we must leave wild animals in the wild. They also made their own discoveries along the way, and I tried to follow their lead.

Soon after our desert tortoise project, Amber brought in a salamander that she found in a dog dish. He had a bite taken out of his tail. Amber and her mother knew we would all be interested in creating a good home for the salamander. We all had to read up on salamanders, for these were unknown to all of us. A second salamander and a newt soon joined Notched Tail (and they are still thriving today).

After Halloween, instead of throwing out our decaying jack-o-lantern, we decided to keep it and observe what would happen. We had just read *Mousekin's Golden House* (Miller, 1990), where a mouse discovers a discarded jack-o-lantern and moves in for the winter. As the pumpkin decomposes, the jack-o-lantern eyes, nose, and mouth close, providing Mousekin with a home sealed up from the winter snow. We wondered if the eyes of our jack-o-lantern would also close. I had the children draw pictures of their predictions. We listened as the children explained their theories, and then we began a daily journal, recording our close observations of the pumpkin.

Group projects were generated from the children's wondering and questions. A colleague of mine noticed the children talking about worms after a rainstorm. As she joined in their conversation, she learned that some children were stepping on the worms. A project on worms was in the making, not based on one day's discussion, but on a sustained interest in the topic by both teacher and children.

These are only a few examples, but they show how our inquiry and writing and reading were weaving their way through our classroom life from the first day.

## Explorers Club

February arrived and with it, Explorers Club, the opportunity for the children to pursue their personal inquiries in a sustained way within a supportive community.[2] I had begun preparing the children for Explorers Club from the beginning of the school year. In addition to the writing, reading, and inquiring I have described already, we had many discussions about what we would like to learn about, what we were curious about, what we were interested in. Now we began more formal inquiry by generating a list of possible topics. The list grew over several days. Then I started interviewing the children individually to better understand their thoughts. I asked them to tell me three things they might be interested in and why these were personally important to them. I asked them what they already knew about these topics and what they wanted to know. Here's what some of them told me.

> *Lawrence:* "I'm curious about potions. How do they mix stuff?"
>
> *Courtney:* "The stars and the moon. I know some stars shine brightly, because I've seen them. How do they make stars? How does the moon change shape?"

*Rachel:* "I want to know about deer and elk because I see them a lot when I'm coming home. I know they know how to run fast. I know they can jump over the fences fast. I want to know what they eat and where do they have babies?"

*Sydney:* "Ocean and beaches. I know how the water got there. Somebody spends all their life getting buckets of water and pouring it there. But I don't know how the sand got there."

*Robert:* "I want to study dinosaurs. I know about Ankylosaurus and Tyrannosaurus Rex. I know dinos kill other dinos. I want to know how they died."

I asked the children to choose their favorite topic, and I then grouped the individual topics into more general categories (so that the children could work in groups, while still pursuing their individual interests). I made these public by putting the children's names on sticky tabs under the appropriate category. The movability of the sticky tabs was important. I wanted to give the children a chance to change their topics if they wanted to. I knew that some of the children might want to change topics in order to work in the same group as special

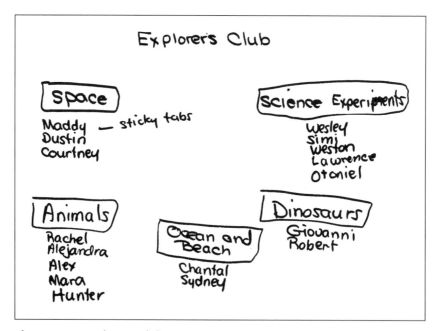

**Figure 7.8**   Explorers Club Groups

friends. After three days, the children knew that they had to literally stick to one topic. The chart became permanent.

I typed the children's questions and sent them home to the parents with an accompanying letter:

Dear Parents,

Our class is beginning a research project. I have been asking the children what they are interested in studying and what their personal questions are about their choice of study. We have come up with the following topics:

| | |
|---|---|
| Dinosaurs | Space |
| Science experiments | Ocean and beach |
| Animals | |

We will be forming study groups to uncover the answers to some of our personal questions, with hopes that more questions will be generated. For example, Mara is interested in deer, elk, and household cats. She wants to know when and where they have their babies. Her animal study group has different questions about other animals. We will go to the library to gather books on these topics; the study group will use their "text set" to find some of their information.

There are, however, lots of ways to obtain information. We can go to people who are experts, we can watch videos on animals, etc. I hope to employ some first grade scientists to teach our kids about science experiments. Our geology experts in the fourth grade could help Chantal with her questions about oceans and beaches.

Please read through each child's area of interest and their personal questions. If you have information about any topic, please send it in to add to any child's text set. For example, if you have a poem on space, or if you have a book about elementary geology, or if you are an expert on one of these topics, please send us a note and we will invite you to speak to the study group.

Wish us luck on our research!

Love,
Patti and the Kids

Parents responded by sending in books, poems, collections—and their good wishes. We began by painting book boxes for our text sets. Individual groups of children went to our school library with a parent to gather books on snakes, birds, animals, and so on. Throughout our study (which lasted approximately four weeks), the children took on great ownership of their book boxes. They generously shared their books with other groups, but each group respected this "property" of others.

We obtained information from many sources in addition to books. Our resources included people who were experts (adults and children), videos, trips to make observations about our topics. We set out to get information from people by writing notes and using the phone. Mara had had very little phone experience, since her family lives in a tepee on the mountain. Mara was interested in deer because she saw them quite often at her home. She and the others in the Animal Group called our Environmental Studies Center. One group member wrote down the phone number while another dialed. Mara chose to speak, showing an amazing ability to introduce herself, to summarize what she needed from the Center, and to make arrangements for their visit. Other children wrote notes to teachers, requesting their help with science experiments. Some children wrote to other children who they knew were experts on a specific topic. Our "mentors" arrived in the classroom at different times during our study. They first met with the study group, and then often shared information with the whole class. Reid was studying spiders and had invited Dale from our Environmental Center to visit. Dale brought a tarantula that he first shared with Reid privately. Then Reid proudly held the spider on his arm and informed the rest of the class about what he had learned.

Once the books had been gathered and our mentors were lined up, we started each morning working on group drawings that were on big pieces of Kraft paper. As the children's knowledge base expanded, their drawings were revised. In America we often use art as a culminating activity for a unit of study.[3] But in Explorers Club the children were using their drawings as a way to make meaning. The revisiting of their drawing each day was a revisiting and revising of their knowledge and understanding.

Drawing and writing were not the only sign systems that were in place during our study. We used clay to help make meaning throughout our study. As with our drawing, instead of waiting until the end of the study to make a clay piece, we used the clay throughout the process. For example, Giovanni's many pieces on dinosaurs helped him to make sense of the proportion and function of tails, necks, solid legs, armor, and so on. Our environmental science teacher and our art teacher helped some of the children express their understanding of their topic by creating a papier mâché solar system along with a cardboard tube for a space ship big enough for two children to get into and blast off.

The children's research projects spilled over into our Writing Workshop. I began noticing a crossover among certain groups: Some children were writing about topics that were being studied in groups other than their own. These crossovers showed me that children's lenses can be widened when they are exposed to other passionate children. If Power Rangers are the only thing they see as interesting to their peers, then that is what they become interested in. If, however, children have opportunities to pursue other passions, another world opens up not only to one child, but to many other children as well. A classroom of inquirers feed off one another; they create and recreate each other (Harste, 1992).

What were the children learning in Explorers Club? Were they just learning facts as they had done in the past? Or were they making meaningful connections to their own lives? Because the children had a personal interest in their own topics, they had a personal interest in their own learning. I watched them use their topics

- to work on cognitive issues that were important to them;
- to explore reading and writing and other sign systems;
- to collaborate with colleagues and co-construct their knowledge.

I hope they were learning, too, that school is a place to follow their natural curiosity and to do so *joyfully*.

## Reflections

I have been doing Explorers Club in my kindergarten for four years. I still begin with the children telling what they want to study and why, and each year the individual questions and the areas of study are different.

> *Kyle:* "Planes!  My dad works in the control tower. I want to know what buttons turn on the engines in the cockpit. What do the other buttons do? I know all the names of planes, but I don't know what the buttons do inside."
>
> *Maggie:* "Science stuff! I have a little set of Doctor Dreadful's Food Lab. I've made monster skin. I want to know which [experiment] explodes and which one doesn't."
>
> *Haley:* "My friend Jessica has a ferret and I really like it. I know they eat prairie dogs. I want to know how they do that. How do they run so fast? How do they take care of their babies?"
>
> *Lili:* "I want to know about panda bears. Why do poachers kill animals? I know they want to kill animals to sell them. Maybe I should tell everybody to be nice. Somebody could go there to everybody to [tell them to] stop killing panda bears. I want to know where they live. I know they climb trees with their claws and eat bamboo. Can they go some place where poachers can't kill them?"

*Trent:* "Snakes! I like the way they slither and stuff. How do
rattlers kill the people? I know some snakes live in the
desert. I know rattlesnakes and cobra snakes. I want to
know other snakes that have poison."

We continue to explore our inquiry topics in a variety of ways. Several
groups have made 3-D murals to facilitate their play, and several other
groups have conceived and made costumes. Briana's castle study
involved turning the playhouse into a ballroom for dancing (and a
chance to dress as a princess). Our play structure became the castle
where maps were made, and the top of the play structure became a
lookout tower. Morgan was in the Plane Group, but he made a tunic
costume at home and brought it for the castle. The kids loved the idea,
and with the help of a parent, we turned white pillow cases into tunics
to facilitate play. Briana's one-person castle study eventually involved
the entire class in the play. The whole class was also involved in our
field trips. Over the years we have visited the airport, a ranch (to
observe horses), and beehives for Annabelle's bee study. Some individual groups have gone to second-grade classrooms to learn about
bats, and others have gone to the first grade to hold a boa constrictor.

Now I end each inquiry study by asking the children to evaluate
it. Here is what a few of the children have told me.

*Gerald:* "I feel good because I liked the dry ice experiment.
When we put the dry ice in a cup, smoke came up and it
was pink. Carbon dioxide made it change color. The journal
was the best. You get to write stuff in it. I'd do computers
next so I could go to my sister's class again."

*Jackie:* "I liked learning about dolphins coming up to the surface and blowing air through the hole. I liked the play: We
talked about dolphins. It was fun. Moms pushed the babies
up to the surface. Sometimes they ride on their mom's
back. They drink milk from their mom. I'd do mermaids
next."

*Ricky:* "I liked getting the books from the library. I learned a lot
from the second graders. The flying fox bat has the biggest
wing span in the world. I liked the video where the guy
went into the bat cave with all those bats. That was the
best. I'd do aliens next. How do they stay on earth?"

As I reflect back over the past four years of doing Explorers Club
with my kindergartners, I often think of that first year . . . and of
Giovanni, a beautiful boy with dark eyes and olive skin, ever so full of
energy. From the beginning, I noticed how he always seemed to be

exploring off on his own. I lost Giovanni on the playground one day early in the year. The lunch recess bell rang and all the children lined up . . . except Giovanni. Eventually we found him barefoot in a distant sand box area. He was unaware of the bell and had no idea where his shoes were. I wondered if Giovanni should be in kindergarten. He seemed immature, not ready for a kindergarten setting. He seemed unable to join the group during those times when we gathered together. I worried about taking him on our many excursions; he was difficult enough to keep track of just in the classroom. I contacted his preschool teacher and she shared my concern—and had even recommended that he spend another year in preschool. But his age qualified him for kindergarten, and that is where he would stay. I knew that I would have to begin viewing Giovanni in a new way, letting him show me how best to capture his attention. Fortunately, I soon discovered his interest in science.

Although Giovanni was not always focused or productive during our writing time, I could see that he was continually absorbing information and using his own writing to help unlock the mystery of reading. When we began Explorers Club in February, Giovanni chose dinosaurs as his inquiry focus: "I'm interested in dinosaurs. I know about Tyrannosaurus Rex, and I know they eat leaves and fruit and meat. I want to know where they lived."

Giovanni went to his book box every morning and pored over his books on dinosaurs. However, it was not until our study ended and we returned the books to the library that I understood how much these books meant to Giovanni. His mother called to tell me that Giovanni didn't want to come to school anymore: His dinosaur books were no longer in the classroom. Of course we immediately went to the library to retrieve the books. Giovanni had taught me that for some children, inquiry studies are never finished. (Now I ask the children's permission to return the books, instead of assuming that everyone is finished at the same time.)

Not only did Giovanni read about dinosaurs; he wrote about them too. When we wrote poetry in Writing Workshop, Giovanni wrote:

> Dinosaur eggs
> Crack, crack
> Dinosaurs
> Pterodactyl
> Rex is mad—blowing fire.

He chose to publish a two-page book about dinosaurs.

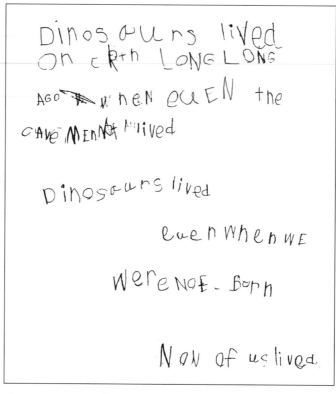

*Figure 7.9* Page from Giovanni's Book about Dinosaurs

My three February/March anecdotal notes on Giovanni's "Things I Can Do List" hint at the way Giovanni's literacy skills were developing as he pursued his personally meaningful study of dinosaurs:

2-19: My books have interesting topics. I can write a whole book about the same topic.

2-23: When I get interested in a topic, I can stick to my work for a long time.

3-24: I'm still working on dinosaurs. I look at books for a long time and then I write the information in my books. I'm reading!

At the end of the year, Giovanni wrote me a poem as a "thank you" note.

Whales go by two by two.
Thank you Patti for teaching me to write.

No, Giovanni. Thank *you* for showing me how to teach.

## Notes

1. Former students, now in the first grade, come back to my kindergarten to share their writing. This self-initiated share time has been the most powerful teaching tool in my classroom. The kindergartners ask real questions such as, "How did you do that?" or "How did you get so good?" The first-graders answer with honesty and a real desire to help their younger counterparts. Their words "I just write all the time," or "I take lots of books home to read every night" carry more weight than any words of advice that I might have for my students.

2. This idea was developed by Carolyn Burke and adapted in a fifth-grade classroom by Joby Copenhaver and Rise Paynter. I then further adapted it for my five- and six-year-olds (Copenhaver, 1993).

3. One year I hung the group drawings up on clothesline with clothes pins, just to get them out of the way when they weren't being used. I found that once I hung them up, the children lost interest in them, apparently assuming that once a work is displayed, it is finished.

## References

Boyd, C. (1993). Creating curriculum from children's lives. *Primary Voices K–6*, Premier Issue, 22–27.

Copenhaver, J. (1993). Creating curriculum from children's lives. *Primary Voices K–6*, Premier Issue, 6–14.

Harste, J. (1992). *Literacy as curricular conversations about knowledge, inquiry, and morality.* Paper presented at the NCTE Annual Convention, November, Louisville, KY.

Harste, J. (1993). Inquiry-based instruction. *Primary Voices K–6*, Premier Issue, 2–5.

Miller, E. (1990). *Mousekin's golden house.* New York: Simon & Schuster.

Short, K. G., & Burke, C. (1991). *Creating curriculum: Teachers and students as a community of learners.* Portsmouth, NH: Heinemann.

Smith, F. (1988a). *Insult to intelligence: The bureaucratic invasion of our classrooms.* Portsmouth, NH: Heinemann.

Smith, F. (1988b). *Joining the literacy club: Further essays into education.* Portsmouth, NH: Heinemann.

## Bibliography

### Patti Seifert

*Professional resources that have been especially important to me include:*

Calkins, L. M. (1983). *Lessons from a child: On the teaching and learning of writing.* Portsmouth, NH: Heinemann.

Calkins, L. M. (1986). *The art of teaching writing*. Portsmouth, NH: Heinemann.

Edwards, C., Gandini, L., & Forman, G. (1993). *The hundred languages of children: The Reggio Emilia approach to early childhood education*. Norwood, NJ: Ablex.

Harste, J. C. (1993). Inquiry-based instruction. *Primary Voices K–6*, Premier Issue, 2–5.

Hindley, J. (1996). *In the company of children*. York, ME: Stenhouse.

Katz, L. G., & Chard, S. C. (1993). *Engaging children's minds: The project approach*. 2nd Ed. Norwood, NJ: Ablex.

Short, K. G., & Burke, C. (1991). *Creating curriculum*. Portsmouth, NH: Heinemann.

***Children's books that I especially enjoy using with children include:***

Chermayeff, C., & Richardson, N. (1994). *Furry facts*. San Diego: Gulliver.

Garelick, M. (1988). *What makes a bird a bird?* Greenvale, NY: Mondo.

Heller, R. (1982). *Animals born alive and well*. New York: Grosset and Dunlap.

Heller, R. (1984). *Plants that never bloom*. New York: Grosset and Dunlap.

Heller, R. (1986). *The reason for a flower*. New York: Grosset and Dunlap.

Lovel, S., & Snowball, D. (1995). *Is this a monster?* Greenvale, NY: Mondo.

Mazer, A. (1991). *The salamander room*. New York: Alfred A. Knopf.

Seifert, P., and Doherty, P. (1994). *Exploring tree habitats, fresh water habitats, sea water habitats, land habitats*. Greenvale, NY: Mondo.

# 8 Finding Our Way: A Year of Learning with Maps

**Mary Kenner Glover**
Awakening Seed School, Tempe, Arizona

On the last day of school before letting out for summer, seven-year-old Kinley sat in the author's chair ready to share his just-completed book. It was a story he had worked on at various times throughout the year about his family's trip to the wedding of his birth mother. It was a powerful moment to witness this private, sensitive boy revealing the specifics of such a significant event in his personal life. His story and exceptional illustrations recalled the details of his trip: riding on the elevator at the airport as planes landed overhead, the construction equipment he observed after they'd arrived at their destination, jumping on the trampoline at his cousins', the balloons Kinley and his brother played with at the wedding reception.

Among Kinley's illustrations were two maps—one of the trip itself and one of their hotel room. Seeing his maps on the last day of school carried me back to the beginning of the year when we first started our journey together. Contained in Kinley's story was a thread of a study we began on the first day in September. He had taken it on as his own and used it to tell his story.

Our study of maps actually began in August before we gathered as a class. Each summer I try to look for clues about how to start the new school year with my first and second graders. I liken this to Don Murray's idea of "finding the line" in writing: "The line is a word or a series of words that points toward a potential meaning . . . the line is often made up of code words that have private meanings that appear general, vague, or cliché to other readers but which are loaded with precise meanings for the writer" (Murray, 1989, p. 41).

My "line" for the school year initially came during our summer vacation in Maine. My friend's ten-year-old son, Scotty, told me about the country he had made up called Flowel. It had begun as a two-week assignment in school, but he developed it much further. In addition to the dozens of buildings he had designed in a notebook, Scotty showed me a tattered map he had drawn of the country itself (Figure 8.1). I was

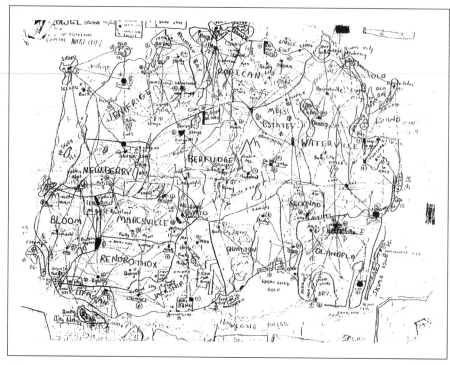

**Figure 8.1**   Scotty's Map of Flowel

impressed with his creativity and passion for his work. I stored the idea away as a possibility for a future classroom project.

   Several weeks later, just a few days before school was to begin, I still hadn't decided how to start the year. Of course, I had in mind all of the math concepts we would need to cover, the general mini-lessons I'd provide for reading and writing instruction, and a few of the chapter books I planned to read. What I was lacking, however, was my big idea, my "line" for the next nine months. Avoiding all the things I knew I should be doing to prepare for school, I went to a book store "just to get ideas." I often do this when I'm in the process of coming up with a new teaching idea. Book stores not only provide numerous possibilities, but just getting away from the classroom sometimes frees the mind of school thinking so that new and creative ideas can come. In the children's section that day, I picked up a new book I'd never seen before called *My Map Book* by Sara Fanelli. I knew the minute it touched my hand that I'd found my line for the year. I knew how we would begin.

On one of the first days of school, I read *My Map Book* to the class. After discussing its brightly colored illustrations and innovative maps, we made a list of what a map is and what it does. These are some of the children's main ideas, which I wrote on a large piece of chart paper for future reference:

A map:

- shows you where to go
- is a drawing of an area
- shows you where things are
- gets you unstuck when you're lost
- shows you directions
- helps you get information
- teaches you about places

When organizing a new content study, I always try to keep in mind the children's thoughts and prior knowledge. Over the years, I have learned to trust my students' ideas and to use this information to build the study and guide its direction. This type of thinking tends to hold a study together conceptually, keeping it whole instead of its being just a series of isolated activities. Brainstorming together also sends an important message to children: Their ideas are valuable and deserving of our attention.

After hearing the children's ideas about maps, I thought it made sense to begin where we were—in our own classroom. We divided the classroom into quadrants and mapped our room. Each small group was responsible for including all the details of its section of the room. As the children drew, they talked, argued, and negotiated what should be in the map and how it should be illustrated. The wall above the cubbies in our classroom was soon covered with this large, elaborate map drawn with markers, crayons, pastels, chalk, and watercolors. We were well on our way as learners together.

During the same time that we worked on the classroom map, I asked the children to make maps of their bedrooms as a homework assignment. I deliberately didn't mention the idea of a "bird's eye view" because I wanted them to use their own thinking and not be restricted by someone else's concept of a map. I find it important to keep this kind of openness to possibilities in all aspects of my teaching. It not only provides me important information about the children's cognitive development, but it also encourages them to trust what they know and how they are going about their own learning process. Their

**Figure 8.2a**   Richie's Map of his Room

**Figure 8.2b**   Caity's Map of her Room

maps were varied, as you can see in Figures 8.2a and 8.2b. Richie was able to draw his room from a slightly aerial view, while Caity's map, which primarily showed where she and her two sisters slept, included wonderfully detailed drawings of many items in her room.

For another homework assignment, the children brought in an actual map of a significant place or event in their life. First I asked the children to tell stories about their maps. I helped them begin by giving a mini-lesson using my map of Boston, the place I'd visited just weeks before school started. I showed them my map of Boston Commons and told them about my excitement at seeing the swan boats in the pond—the same swan boats I'd read about in E. B. White's *The Trumpet of the Swan*. I talked about sitting by the pond in the early evening, listening to the sound of the ducks taking flight off the water. The children began sharing their maps and stories. They were as varied as their bedroom maps. Robert brought a huge topographical map of Arizona and told of visiting Meteor Crater. Richie's map was of Wonderland, where Alice had her adventures. Cynthia brought a world map and pointed out Japan, her "favorite place in the world." Emily shared a map of Venezia and told us about the waterways there instead of streets. Our map study was already producing a rich collection of stories from which to venture in other directions as the school year progressed.

The next step for the map stories was to write them down. Once told, each child recorded his or her story on paper and attached it to a copy of the map. For example, Nick created a map and brief description of his trip to Florida and the Kennedy Space Center. It not only told about his trip but also revealed his passion for outer space travel and UFO's, which remained a significant interest throughout the year. For him, this initial story was just the beginning of many other pieces of writing about outer space. Although the stories were not fully developed when written down, they served as a beginning for this process. In other words, these early stories, put into writing, served as a foundation for learning how to transform spoken words into print.

Maps took on a life of their own and seeped into many other parts of our daily living. When we visited the Phoenix Art Museum to see the Latin American Women Artists Exhibit, we prepared ourselves by viewing slides of several pieces from the exhibit, as well as a map of the artists' countries. We even mapped our route to the museum. What I'd thought would be a ten-minute discussion using the overhead projector ended up being a half-hour exchange of observations of our map of metropolitan Phoenix, including the location of the airports, the Phoenix Zoo, and other local attractions. At the time, I was surprised by the amount of talk generated by the Phoenix city map.

**Figure 8.3**   Todd's Map of the Playground

Looking back, I think the discussion was so well-developed because the children understood the significance of a map and were eager to share what they knew. Furthermore, because they had previous map knowledge, they felt confident applying it to a real-life situation—finding our way to the museum.

Our map study began to spill over into several areas of the curriculum. We became involved in a math study of measurement, and I asked the children to make maps of the playground as an introductory assignment. Although some of them never got around to measuring the various playground items, they drew wonderfully detailed maps that included the climbing structures, trees, tire bridges, and the asphalt bike riding area. Todd's map of the playground (Figure 8.3) even included a legend for picnic tables and other significant playground components.

Spontaneous reading and writing inspired by the map study also took place. Kinley jumped up excitedly and came to show me the map he'd found in the book *Castle* (Macaulay, 1977). In addition to the map he drew of the castle, he also worked for several hours on a map of the route from his house to school. In his own way, he was showing me the way to his house and also a way to know him as a learner. His

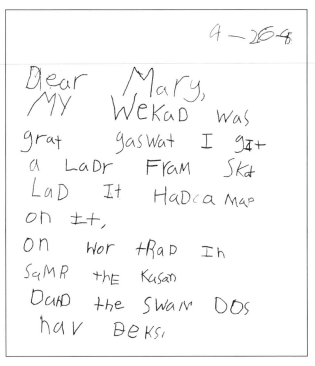

**Figure 8.4** River's Journal

map and the way he approached map making revealed that he is a child who will include details in his work if given the time to develop them. Additionally, he was telling me without words that he was willing to show me the details of himself as long as I was entrusting him with the time to do so at his own tempo.

In his journal, River wrote to me about the map he had just received from Skateland, a local roller skating rink, and also made a connection with the map story I'd told about the birds in Boston (Figure 8.4). River took on the map study more seriously than most of his peers. One day he exclaimed, "Everything's a map . . . the world, streets, a day. . . ." In the middle of our measuring study, he approached me with a ruler in one hand and a world map in the other and asked, "How big is the world?" After I showed him how to find maps on the CD-ROM encyclopedia, I noticed he'd made a copy of a map of Texas. When I commented on it, River said, "Texas is a really sad map for me. My cousins moved to Texas last year." River's sad Texas map eventually led him to write a story about those same cousins.

**Figure 8.5**    Jesse's Map and Note for the Maintenance Man

The concept of a map, along with its power and usefulness in everyday life, began to make sense in my students' minds. They saw potential for maps everywhere they turned, and since they had personal experience as map makers and readers, they felt confident to apply their map skills independently. For example, when Jesse noticed that one of the lights in our classroom was blinking and needed to be replaced, he made a map of our room with a note for the maintenance man. He even went back and revised his map when he realized he had indicated the wrong light fixture (Figure 8.5). During our first visit to a nursing home, I asked the children to make a drawing of something they saw. Brittany brought hers to me and said, "I made it like a map!" (Figure 8.6).

**Figure 8.6**   Brittany's Map of the Nursing Home Visit

Maps helped us find our way into literature as well. During our read-aloud of William Steig's *Dominic*, we made a map of Dominic's adventures. After reading a chapter, I would ask one child to draw his or her interpretation of it on a large piece of paper, our story "map." Each day, another child added a section as the story developed. Several chapters into the book, I introduced the idea of tension in story by asking my students to make their bodies tense and then relaxed. I explained that this tightness is called tension and that a story can also have it. We reviewed what we had read so far and looked for places where the story had tension and then relaxed. Each time there was tension, we made a big T on our map. The children loved this process and were excited about knowing the new concept "tension" and being able to identify tense moments in the story. When we finished *Dominic*, we discussed the different kinds of tension in the story. Among the various types mentioned were: fighting tension, listening/wondering tension, creeping tension, and "uh-oh" tension. Jesse offered the most entertaining comment, as we discussed the tension at the end when Dominic met his true love: He said it was "romantic tension."

Our map study naturally led to other studies. We soon began a study of masks. After creating imaginary masks out of recycled materials and making up a story for every mask, each child selected a real

Name ___Nathan___

Draw a map of the place (country, state, or region)
where your mask comes from. Make it detailed,
bright, and colorful. Be sure to label your map.
*(This will be part of your display for the mask exhibit.)*

**Figure 8.7**   Nathan's Mask Display Map

mask from a different culture of the world. They gathered materials, researched information about their masks, and eventually made papier mâché replicas. As a culminating event, we formed a museum for parents and other classes to visit. Each mask was displayed on a panel, along with its description and a map of the country from which it originated (Figure 8.7). We also made a visitor's guide which explained each mask. As visitors to our museum viewed the displays, the children confidently explained what they had learned. The map study provided a strong base from which to build future studies, and it also gave the children an opportunity to use their emerging skills as language users with an air of confidence.

Even after we stopped talking about maps every day, the children continued to make connections with them from time to time. One afternoon when I had finished reading Chapter 4 of C. S. Lewis's *The Lion, the Witch and the Wardrobe*, we were talking about Edmund, who had just stepped into the magical world of Narnia and met up with a witch. Seven-year-old Caitlin commented: "I was surprised the witch was so nice to Edmund. She was really mean in the other book." Another child countered, "She was just trying to play a trick on him. She wasn't really nice." More discussion followed. Then Celina said, "I'm feeling a lot of tension in this story!" She had remembered our map notations about tension when we read *Dominic* and applied it here. The *Dominic* map served as an introduction to the elements of story, and the maps in the Narnia books guided us along on our literary journey through Lewis's magical stories. As we continued with literature throughout the remainder of the year, our knowledge of tension was joined by other elements of story, such as place and time, which were also enhanced by our study of maps.

Individual children found many additional ways to use maps. Following our mask study, Todd decided to do an independent study that ended up being a collection of imaginary masks he created. He drew each mask, wrote a brief description of it, and included a map of where it was from (Figure 8.8). When Daniel published a book and wrote his author description of himself, he chose to include a map to his house (Figure 8.9). In his log for a small group literature study, Nick drew a map to remind himself of the distance between two countries and of their different cultures (Figure 8.10).

As the year came to a close, I realized that our map study had become much more than a clever way to hook children into geography. It was much bigger than an interesting content study to start the year. Maps had become a guide, a tool, for navigating our way through what we wanted and needed to learn, both together and individually.

As a culminating experience, I wanted to see what the children would do with maps as a way to reflect on our year of learning. I asked the children to make a map of their year and left the assignment open-ended as to how they could go about it. As they completed their maps, they took turns sharing. Kaitlin chose to make her map in the form of a book. Each page was a calendar with a month of the school year on it, along with a photograph from that month. Celina's map had a road that traveled along, connecting different experiences we'd shared throughout the year, such as stories and content studies.

**Figure 8.8**  Todd's Description and Map for His Imaginary Mask

Kinley's map was a unique 3-D map. He used recycled boxes and containers for the buildings, which included his house, the home of the family he carpooled with, the nursing home we visited every other week, the Phoenix Art Museum, and the school (which was actually just our classroom and the basketball court outside of our room). When someone asked him why the inside of the school was just our classroom, Kinley said that was the most important part of the school to him. He had, in fact, made a sign on his map explaining that the size of each building corresponded to its importance to him. For example, our classroom was made from a large box and the nursing home was a tiny one. Kinley connected all of the buildings with a road and reported that his four-year-old brother Barry gave him the idea to make the road. Some of his buildings had many details. In our classroom, he made a miniature chalkboard with the daily plan on it, something I do every day. In the box representing the Phoenix Art Museum, he had placed a small

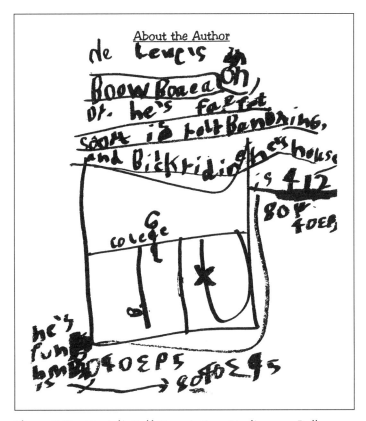

**Figure 8.9** Daniel's Self-Description: He lives on Balboa Dr. His favorite sport is roller blading and bike riding. His house is 412. His phone number is 804-0395.

piece of plastic on the corner of the upper part, intending it to be the large second floor window overlooking the museum's main gallery. Evidently the window had made an impression on him during our various trips to see art exhibits.

Jesse's map was a detailed record of all of the books we'd read together during the year. In addition to the titles, he drew line drawings of characters and events and then watercolored them. Nathan's map consisted of several sheets of computer paper connected together. Each page had a number and a drawing (with a brief explanation) of some significant event that had occurred. Along with all of the events I would have expected him to include, such as the first day of school and our Winter Solstice program, he added something he had learned or done in P.E. class each month (Figure 8.11). This was a surprise to me—I had no idea P.E. was such an important part of his school life.

Date: 4-1-96

Assignment: List why You think the
Japanese Americans were treated the way
they were & they weren't
from this state? ❶ Because the
way there eye's started to Push
in next to thir nose Like this?
❷ because they talk a difrent
way? ❸ Because thir from a
difrent culture?

it is 6,000 miles from Amirica Across to Jabrin

United
States
of Amirica

Japan

**Figure 8.10**   Nick's Literature Log Entry

Thinking back on our first discussion about maps and how they show us where to go and where things are, I realized that they also show us where we've been. The maps created at the end of the school year revealed what was important to each child. I learned how significant the stories were to Jesse, how much Kinley paid attention to the architecture at the art museum, and what a passion Nathan had for P.E. The maps had served as a guide for me to understand and remember my students in yet another way.

Maps became my line for teaching that school year, as well as a metaphor for how I think about the work of a teacher. When we're really teaching, we're giving our students maps so they can find their way, and at the same time, we're showing them how to design and

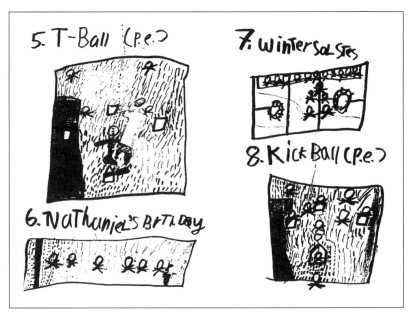

**Figure 8.11**   Jesse's Map of the School Year

make their own. We give them maps in the form of language so they can name what they encounter in the learning process. We give them maps by reading them stories that will inspire a sense of wonder and awe. We give them maps by asking questions and joining them in the process of trying to find the answers and meanings.

It is my hope that we can begin to use this map metaphor to become more trusting of children's thoughts and ideas. When we made our original list about maps, the children suggested that one thing maps do is help us get unstuck when we're lost. By placing the map in their hands, perhaps they will show us a way to get "unstuck" from practices that are meaningless and irrelevant to all of our school lives. Allowing them to help design the map may release us from looking at teaching as a series of activities and help us see the greater, more significant destinations we need to reach on our school journeys. In so doing, we may find ourselves on adventures even more wonderful and charming than those experienced by the children who stepped into the wardrobe and entered the magic of Narnia. And finally, we may come to know our students in a new way, a way that will help us guide them further along a path leading toward their highest human potential.

## References

Fanelli, S. (1995). *My map book*. New York: HarperCollins.

Lewis, C. S. (1950/1994). *The lion, the witch and the wardrobe*. New York: HarperCollins.

Macaulay, D. (1977). *Castle*. Boston: Houghton Mifflin.

Murray, D. (1989). *Expecting the unexpected: Teaching myself—and others—to read and write*. Portsmouth, NH: Heinemann.

Steig, W. (1972). *Dominic*. New York: Farrar, Straus and Giroux.

White, E. B. (1970). *The trumpet of the swan*. New York: Harper & Row.

## Bibliography

### Mary Kenner Glover

*Professional resources that have been especially important to me include:*

Fletcher, R. (1993). *What a writer needs*. Portsmouth, NH: Heinemann.

Glover, M. K. (1997). *Making school by hand: developing a meaning-centered curriculum from everyday life*. Urbana, IL: National Council of Teachers of English.

Graves, D. (1983). *Writing: Teachers and children at work*. Portsmouth, NH: Heinemann.

Heard, G. (1995). *Writing toward home: tales and lessons to find your way*. Portsmouth, NH: Heinemann.

Murray, D. (1989). *Expecting the unexpected: teaching myself—and others—to read and write*. Portsmouth, NH: Heinemann.

Paley, V. (1992). *You can't say you can't play*. Cambridge, MA: Harvard University Press.

Peterson, R. (1992). *Life in a crowded place: making a learning community*. Portsmouth, NH: Heinemann.

*Children's books that I especially enjoy using with children include:*

Frasier, D. (1991). *On the day you were born*. San Diego, CA: Harcourt Brace Jovanovich.

Lewis, C. S. (1950/1994). *The lion, the witch and the wardrobe*. New York: HarperCollins.

Marshall, J. (1973). *Yummers*. Boston: Houghton Mifflin.

Nye, N. S. (Ed.). (1992). *This same sky: a collection of poems from around the world*. New York: Maxwell Macmillan International.

Steig, W. (1972). *Dominic*. New York: Farrar, Straus and Giroux.

Steig, W. (1976). *Abel's island*. New York: Farrar, Straus and Giroux.

Sullivan, C. (1989). *Imaginary gardens: American poetry and art for young children*. New York: Abrams.

# 9 Fueled by Surprise

**Phyllis Whitin**
Dutch Fork Elementary School, Irmo, South Carolina

Our daughter Becca was not quite two when she taught me some important lessons about surprise. She and her two older brothers were sprawled on the floor making get-well cards for a family friend named Becky. Becca had decorated her paper with bold orange and red scribbles. Suddenly, she tossed the orange crayon to the floor and carefully selected a black crayon. She began to make deliberate long and short, vertical lines in the lower corner of her paper, muttering, "Becky." I was stunned. Becca was no longer drawing; she was writing.

I remember stopping in my tracks and staring at Becca as she worked. The determined strokes and the commanding tone in her voice signaled the value that she gave to this authoring decision. In one brief, miraculous moment, I had a window into Becca's literacy. My surprise led me to pause and reflect. I realized that she must have been sorting out the role of illustrations and print for a long time and that she had selected a black crayon because it signified a writing tool to her. The marks that she made with the black crayon were different from her drawing. She had made decisions in her mind about the functions of writing and illustrations while she watched the family read aloud and write for numerous purposes. I could see both the wonder of the human mind and the power of social context in her learning. I made a vow that day to watch her even more closely from then on so that I could continue to learn more. Becca was teaching me about the energizing potential of surprise: Surprise slows down our teaching so that we can listen, look closely, and reflect. In fact, I have come to realize that without surprise the lifeblood of my teaching would drain away. It is surprise that fuels my teaching.

Becca helped me learn to believe in the importance of watching and reflecting upon surprise. Once I came to value surprise, I made a conscious decision to look for its many dimensions. With Becca, surprise led me to recognize signs of developing literacy. On other occasions, children's surprising comments and observations have encouraged me to examine my teaching practices. Over time, I learned that if surprise were important for me as a learner, it would be equally important for my students. I have therefore developed and used specific strategies and conditions to ensure that surprise will be an important dimension of my classroom. The stories that I tell will reflect both the lessons I have learned from surprise and my intentional plans to include surprise in my day-to-day teaching. These stories are drawn from my work in elementary and middle school.

## Redirected by Surprise

Even a casual comment or question by a student can catch me by surprise and cause me to take a hard look at the implications of my teaching decisions. One fall I learned an important lesson about children's writing by examining the implicit message of an unexpected student comment. For many years, I have displayed posters of poems around the room. I recite the poems, and I invite the children to say the poems alone or chorally. Enjoying poetry together has always become an important ritual for my classes, from preschool through middle school. At the beginning of this particular year, I created a bulletin board showing work from previous seventh graders as a preview of possible projects for the current year. On one of the first days of school, I asked the children to nominate a poem to recite chorally. Andy pointed to the board of student work and asked, "Can we say one of those poems?"

Andy's question was unexpected, and instantly I realized the message I had been sending inadvertently. The poems I recited were from published, famous authors. Although I regularly provided time for students to celebrate their written work, I never had encouraged my students to recite, read chorally, or memorize student work. In my mind, I had separated the two groups of authors, yet I had been in the habit of calling the students "authors," calling our group conferences "authors' circles," and calling our sharing time "authors' celebration." Andy's comment brought this inconsistency to my attention. With all these thoughts racing through my mind, I smiled, weakly, "Yes," and Andy recited a student-authored poem. Andy changed my thinking and my practices from that day forward. I still have many posters of published poets, but alongside them are poems by students. The children and I recite them all, naming the title and author of published and unpublished poems with equal dignity. How the children love to hear their classmates say by heart a poem that they have written. Thanks to Andy, now the children can believe that they are valued authors in my class.

At other times, when I listen to children, and when I read their silent messages, I find that I need to change my expectations for a single lesson or experience. One such instance occurred in my fourth-grade class the day after winter vacation. I usually start the day after this two-week break with an open-ended writing time. I suggest some broad topics: a time I was surprised over vacation, a snapshot of a moment, a time I felt particularly happy or sad, and so forth. We all return to the class bursting with news, and by writing about our experiences, we have some potential drafts for further writing. We follow the writing time with informal sharing so that the class can catch up with each other's news.

On this particular occasion, after a fifteen-minute silent writing period, we gathered on the floor in our circle. I reminded the children that we could share all, some, or none of our writing. We proceeded to take turns, with most of the children describing visits with relatives, special gifts, and the results of some exciting college bowl football games. I, too, was eager to share, and my own self-centeredness almost made me miss a surprise I needed to heed. When it was Colby's turn, he chose not to share, but just before we concluded our group time, he said, "I'll go." The topic of Colby's piece was similar to his classmates', but his voice did not match the content. "I was surprised by the score of the Florida game . . ." he read in a jerky, hesitant monotone. I leaned a little closer, puzzled. Colby continued to give a few football scores, took a breath, paused, and muttered almost inaudibly, "And I was surprised when my dog died."

The importance of gifts, traveling, and relatives paled in significance. Colby needed to know that we had really heard his message. My role was to gather the group together in his support. Quietly I said, "I'm so sorry. It's so hard to lose a pet that you love." The children took my cue, and we sat in silence. Finally Colby added details. He had watched as his dog was struck by a car. Listening, we all remembered the happy stories Colby had written in the fall about his dog.

Breaking the long silence, Jennifer spoke. She, too, had lost a dog earlier in the year. Now she explained how her dog had been part of the family since before she was born. Her dog had protected her as an infant and had remained as her fast companion for these ten years. Fighting tears, she said, "When my dog died, I cried and cried. I cried every night for a long time."

Laura Jane, Ross, and others quietly shared their stories of grief over pets they had lost. In between the stories, the children and I sat in silence or wiped away tears. I moved to pat or hug the children who had spoken. Finally, I thanked all the children for understanding how hard this time was for their classmate. We would all support Colby on this difficult day.

The conversation was not one that I had anticipated, and, sad as it was, it taught me more about surprise. I need to know my children well so that I recognize surprising cues. I need to let surprise change my preconceived notions of a lesson plan. Letting surprise lead me can help me to support individuals and build community.

## Growing through Surprise

One of the measures I use to judge if my classroom is thriving is my own development as a learner. When I feel my own thinking stretched, I believe that my students are challenged as well. I grow as a learner myself when the children surprise me with a comment, observation, or question. I have come to appreciate the interdependence of my learning and the children's. I therefore have come to plan intentionally for this dimension of teaching.

One day Deidre stayed in from recess to share her thoughts about some science observations she had made. A pair of bluebirds had been building a nest in a box behind our portable classroom. The children had recorded the length of time between nest-building trips for several days. When Deidre studied the data, she noticed that the female had made many more frequent trips earlier in the week than at the latter part. This change in pattern interested her, and she wanted to talk about it.

At one point during our conversation she mused, "Maybe the female bluebird is trying to get exercise because she has to get on to the nest for a long time."

Although I, too, had known that the bird was coming less often, the thought of her needing exercise had never occurred to me. I was intrigued. I began to think of a human female and the importance of exercise and nutrition during pregnancy. I commented that for a human, a developing baby takes a lot of energy. Deidre answered, "Like she has to feed two."

"Right," I replied. "So this bird is feeding up to five or six. So maybe she's out getting nourishing food, to get the right proteins and things to get in the eggs to make them strong . . . maybe . . . you know how animals eat a lot before they hibernate? Maybe her system is saying . . ."

"Eat," Deidre continued. "Kind of like hibernation. Because she has to sit on that nest a long time."

"Maybe the reason might be partly for exercise and partly for food," I wondered.

Deidre extended the idea of my analogy. "Just a few days instead of like months . . . but she still has to eat." Deidre and I smiled at our collaborative theory, and I made sure that she realized how her thinking had impacted mine.

As I reflected upon this brief interchange, I was struck by the way we developed this idea. Deidre had first wondered why the female bluebird spent longer periods of time away from the nest. She developed a tentative theory that the female needed exercise before she began the long incubation period. Deidre's theory was based upon her knowledge that the female bluebird singularly incubates the eggs, while in other species both sexes incubate. Her idea caused me to think about my own experiences as a mother, with special needs for exercise and nutrition. Deidre's next comment, "Like she has to feed two," led me to contrast a bird's brood with that of a human. A large number of babies made me think of a larger volume of food, which led to the idea of hibernation. Finally, Deidre brought my far-fetched idea of relating incubation and hibernation into balance by emphasizing the proportional relationship of "a few days instead of months." Neither Deidre nor I could have developed these ideas on our own. Each of us contributed our knowledge, experience, and perspective.

Once again, I saw new value in surprise. When I am ready to be surprised by my students' thinking, I am cast in the role of co-learner. I help my students make connections, and they do the same for me. I delight in this generation of new ideas, and my students see this delight in action. At these times I am at my best as a teacher because my students see my joy in being a lifelong learner. My demonstration speaks more loudly than any of my words. Through such experiences, I affect students like Deidre from another perspective as well. When I acknowledge the impact that my students have on my thinking, I empower them as learners. They see their ideas as meaningful, valuable, and important. Developing hypotheses and theories with my students is one strategy that supports this empowerment.

## Nurturing Surprise

Another strategy that I have found to nurture surprise in my classroom is to provide opportunities to express ideas in multiple ways. Written language is privileged in schools, particularly in post-primary grades. While reading a story, for example, many teachers ask their children to answer written questions, to create essays according to guidelines, or to follow specified prompts. A refreshing change from these routines is the Sketch-to-Stretch strategy (Short & Harste, with Burke, 1996; Whitin, 1996). It is this shift in responding from writing to art that generates surprise.

Sketch-to-Stretch is simply an invitation to put one's ideas about a story into a visual form. In sketching, learners draw what the story means to them rather than illustrate a scene. I usually ask students to think of important ideas or feelings in a story or poem, and then to brainstorm colors, shapes, textures, lines, or symbols that might show those ideas. For example, if someone says that a feeling in a story is sadness, I ask what color might stand for sadness. Usually someone will suggest blue or gray, but I always ask, "Who has another idea?" I want to be sure that from the start we all understand that multiple interpretations are welcome, although I do ask students to give reasons for their ideas.

Once acquainted with the strategy, children often choose to sketch in their reader's response journals or collaborate to create group sketches. The generative power of collaboration is a constant source of surprise and delight for me. Recently I was particularly fascinated by the thinking of a small group of boys who were creating a poster in response to the novella, *Sarah, Plain and Tall* (MacLachlan, 1985). In this turn-of-the-century story, Sarah leaves her home on the coast of Maine in response to a newspaper ad for a prospective wife and stepmother. Children were amazed at this historical practice, and from their own perspective of divorce and separation, they empathized with the stresses of trying to establish a blended family. While reading and discussing the book, the children talked regularly about the theme that we came to call "building a family." They identified key events in the book that helped to draw the family closer together and lessen Sarah's homesickness.

After completing the book, I asked each small group to create a sketch that would show a time line for a theme in the book. One group of boys wanted to illustrate how key events slowly strengthened the new family's relationship. After some discussion, the boys decided to draw a large flower to show changes over time. They developed some initial ideas during the first work period. In a class meeting, Joseph explained why the group chose a flower as a symbol. He described that when a person plants a seed, the plant grows in stages. "Like the characters," he continued, "they have to keep growing. As the flower is growing, it picks up memories. The petals stand for the memories now growing, but the center is where they are closed up. Your brain is inside your head; memories are on the inside so they can't get damaged."

Alex added, "Like water and minerals are inside a cactus. They are kept on the inside." Alex remembered our study of the desert the month before and related the idea of protection to this special plant.

Jason also elaborated upon Joseph's idea. Folding his arms over his chest for emphasis, he explained that on the inside, the memories would be "close and captive. You don't put memories on the outside where they can get damaged."

I was fascinated by the boys' differentiation between the inside and the outside of the flower, and how they related it to the fragile nature of developing memories that would build a family. Joseph's and Alex's comparisons added a scientific perspective to the idea of protection, while Jason's poetic phrase, "close and captive," along with his gesture, added an aesthetic dimension. Giving the boys a chance to talk about their thinking to the class before they had finished their poster allowed them to generate new ideas. The idea of protecting good memories was becoming more important to them. Even though I had seen this generative power of talk and drawing before, I was still not prepared for the surprises of the next day.

When the boys returned to their group, they developed their idea of protecting the most important memories. Looking through their journals and notes, they agreed upon four key events of the story that were the most precious new memories for the family: swimming in the cow pond, sliding on a haystack "dune," singing, and eating together at the table by candlelight. Finding these key "good" memories led them to contrast these events with Sarah's sadness and homesickness. As they sketched the positive scenes, they began to talk about how people deal with bad memories, and how the good memories in the book became stronger than the sad memories. Meanwhile, the idea of a flower made them think about bees, and Joshua began to sketch a bee. Connecting their ideas together, they decided that the pollen could represent the bad memories, and the bee came to take it away. "Yes," exclaimed Alex, "and the bee takes the pollen away and makes it into honey. So the bad memories can be made into good memories." This new idea of the bee helped the boys strengthen their premise that the good memories developed a strong family relationship despite some sad times. Their final commentary for their poster read:

> In the middle [of the flower] is the main memory of Sarah. The petals are protecting the main memory from the other bad memories of Sarah. The pollen around the flower is the bad memories. The bee is the bad memory taker awayer.

I was amazed at the way the boys extended the metaphor of the flower to explain Sarah's internal conflict. As they elaborated upon the parts of a flower, the way it grew, and how it related to other forms of life, they analyzed the ideas in the story more deeply. I doubted that they would have developed these ideas without the opportunity to express their thinking in the less-traditional way of sketching. If they had merely responded to a predetermined set of questions with implicit correct answers, there would have been no surprises. Through sketching and talking, they grew as literate people, and I appreciated both their personal thinking and the sophistication of their collective literary analysis. Like Becca, these boys showed me the wonder of human minds and the power of social interaction.

## Planning for Surprise

I have also found that encouraging metaphorical connections in other disciplines can lead my students and me down surprising paths of thinking. This third teaching strategy actually grew out of my interest in sketching in response to literature. Every sketch is a metaphor, such as a flower that represents building a family. I discussed my ideas with my husband, with whom I collaborate. We began to search for opportunities to capitalize upon the use of metaphor in all subject areas, particularly in mathematics and science (Whitin, P. & Whitin, D. 1997).

While working with fourth graders in mathematics, we noticed that the children naturally described mathematical patterns in metaphorical terms. Danny, for example, was coloring a pattern of multiples of four and eight on a hundred-square board. He noticed that every other number in the multiples of four (4, 8, 12, 16, 20, 24), was also a multiple of eight (8, 16, 24). He commented that four was like eight's "little sister" because "she follows him wherever he goes." His metaphor captured the "tag along" quality of the two sets of numbers. Intrigued by Danny's idea, we began to ask the children intentionally, "What does this number pattern remind you of? What is it like?"

We found that asking these questions opened the door to other surprising connections for mathematical ideas. While studying fractions, we talked about the confusing relationship of denominators getting larger while the size of the fraction gets smaller (one-half is greater than one-eighth, even though two is smaller than eight). Amanda explained it this way: "One-half is bigger than one-eighth because the one-eighth came from the one-half. For example, if you were just born, you can't be older and bigger than your mom because you came from her." Amanda demonstrated her point by showing that four one-eighth pieces covered the same area as one-half in a manipulative model. I was surprised by her insight and realized that the use of this analogy allowed Amanda to explain a difficult relationship in a personally inventive way.

On another occasion, exploring equivalent fractions led Ryan to create a comparison that showed his personal perspective. After listing numerous names of one-half (one-half, two-fourths, four-eighths, eight-sixteenths, etc.), we asked, "How can there be so many fractions that equal one-half? What does this idea in fractions remind you of?" Ryan suggested, "It's like culture. There's a lot of cultures in the world. But all the people are God's." One of Ryan's favorite subjects was social studies, so he naturally used a cultural referent to explain this mathematical idea. Jon, on the other hand, was an avid rock hound. His metaphor reflected his own interest: "They're [equivalent fractions] like optical calcite and green calcite. They're both calcite, but they look different." Consciously inviting the children to create these metaphors encouraged them to make surprising connections between their own experiences and abstract ideas. They made sense of mathematical ideas for themselves, and as a teacher, I learned to value their unique thinking through these unexpected metaphorical images.

Setting the spirit of searching for metaphors or analogies proved to be an important dimension of science class as well. Jonathan, for example, compared the clashing of cold and warm air masses in weather to people fighting. When a cold air mass pushes a warm air mass out of its way, the "bully" cold air mass has "won." On another occasion, Lauren was studying a picture of a Minnesota lake in early spring when the ice was breaking into shards. She compared the relationship between the ice shards and the lake water to plate tectonics: "Instead of water, magma comes out. The ice is like the plates of the earth when they crack and move. The icicles [shards] are like thin crust on the magma." Her comparison helped her to make sense of weather conditions and geology from a fresh perspective. Whitney, on the other hand, used her personal experience to describe the sound of a bird at our class feeder. She said, "It made a sound like a jumping rope."

Jonathan, Lauren, and Whitney were using what they knew about one experience (squabbles, plate tectonics, and jump roping) to make sense of other experiences. Personal interests and experiences became valuable assets to the children as individuals and to the group as a whole. Making a wide range of ideas public encourages learners to make even more connections. And the cycle that surprise sets in motion continues.

## Reflections on Surprise

These stories have led me to be even more determined to seek surprise in my teaching. First, I need to watch and listen to my students closely. I always find valuable opportunities to reflect upon teaching and learning by being ready for surprise. I want to use surprise to understand learning processes more deeply. I also grow by using surprise to alter my teaching practices, whether it is for a day, a year, or a lifetime. I need to capitalize upon instances of surprise so that I can honor my students as individuals and build community.

Ironically, I cannot leave surprise to chance. I need to plan for surprise. I want to leave room for the unplanned. I am not promoting a classroom that is unplanned and aimless; such are the conditions for chaos. However, I am advocating a classroom that celebrates and nurtures surprise. Such a view of teaching expands the traditional definition of planning. Part of planning becomes the deliberate, conscious awareness of setting conditions for a classroom environment that embraces the tentative and the playful, because in such a climate teachers show themselves as learners. Surprise needs to be part of teaching because it is part of learning itself. Teachers can plan for surprise by inviting children to hypothesize about themes in literature, patterns in mathematics, and observations in science, and then to join the conversations themselves. Teachers can plan for surprise by creating open-ended opportunities to express ideas in multiple ways. Teachers can regularly ask students, "What surprised you?" and listen hard to what they have to say. Through surprise, we can be both lifelong learners and lifelong teachers. We can be fueled by surprise.

## References

MacLachlan, P. (1985). *Sarah, plain and tall*. New York: Harper & Row.

Short, K., & Harste, J., with Burke, C. (1996). *Creating classrooms for authors and inquirers* (2nd ed.). Portsmouth, NH: Heinemann.

Whitin, P. (1996). *Sketching stories, stretching minds: Responding visually to literature*. Portsmouth, NH: Heinemann.

Whitin, P., & Whitin, D. (1997). Ice numbers and beyond: Language lessons for the mathematics classroom. *Language Arts*, 74, 108–115.

## Bibliography

### Phyllis Whitin

*Professional resources that have been especially important to me include:*

Barnes, D. R. (1976/1992). *From communication to curriculum*. Portsmouth, NH: Boynton/Clark.

Doris, E. (1991). *Doing what scientists do: Children learn to investigate their world*. Portsmouth, NH: Heinemann.

Eisner, E. (1992). The misunderstood role of the arts in human development. *Phi Delta Kappan, 73*, 591–595.

Graves, D. (1991). *Build a literate classroom*. Portsmouth, NH: Heinemann.

Harste, J., & Short K., with Burke, C. (1988). *Creating classrooms for authors: The reading–writing connection*. Portsmouth, NH: Heinemann.

Smith, F. (1979). *Reading without nonsense*. New York: Teachers College Press.

*Children's books that I especially enjoy using with children include:*

Fendler, D. (1978). *Donn Fendler: Lost on a mountain in Maine*. Sommersworth: New Hampshire Publishing Co.

MacLachlan, P. (1985). *Sarah, plain and tall*. New York: Harper & Row.

Prelutsky, J. (ed.). (1983). *The Random House book of poetry for children*. New York: Random House.

Taylor, M. (1975). *Song of the trees*. New York: Dial.

Yashima, T. (1986). *Crow boy*. New York: Viking.

# 10 Getting Real with Students

**Mary M. Kitagawa**
Mark's Meadow School, Amherst, Massachusetts

In the popular press, and even in some professional publications, there is an enormous misconception about where the demarcation line is between "whole language" and other philosophies of education. Contrary to impressions from the media, the place of phonics in the curriculum is not the dividing line. The distinction is easier to see in upper elementary grades where the red herring issue of phonics does not obfuscate the picture. What marks a whole language classroom is teachers who take the political stance encapsulated in this maxim: Get real with your students so they can really learn.

I kept a journal in 1996, while teaching a fifth-sixth grade class, but I have always been a sporadic diarist, so it was usually the exciting or frustrating days that I recorded. As I now look back over the entries, I find that what probably keeps me in teaching after over thirty years of "trying to get it right" is the challenge of trying to lead by following. "Following," in this sense, is not the least bit passive, however, for my role is to give back to students the exploratory zeal they had as toddlers.

The best learning occurs when I loosen the reins so that students interact more freely with me and more collaboratively with each other. Ten- to twelve-year-olds, whose interests are almost riveted to those of their peers, take to the approach with enthusiasm, and as my journal shows, the teacher who goes along for the ride is in for a lot of excitement, too. One of the subtle but essential ways a teacher can loosen the reins is by altering her discourse patterns with the students.

There is a great deal of research about classroom discourse (Cazden, 1988) that describes teacher–pupil exchanges in the recitation mode: IRE—Initiation, Response, Evaluation. The traditional pattern is that the teacher *initiates* the exchange with a question addressed to the class or an individual, gets a *response*, and *evaluates* it before initiating another exchange. Although such a pattern of recitation may be less prevalent today than previously, it still appeals to teachers who want to control on a micromanagement level. It feels like "getting it right," and to a passerby it looks like orderly learning, but it is a perfunctory way to "cover" the curriculum with little real learning for most students.

There is no doubt that teachers *are* responsible for their students' learning, but to achieve long-term effects, schooling must be team action at center court instead of a spectator sport. One of the most effective ways to engage students in their own learning is to replace many of our IRE exchanges with the egalitarian discourse patterns that are typical outside of school.

Years ago, in a seminar in England led by Peter Medway, what might seem obvious to others dawned upon me for the first time: *"Where, other than in classrooms,"* he asked us, *"would people tolerate being asked questions for which the questioner has a predetermined answer in mind?"* Doing so out of school sounds condescending or sarcastic unless it is clearly only a rhetorical device.

I began to monitor myself, trying to reduce the number of what I call "teacherish" questions—that is, the questions only a teacher asks—and replacing them with challenges and open-ended tasks in which students' responses are a matter of my genuine inquiry. Besides monitoring the nature of my questions, I structure much of the school day into interactions in which my contributions are to be given no more validity than the students'. I tell them up front that this is my goal; I invite them to help me, and I demonstrate that I mean it. There are many small but significant ways I do this: being as real in dialogues as I would be with an adult, bending over backwards to accommodate their suggestions, and frankly seeking their advice on matters that they can help me decide. Some areas of the curriculum lend themselves more easily to genuine dialogue than others, but in every context my primary goal is to nurture student initiative. When they take the initiative, learning happens.

In literature study circles my students delve more deeply and personally into their novels during discussions when I completely restrain myself from teacherish talk. Although they know that I am passionate, not *laissez-faire*, about the quality of our discussions, they expect of me genuine discourse (including the times when I spontaneously react with jealousy that they noticed something I missed!). And by constantly treating their interpretations with respect, I build a level of rapport that allows me to present some of my own views without overwhelming the students' confidence in their own.

If I ever toss a comprehension question into an interpretive discussion (e.g., a question about the novel's literal information), it is alarming how fast students revert to the recitation model. (The only exception is when they know that I am truly seeking personal edification, as with L'Engle's books, which my students handle better than I do!). The recitation mode is easy to recognize: Students shift their gaze to me instead of looking at the classmate who is speaking, and they overly attend to whatever I contribute. Turn-taking slows to a crawl because students pause between speakers and look to see if I want a turn. In genuine literature-study conversation, without the recitation component, I find myself competing for turns like everyone else. While discussing Natalie Babbitt's *Tuck Everlasting*, a group of students was debating the ideal age to drink the magic spring water that prevents either aging or dying. Some were arguing for 18 and others insisted that 21, 25, or even 28 would be better. I was desperately trying to convince them that the real question was whether to drink the water in the first place, saying that I personally wouldn't touch the stuff. They suspended their argument only long enough for Lupita to resolve that discrepancy with a single sentence: "That's because you've already passed all the good ages." I have been thinking about using that as my epitaph: "She died because she had already passed all the good ages!"

Genuine questions are also quite natural in writing workshop conversation, within conferences and during group sharing sessions: "How did you come up with this character for your story?" I ask, or "Have you decided on a title for this poem?"—inquiries that only the author could answer. Because students know that their decisions drive the content of their writing, they find it natural to explain those decisions authoritatively. (I will admit that this is one of the harder tasks for me, however—to keep from "fixing" their writing my way!).

It may sound as if all I do is "hang out" with my class as one of the gang, but that is absolutely not the case. Much of the day I am clearly an instructor rather than a co-participant. A commitment to genuine conversation does not mean that teachers can never instruct. When there is a lesson that is best imparted through direct instruction, they should be up-front about what they are doing and engage in a straightforwardly instructional mode. To me, the instructional mode has to contrast with the co-participant mode, but even when I instruct, I try to avoid teacherish IRE patterns, such as pretending to elicit information from students as a ploy to hold their attention. For example, if the point of the instruction is to remind students of what has been taught previously, I think it is more honest to say something like, "It looks like you need a review of dialogue punctuation; I'll go over it for you now" rather than teasing them with, "Now what punctuation rules are needed for a dialogue?" when you are already convinced that they have forgotten or never understood it in the first place.

Also in whole-class instruction, I prefer to be direct when presenting knowledge as the authority instead of worming approximate answers from students and correcting their responses. For instance, if I plan to teach the formula for finding the area of a circle to students who have recently learned to find the circumference, I might straightforwardly ask them if they need to review what *pi* is, or, if I were determined to review it anyway, I would just do so. I personally believe that students attend to direct instruction best when it is presented as that, and furthermore, that they appreciate an up-front approach about the fact that I have something to teach. They know that they are not being tested, because I am not engaging in questioning but rather in telling or demonstrating. They can safely reveal any confusion because it is obvious that my goal is only to help resolve it. Their energy can be shifted from trying to be "right" to asking the questions they would really like to have answered.

Beyond language arts, in fact throughout the curriculum, genuine questions foster richer dialogues with students than teacherish questions do, for questions with right and wrong answers signal students to be performers. When answering a question feels like a performance, it is normal to pull back from risk-taking. Once freed from the obligation to perform, students' talk is one of the key ways they can bring to the surface what it is that they almost know.

On the first day of school, according to my journal of 1996, I asked my class, "What do you think it is that makes a poem a poem?" It wasn't the first class I had ever asked that question, but the potential array of answers is too large to make it anything but a genuine query. After they looked at some poems written by the class of the previous year and brainstormed awhile, I asked the students to go home and list ten attributes of poetry. Philip's "a poem is a song without a tune" seemed to put the other students into a positive mood for the assignment. The next day they got together in groups of four or five to narrow their forty or fifty contributions to ten that they felt best described the nature of poetry.

Lest anyone think the group processes were smooth on that second day of school, let me digress with a description from my journal entry made that evening:

> Alan was sabotaging his group's efforts by flippant strategies such as closing his eyes and aiming his pencil at the list for a blind choice (until I called him aside and asked for more positive leadership, he being one of my former fifth graders—now sixth); and another group decided that the democratic process was to let each member select their own best two, a quick strategy that

bypassed most of the fruitful discussion I had envisioned. But the other four groups did negotiate their choices, and two of those groups debated so extensively that they required far more time than I had planned, creating boredom and consequent misbehavior among the fast finishers.

That second night I typed a list of the sixty "winners" from the six groups, and the next day we had an election. I recorded votes on an overhead transparency of the list. After we pooled votes for the ones that seemed like restatements of the same attribute, we settled upon these ten, in order of popularity:

**Poetry**

- can express feelings
- is like a song without a tune
- creates a picture in your mind
- has a rhythm
- sometimes has metaphors that express ideas
- is often descriptive
- says a lot in just a little
- can be in groups of phrases (not necessarily sentences)
- can be fiction or nonfiction
- creates a way of looking at things differently

The last one actually tied with "sometimes rhymes," but the students left it off because they said everyone knows that.

I judge that this series of lessons was effective because we got from it a "consensus" to put on a wall chart, and immediately afterwards about half of the class dived into poetry books to do some reading while the rest grabbed pencils and began to draft poems. Part of restraining my teacherish voice had been to let stand their contribution "fiction or nonfiction" rather than bargaining with them for "fantasy and realism," which I suspected they meant. Had I chosen to bargain, it would have been easy to ask for clarification, but this was early in our relationship, and I did not yet trust them to know that my puzzlement was genuine. On the third day of school, I was leery of having my question taken as an evaluative zinger that would diminish their sense of ownership of the list.

That same day we did a science activity, which I chose as a launch to our mandated Buoyancy and Density science unit and also because I was quite sure it would encourage lively hypothesizing. Though basic principles of buoyancy are involved and I had done this lesson before, something beyond my expectations occurred, so I found it easy to contribute my genuine questions to theirs.

Pairs of students dropped unpopped kernels of popcorn into water, wrote observations, then added Alka Seltzer tablets, speculating on paper about causes for the results. I asked them to do a double column list: observations and hypotheses. It was noisy but productive, and some groups had time to add raisins to see if the results were different. During discussion, they debated why there were bubbles on the popcorn kernels that sank in the water even before the Alka Seltzer was added. About half thought that air above the water line caught onto the kernel and rode down with it, and others maintained that there was air emerging from inside the kernel. Since most students felt that the fact that the kernels sank proved their solidity, and further study of kernels showed no visible airholes, there was a lively debate. About the raisins, some students suggested that we should have tried it with grapes, with Juanita arguing that raisins are also grapes so they would behave alike, and Taylor convincing her that the difference in water content would be a variable.

I had to fight my urge toward closure and not end the lesson by giving or eliciting a teacherish conclusion, but that was not as hard for me as it would have been had I not been genuinely surprised by the air bubbles and equally curious about the effects of some of the variables they suggested, including using soda pop instead of water. (Just writing this, I realize that we should have tried popping the kernels after the experiment.)

The first read-aloud book of the year led to a long series of creative drama experiences in which I got to be more a tracker than a controller of the students' learning. In *The Girl Who Owned a City* (Nelson, 1995) the characters are children who must survive without adults because some plague has wiped out everyone over the age of twelve. Our discussions were so rich, and the novel was so popular, that I launched a three-session survival simulation that actually occupied us for about thirty minutes a day for the next three weeks. We were twenty-seven children shipwrecked on a tropical island with no hope of rescue.

I had read about what is variously called creative or spontaneous drama (especially Johnson & O'Neill, 1984) in which the only performance is cooperative exploration through role-playing. I had tried some such events off and on, but this turned into the most extensive creative drama any class of mine had undertaken. My role was to establish the setting and our plight, as well as to challenge the students to join me in speaking only in character during the co-creation of our ad-libbed drama. From the beginning, both while they acted in character and during debriefing sessions, the students insisted that no leader was necessary and that electing a leader would just make others jealous. I tested their determination by playing my part in role as someone dense enough to keep talking about a leader and asking how one should be chosen, but they did not budge.

By the third episode, the group, with everyone speaking in role as survivors, had decided what task subgroups we needed: explorers, firemakers, shelter builders, food gatherers, doctors, and so on. Taylor volunteered to run the meeting in which jobs were given, and, although he was told not to assume leadership, he was allowed to coordinate turn-taking. As a minor character, a sleeping-mats weaver, I could act helpless when anyone sought to use me as a resource while we were in role. When, for example, the firebuilder asked me how he was going to start a fire without matches, I simply shrugged. When students complained about the behavior of others, I usually sympathized without coming to their rescue. (I did, however, set game rules during debriefing sessions, such as suggesting that it would be fair to look up survival information between role-playing episodes. And twice, when serious horseplay threatened the role-playing of others, I did break everyone out of role to reiterate rules about sincere participation.)

Every two class periods were one day on the island. The first was daytime, and students worked together in groups according to their roles. To my surprise, they never solved problems with unrealistic ease. In fact, though they were just talk-acting their parts in most groups, the shelter builders' attempts regularly fell down in spite of elaborate variations that they pretended to attempt, and the firebuilder never did figure out how to get a blaze going in spite of plenty of advice from others. (Fortunately, our food gatherers never brought us much but bananas and coconuts, so there was nothing to cook.)

After the third of these daytime simulations, I wrote in my journal these observations about the differences between the small groups:

> Some seemed more like kindergartners than upper elementary, but no one seemed to consider it beneath their dignity. The doctors did more playacting than talking, making leaf bandages and foraging for "medicines" on the playground lawn, while most of the other groups only "talk-acted" or drew diagrams about what they were doing. Yet even the talk-actors would sometimes wander over to the doctors with a physical need to be "treated" and then go back to the small group work that was

mostly verbal. My sleeping-mats teammates were another physically involved group; they looked up raffia between sessions and, when the encyclopedia description did not suffice, went to the art teacher for actual materials to make miniature sleeping mats.

The class periods that alternated with "daytime work" were whole-group discussions around the (unlit) campfire where the survivors presumably met every evening. Taylor continued as discussion leader, but the group constantly reminded him that his position did not include decision-making powers, which frustrated him and caused friction because of his violations. Every campfire seemed to be a different governing experiment. David argued for rotating leadership, including the running of meetings, but was outvoted. Finally they resurrected a suggestion someone had made in the first days, when the group committed themselves not to have any single leader: They would have a council. Each subgroup that worked together on survival needs, such as shelter builders, would send a delegate to the council at campfire time. Council members, sitting in an inner circle, could speak freely, while Taylor would sit in the outer ring and occasionally call on outer ring members if they had something to say to the council. It did not work well at all, but it was fascinating to see them struggle with the logistics of governance.

Once, in processing after a session, students asked me to regulate some of the off-task horseplay and insincere comments that were interfering with the role-playing during campfire sessions. We all knew what they meant. I suggested that I would be a sandman, and, if someone's behavior was unproductive, I would signal that person to "fall asleep" by leaving the circle. I guess they were serious about the success of this game because everyone whom I later had to signal for a nap dropped out without objection. They would just say something like, "Well, it's been a hard day," and pull back from the group.

An observer might think my role was too passive, but actually I believe that my mere presence (even playing a minor role among the stranded children) kept the game from turning into a *Lord of the Flies* simulation! I contributed a behavioral bottom line, which enabled them to maintain enough sincerity to struggle genuinely with the conflicts of independence versus interdependence that seemed to underlie most decisions. In their journal entries, many students indicated that, though they did not want to give up their Utopian ideas of a society that needs no leader, they realized that this group was headed for a split that might have been prevented had a leader been chosen.

Our survival game, as we called it, was an occasion of experimentation for all of us. I was "teaching by ear" just as much as they were "learning by doing." I had secret doubts on many occasions. Once, when the explorers told us at campfire that they found two skeletons with swords stuck through them (I don't know why their assailants had left their swords behind; perhaps each of them had killed the other simultaneously!), I was nervous that our role-play would take a violent or whodunit turn, but that campfire session was one of the most focused discussions of all. The swords were too rusted to be of any use, it was reported, but the group debated the ethics of using human bones to aid our survival. Some argued that we could make a trap from the rib cages or could sharpen bones for tools. To those who thought the skeleton parts should not be used, out of respect for the dead, others said, "Whoever it was would probably want us to use what we could," and "It would be sort of like an organ transplant." Philip argued that, after the soul had departed, the use of the remains was no different from use of animal remains. I was amazed at the focused but dispassionate involvement of the whole group. No one had to be put to sleep during that campfire!

Since a simulation is artificial by definition, what did the survival role-playing have to do with genuine questions? I think it had everything to do with my underlying assumption that students have to see the teacher as being open to their thinking rather than as steering them toward predetermined outcomes. If I were standing in front of them with a teachers' manual to which I could refer for answers or next steps, their participation would probably have been to subtly, or even overtly, sabotage the process. Genuine questions and co-constructed simulations allow students to provide direction to the concepts they are ready to handle and force them to use each other as resources. And the level of the learning that accompanies this "loosening of the reins" is shown clearly by an examination of the results.

Looking back upon the year as a whole, I know that, even though interpersonal dynamics remained thorny right up until summer vacation, community building *did* occur in those early months, and I attribute much of the credit to our role-playing. My assessment has to be in the Good News/Bad News format:

> GN = The class as a whole remained accessible to each other in many peer consultation situations, such as in excellent writing conferences between peers (some of the best I have ever overheard) and collaboration in math, science and social studies.
> BN = The handful of students who dealt with their peers disrespectfully at the beginning of the year continued to engage

in serious putdowns except when I was involved as a direct witness, a buffer, or a threat. Most of the verbal attacks occurred on the playground or at least out of my earshot, but the repercussions constantly spilled back into the classroom, so I knew that I was only keeping the lid on rather than actually shutting off the heat. GN = The class eagerly engaged in another simulation in December, a model United Nations which accompanied our World Regions and Contemporary Issues unit. Although we had never spoken explicitly about how our governing attempts on the island compared to those of actual societies, it was obvious that students had absorbed concepts about government by role-playing the formation of a mini-society on the tropical island.

When I chide myself about "getting it right" so I can retire in peace, I am not really serious. Actually, I believe that since "getting it right" is "getting real," I have to accept the risk of "getting it wrong": Tidy structures and predictable outcomes have to be sacrificed in order to achieve the often disorderly process by which concepts grow in experiential contexts. There is no threat to my high expectations and standards when I tip the balance away from teacherish to genuine questions and from prepackaged curricula to open-ended opportunities. The quality of the students' participation and learning has always exceeded my most optimistic expectations.

## References

Babbitt, N. (1975). *Tuck everlasting*. New York: Farrar, Straus & Giroux.

Cazden, C. B. (1988). *Classroom discourse*. Portsmouth, NH: Heinemann.

Golding, W. (1954). *Lord of the flies*. New York: Coward-McCann.

Johnson, L. & O'Neill, C., (eds.). (1984). *Dorothy Heathcote: Collected writings on education and drama*. London: Hutchinson.

Nelson, O. T. (1995). *The girl who owned a city*. Minneapolis, MN: Runestone.

## Bibliography

**Mary M. Kitagawa**

*Professional resources that have been especially important to me include:*

Britton, J. et al. (1975). *The development of writing abilities 11–18*. London: Macmillan.

Mitchell Pierce, K. M., & Gilles, C. J. (1993). *Cycles of meaning*. Portsmouth, NH: Heinemann.

Moffett, J. (1968). *Teaching the universe of discourse*. Boston: Houghton Mifflin.

Routman, R. (1996). *Literacy at the crossroads*. Portsmouth, NH: Heinemann.

Shannon, P. (Ed.). (1992). *Becoming political: Readings and writings in the politics of literacy education*. Portsmouth, NH: Heinemann.

**Children's books that I especially enjoy using with children include:**

Alexander, L. (1964). *The book of three*. New York: Holt, Rinehart and Winston.

Alexander, L. (1965). *The black cauldron*. New York: Holt, Rinehart and Winston.

Alexander, L. (1966). *The castle of Llyr*. New York: Holt, Rinehart and Winston.

Alexander, L. (1967). *Taran wanderer*. New York: Holt, Rinehart and Winston.

Alexander, L. (1968). *The high king*. New York: Holt, Rinehart and Winston.

Babbitt, N. (1975). *Tuck everlasting*. New York: Farrar, Straus, and Giroux.

Collier, J., & Collier, C. (1978). *The winter hero*. New York: Four Winds Press.

Hamilton, V. (1974). *M. C. Higgins the great*. New York: Macmillan.

Lunn, J. (1996). *The root cellar*. New York: Puffin Books.

# 11 "I Can Hear You Thinking": Talking and Learning in a Multiage Classroom

**Kathryn Mitchell Pierce**
Glenridge School, Clayton, Missouri

I teach in a primary multiage classroom with children in grades 1, 2, and 3. Most students join our group as first graders and stay for three years. Recently, I listened in as a multiage group of students—Evan (age 9), Laura (age 7), and Michael (age 8)—were working at a table. After a long pause during which the three were deeply engrossed in independent thought, Michael said hesitantly, with a slight rise in intonation, "OK . . ."

> *Laura:* I can hear you thinking.
>
> *Michael:* Huh?!
>
> *Evan:* I'm going to get some Wite-Out.
>
> *Michael:* How come you always use Wite-Out?
>
> *Evan:* I usually write in pen and I usually screw up.
>
> *Michael:* Oh. Then you'll always need it, I guess.
>
> *Evan:* Yeah. 'Cause one time I tried to erase it and I ripped a hole in my page.
>
> *Michael:* [laughing]
>
> *Evan:* I just have to write over it [as he covers his error with daubs of white liquid].
>
> *Laura:* But it works!
>
> *Evan:* Yeah. It's gone now!
>
> *Michael:* Yeah. It went right through the page!
>
> *Evan:* OK. Let's see . . . [as he returns to his work].

Their conversation intrigued me. At first, I wasn't even sure why. Since I had taped this as part of the other work going on at the table, I had the chance to revisit the conversation several times as I attempted to sort out why it had captured my attention. Listening to the tape for the second and third time, I found myself smiling as I thought of Evan—how much he had grown and matured since I first met him several years ago. Now he was one of our "big kids" and already thinking about life next year in fourth grade. Laura and Michael, younger members of our group, looked on with admiration as Evan used the Wite-Out. Evan is just about the only one in our room who uses Wite-Out; the others seem to view it as a privilege Evan has earned by virtue of his status as one of the big kids and a passionate writer. Evan seemed so confident as he explained his use of the magical disappearing liquid—and so confident as he said, "and I usually screw up." The others didn't laugh at this or respond negatively in any way, and Evan seemed to know that they wouldn't.

Fleeting conversations like this one happen all day every day in our classroom. Most of them register momentarily and then are lost to my memory, but the tone remains. Listening in on these "peripheral" conversations is one of the ways I keep my finger on the pulse of our classroom. Talk is an essential way that we establish, maintain, and assess the social and intellectual health of our classroom as a community.

## How I Foster the Children's Exploratory Talk

For years I read about "The Language Arts" as being composed of reading, writing, listening, and speaking. For me, the term "speaking" conjured up images of public speakers, podiums, speaking engagements, speeches, and other formal situations. When I first began teaching two decades ago, our language arts curriculum (that is, the teacher's manual for the language arts basal series) had lessons on teaching "listening behavior," "listening comprehension," and "general listening skills." The textbook also included lessons on speaking, such as making introductions and presenting a well-organized speech to persuade, to explain, or to summarize. I don't remember any lessons on group work, responding to a conversational partner, or using talk as a way of creating new understandings or socializing in the way Laura, Michael, and Evan were doing.

Today, it is exploratory talk that lives at the heart of my classroom. Rich, exploratory talk (Barnes, 1975)—the informal, rough draft talk that supports learning—does not just magically happen in our classroom. I deliberately work to foster it. One of the important ways that we establish and sustain our learning community is through talking about our lives. At the beginning of the school year, I build in time for us to get to know one another, even though two-thirds of us are returning to the same classroom. We introduce our special buddies (the new students), tell family stories that will eventually become writing pieces, get caught up on what we have done over the summer, and make shared plans for what we will do together. This start-up time is essential, for this is the time that I signal to the children that all our personal stories are valued, and I demonstrate how members of a caring community listen to one another. During this time, we read and discuss books that help us think about ways we want to live and learn together in our classroom community, books like Leo Lionni's *Swimmy* or *Alexander and the Wind-Up Mouse* or *Frederick*. These books help us generate a list of words that describe a caring classroom community. This year our list included: caring, sharing, helping, respecting, cooperating, risk-taking, persevering. As a class, or in small literature groups, we discuss books like *The Hundred Dresses* or *Crow Boy* that help us think about ways we can invite others into our learning community. The books provide a starting place for our discussions and offer us new perspectives to consider as we make our plans for living and learning together.

I gravitate toward providing opportunities for students to work in pairs and small groups rather than having them listen, as a whole group, to the presentation of information. When deciding whether and how to group students, and how to support and focus their group work, I select strategies and experiences that seem most likely to encourage exploratory talk. One example would be the strategy, Say Something (Short & Harste, with Burke, 1996). Say Something involves two students reading a shared selection. They stop periodically throughout the reading to "say something" to one another about their reading. I have used this as a formal strategy to help students work through difficult reading material or learn important discussion skills. I might say at the beginning of a work period or small-group lesson, "Read this material aloud or to yourself, stopping at places you feel are important to say something to your partner about what you are thinking."

Most times, however, Say Something is one of the many strategies I carry with me in my head, that I pull out when it seems appropriate for an individual or a group. For example, when Meaghan was moving into an independent reading phase from an emergent phase, I encouraged her to "turn and talk with your neighbor about your book" to help her maintain a focus on meaning and response while she also wrestled with her new decoding skills. Partner reading, a strategy that we use almost daily, is an informal extension of Say Something that invites students to stop and talk informally about their reading and encourages them to keep their focus on meaning making and responding.

Once specific strategies like Say Something and partner reading have been introduced to even a small group of students, all the students begin to use them informally. In fact, these strategies have become so embedded in our classroom interactions that they no longer feel like "strategies" at all. Literature discussion groups (small group discussions of a literature book) occur formally as scheduled parts of our work, but they also occur informally as students gather together spontaneously in comfortable groups to talk through issues that have emerged in their reading.

Other strategies that have become "invisible" include:

- An Agenda. Brainstorm as a group what you could do next and then decide where to start, or make a list of the ideas you want to discuss during your next group session. (I learned this strategy from Carol Gilles.)

- Sketch to Stretch. Represent responses to texts or experiences through art. (Margie Siegel and Carolyn Burke first introduced me to the power of this strategy.)

- Learning Logs. Record what you did and learned.

- Group Reflections. Include, in your group learning log, your plans for your group's next experience.

- Three Pluses and a Wish. Identify three areas of recent growth and a wish for growth in the near future. (Heidi Mills and Tim O'Keefe first shared this with me based on their work with three-, four-, and five-year-olds.)

When students spontaneously use these strategies to support their own work, then I know they are beginning to value the power of language in learning.

I also work to create situations in which students can move between the roles of supporter and supported, expert and novice, confident risk-taker and hesitant stepper. We spend time talking about how to respond to one another in various group experiences. We reflect on what we have learned from others and what we feel we have contributed to the learning of others. Near parent conference time and progress report time, we talk in pairs and small groups as we share our working portfolios, self-evaluations and learning reflections, to help one another see evidence of risk-taking, growth, and confidence.

In all these ways, then, I deliberately foster the children's exploratory talk. I cannot leave it to chance, for this talk is too important in our learning community.

## Why I Foster the Children's Exploratory Talk

Exploratory talk supports children's learning in our classroom. Nothing could be more important than this. But it helps me learn too—about my students and how they are building their understanding. As I listen to the children, I hear the typical characteristics of exploratory talk—periods of silence, false starts, tentative language, musings—all indications that the materials and the conversation are stimulating new ideas and offering new perspectives. I tape discussions, listen to the tapes, and sometimes transcribe portions of them so that I can examine the children's talk more closely and better "hear" what the students are thinking individually and collectively. Here is an example. It comes from a three-week inquiry into geometrical 3-D shapes. During this study, I had observed students working in small multiage groups on various tasks and open-ended problems. As I observed them, I realized that the context required the students to simultaneously juggle:

- working cooperatively in a small group that was responsible for accomplishing a shared task;
- using talk, sketches, rough drafts, and pooled resources to invent (or recreate) geometric understandings;
- using fine motor skills to carry out the plans for drawing, cutting, folding, and gluing complex shapes.

I was impressed with the ways students handled these complex tasks, and I began making tapes of their discussions in order to better understand how they supported one another in these small-group settings. The following is an excerpt from one of these tapes. Cory (age 6), Seth (age 8), and Polly (age 7) are attempting to design a pattern for making a cube and a four-sided pyramid from a single sheet of paper.

> The group has sorted quickly through their ideas about creating the cube, and Polly is busy executing the plan. Using a ruler, sharp pencil, and special paper, Polly is drawing the final pattern for the cube. She is being meticulous about measuring the length of the sides, making the series of squares in a straight row, and creating crisp right-angle corners. The planning required to accomplish the task has been completed, and Polly's job requires time and careful attention to details. Seth and Cory, pleased with the group's first success, carefully watch Polly's work. For several minutes they just watch, although Cory periodically comments on Polly's actions: "I've noticed that you're . . ." or "You seem to be . . ." Polly responds to these observations with brief explanations of her actions.

*Me:* What could you two be doing while Polly is finishing this? Is there anything else that you could do to keep your group moving?

*Cory:* We could start on the other one . . . the . . . what's it called?

*Seth:* Yeah, the pyramid one. We could start on that one.

Cory sketches four tall isosceles triangles in a row "mountain range" style. Seth repeats the drawing on his own page. Cory explains to Seth that they can "fold it around, wrap it around" to make the four upright sides of the pyramid. Seth begins to cut his figure out, and Cory looks back at Polly's work. Polly has stopped mid-cut and is looking at Seth's work.

*Cory:* (gently but firmly) Polly, just get to work!

Cory watches Polly and then returns his attention to Seth's cutting. He continues to look back and forth between them.

*Cory:* You probably won't understand my idea but . . . I think it would be . . . you could cut it over here [pointing to the edge of the paper] . . . we'll have more paper . . . you won't waste so much that way. [They were given a limited amount of "draft paper" and a single piece of "final product" paper.]

*Seth:* Oh! Yeah, I get it.

Seth changes the way he is cutting through the paper to get to the shape he has drawn in the middle of the page. Cory continues to look back and forth between the two older classmates as they work.

*Cory:* (to Seth) Maybe we should make this one [pointing to Seth's drawing] the pyramid one . . . like the cube . . . make them the same.

Cory looks over at Polly again, watches her for a minute and then looks back at Seth, who is now staring at his unfinished cutting. Cory begins to quickly sketch out his idea [four triangles point out in four directions from a center]. Seth looks on as Cory sketches and then shifts attention to Polly's pattern for the cube. After a minute he begins to draw a new shape that looks like Cory's.

*Seth:* This will work just like the cube. See . . . we can pull this and this and all these sides up [pointing to each point on the four-sided star he has drawn] like on the cube.

Later, Polly invents a way to attach the sides of the cube she has finished cutting and folding. Using a glue stick and small slips of paper, she "tapes" the sides together. [They weren't allowed to use tape, but Polly found a legal way of accomplishing the task.] Next, she applies this strategy to the pyramid created by Seth and Cory. The group ends up creating both shapes within the first time period.

I recognized the informal, hesitant, and tentative language associated with exploratory talk as these children were talking among themselves to create and refine their understandings. The ideas they wrestled with and the conclusions they reached belonged to the group more than to any one individual. While some members of the group may have been able to accomplish this task alone, all members experienced success with the task in large part because of the opportunity to talk about half-baked ideas, to think out loud, and to explore possibilities. They shared observations, asked questions, and suggested possibilities, often phrasing ideas in the hesitant, "I wonder what if . . ." language commonly associated with exploratory talk. As I listen to this kind of talk, I know that the children are learning. And I am learning too.

## What the Children and I Learn from Their Exploratory Talk

I devote a significant amount of my classroom time to listening in as children talk. I listen to hear what they are wrestling with, what they are learning, and how they are using talk to learn with and from one another. In their talk I hear our lived-through curriculum. I listen carefully because their talk helps me see what is happening in our classroom from *their* perspective. I listen informally as the children enter the classroom in the morning, as they move from one experience to another during the day, and as they go about their work and play; and I listen more formally, notebook or tape recorder in hand, to small-group discussions or partner work. I listen as one student from a research group talks with a student from another research group about the relationship between the steppes of Australia and the pampas of Argentina. I listen as two students sort out the similarities and differences among the emu of Australia, the ostrich of Africa, and the rhea of South America.

Anomalies and misconceptions occur on a regular basis. There was a time when these misconceptions and premature conclusions reminded me of how much the children *didn't* know. However, over the years I have learned to celebrate these as evidence of the children's active engagement in learning (Piaget, 1977). When children are perplexed, I am convinced their brains go into warp speed. When one of our bird experts was asked about the nests created by penguins in the south polar region, he struggled to find ways that they could have built nests from branches and twigs in an area that offered no such plant materials. Until that point, he had been recording information about which he felt very confident, information he already knew. His classmate's question challenged him to go further.

As I listen to students working together, I not only discover what they are learning about the topics of study; I also discover how engaged they are with the focus of our inquiry. I want to know if this inquiry has captured their attention in some way, or whether we're pursuing it because I insisted. If students don't seem to be engaged with the inquiry, I stop and reflect on whether I am controlling the direction of the inquiry more than I should. And as students talk about their work in progress and share plans for the next day, I listen to see if they have a sense of a big picture or a shared direction for their work. If they don't seem to have any, then I know we need to talk and get focused again. I know the children have made our current inquiry their own when I hear, "This is what I'm planning to do next" instead of, "What do you think I should do?" or "Is this enough?"

We often take time to reflect on our learning, and this itself is an important learning experience. We talk about how we worked with others to learn, how we used various resources, and what we now understand about our chosen topic. This use of talk involves retracing the earlier phases of the learning process, and it invites learners to evaluate their effectiveness and their current understandings by asking the questions, "Where have we got to?" and "Where shall we go from here?" The following are our reflections on the 3-D geometry unit. As the students talked, I recorded their ideas.

**What did we do?**

- We made little cubes that were 3-D and pyramids.
- We kept doing harder things until we made a shape city out of the 3-D shapes.
- We had a really hard time making a sphere. Every time we tried, it ended up like an oval with points at the top and bottom (the bases).
- People shared ideas to have different ways to make the same shape.

**The hardest part was:**

- When you were trying to make a cube or any 3-D shapes, when the tabs weren't big enough and you couldn't stick them together.

- When you had to think of a strategy that would really work for your 3-D shape.
- Finding all kinds of ways to do it.
- On the last time you glue, it's hard to get it on without something under it that would keep it up. It's hard to put the last thing on when you can't put your finger in it.

**What we learned about 3-D shapes:**

- I didn't know what a prism was, and when Cory asked what a prism was and somebody stood up and showed an example, then I understood.
- I didn't even know you could make most or any of these shapes out of paper because I had never tried before.
- There are lots of different ways to make the same 3-D shape.
- I learned that there was such things as a sphere (I thought it was just a circle).
- It's hard to make a sphere because it doesn't have corners or creases . . . it's all round and different from cubes and other shapes.
- I learned that some of the shapes we are using in our shape cities are really shapes that we have in our city here.
- It was just hard.
- I learned that when you just traced how you are going to make your cube or pyramid, it gets all folded and then it rips or the other side pops out and it kind of like explodes.

**We learned that a cube:**

- was not a square.
- is a 3-D shape.
- can be made lots of different ways and not just one.
- has six sides.
- all the faces on the cube have to be the same size or it won't be a cube.
- has to be folded the right way or it turns out to be a different thing.
- can be made if there is a line of squares, and then one of the squares is on one side and one of the squares is on the other side. If they are both on the same side it won't work.

In our classroom, talk is one of the primary tools that helps learners explore what they already know, but also—just as important—what they are beginning to think about. We often use spiral notebooks to record these beginning thoughts—ephemeral musings—before they are lost. The following are excerpts from several students' spiral notebooks over a two-week period. They were recording "'I Wonder' questions about our world":

> Why did the dinosaurs die?
>
> Why do people kill?
>
> I wonder why Halloween is so scary.
>
> Why do pineapples have green stems but oranges have brown stems?

When students talk with one another, attempting to explain an emerging idea to an eager listener, they are pushed to "collaborative explicitness" (Barnes, 1975). The questions and comments of one learner challenge the other to be more explicit in presenting this new idea. Through conversation, both learners come to know more about what they are working to understand. Later, students refine their ideas as they prepare to share them more publicly with others. Then their talk becomes presentational (Barnes, 1975) as they communicate their thought-through and rehearsed ideas. As anyone who has ever made a formal presentation well knows, new insights emerge as one prepares familiar ideas for this more formal kind of sharing.

Whether the children are working together on some task, or whether they are reflecting together on the work they have done, I know that their talk is supporting their learning. And mine.

## How Talk Weaves the Social Fabric of our Classroom

The benefits of the informal talk that is the lifeblood of our classroom are not only intellectual. They are social, too. Yes, in this talk, "I can hear [the children] thinking," but I can also hear them building social relationships, and these are essential in a learning community where children are encouraged to take risks, to explore half-baked ideas, to evaluate their own learning, and to critique the work of others. Throughout the year I listen carefully to our talk in many contexts to find out who does most of the talking, who seems to never talk, or who talks openly only in a small-group situation. I make note of returning students who seem to be opening up more or to be organizing thoughts more clearly. I also make note of students who seem to be talking less because they are listening more to others. As I get to know new students, I look for those who seem to have a knack for making others feel good about their work or their ideas, those who actively invite others to add their voices to a discussion, and those who seem able to gently support others who struggle to make their stories public. I also listen for the ways students indicate that they are really listening to one another. In discussions, I listen for phrases such as, "Well, this is like what Nick said, but . . ." or "I think I have an answer to what Sloan asked . . ." I try to put students who do this easily into groups with others who are hesitant to share their ideas and might benefit from a classmate's supportive listening.

This community talk reveals how the children perceive the abilities and status of others in our group. I note the praising and validating remarks of older students in recognition of an important learning risk taken by a younger student. Such celebration of accomplishments is initially reserved for those who are younger or perceived to be less able. In October, I observed several students working on a survey project. As I dropped in to listen, group members were writing portions of our class list on their survey recording forms. Evan, the group leader, is famous in our classroom for having small handwriting, the kind that drives me to find a magnifying glass! Mary, a member of Evan's group and one of our young newcomers this year, was writing her portion of the names on the list. As she wrote, Evan looked on like a critical supervisor. "Wow! She's got really good handwriting for a first grader! Look how small it is," Evan commented with genuine amazement and respect. Mary didn't look up from her writing or even slow her pace. But I watched as her eyebrows popped up quickly and a confident grin spread across her face, as if she had been waiting for him to notice that she, too, could write in tiny letters like the "big kids." Little episodes like these help to bring newcomers into our classroom community, as returning students learn about and come to value their special gifts and interests.

Our talk is not always easy and comfortable. I know that issues of race and gender affect the workings of our community. I realize how, early on in schooling, children develop perceptions of what girls can and cannot do, what boys should and should not do. I notice the differences in the ways our children of color are received by white children and by other children of color. Sometimes what I hear in their talk concerns me—even upsets me. These are the uncomfortable times when their talk highlights something that I know must be addressed, something that I know reflects issues that are bigger than our classroom space, something that I feel uncomfortable addressing because I don't want to muck about on the surface of these issues. I know we must go deeper.

This winter we read and discussed *Cat Running* as a whole class read-aloud. The book raises issues of discrimination by others toward the "Okies" from the dust bowl who found themselves homeless and penniless. In this book, white families discriminated against white families. Many of the rejecting stereotypes associated with the label "Okie" could easily be found today in association with people of color. Some of our students could not fathom how a young child could be so cruel to an "Okie," whereas others (particularly those who had felt the sting of that kind of rejection) had little difficulty believing that an otherwise "nice kid" could engage in such behavior. Several years ago, Spinelli's *Maniac Magee* moved us into similar conversations about issues of race and discrimination. Last year it was *The Hundred Dresses*. Each year, it seems, the topic comes up. Each year a different chapter book gets us started talking about these difficult social issues up front and directly.

I'm still sorting these issues out for myself—still sorting out my responsibilities as a teacher. I struggle with the need to address social issues honestly and openly, but I also want to protect some of the joyous naiveté of youth. I hesitate to impose the social concerns of our society on very young children, but I cannot listen to unknowing hurtfulness without some response. So we talk. Mostly we talk about individuals we meet in the safe pages of a book, but even here children have the opportunity to hear others remark, "I would never do that," or "Why did the teacher let that happen?" They have the opportunity to sort out their own ideas and to hear how they contrast with the ideas of their classmates.

## Final Thoughts

Reflecting on the questions I ask myself as I listen to tapes of the children's exploratory talk, I realize that I focus on both social and intellectual aspects of the talk and that the two are inseparable. My listening and notetaking are guided by questions like these:

> How engaged was the talk? Did the students seem to be building on one another's contributions? Did it sound excitedly intense without being stressful? Did their body language suggest that they were deeply involved in the discussion?

> What did they talk about? Did they focus on the task? On the process they were using? On sharing one another's ideas? On real-world connections to the work at hand? Were they talking about things that seemed unrelated to the work at hand? Were they "off task"?

> Who did most of the talking? Who seemed to be leading the discussion and determining the direction it would take? Was this person leading the others to a predetermined conclusion, or asking questions and inviting others to help him or her think out loud?

Who didn't seem to have a voice? Was anyone silent in the group? Was that person giving body language cues of being disinterested? Rejected? Unable to get the floor? Hesitant to contribute?

How does this conversation connect with previous experiences and future ones? Did students make reference to ideas that had been discussed previously? Did they connect to earlier areas of study or propose new ones?

What new understandings were they wrestling with as they talked? Were they pushing at the edges of an anomaly? Arguing different points of view? Attempting to resolve apparently contradictory information? What did they seem uncomfortable with? When were they most hesitant and unsure in their discussion?

How were they using talk to support their learning? Were they offering tentative ideas? Making confident proclamations and waiting for others to challenge? Were they making connections among materials at hand, the current experience, and contributions by others as they talked?

How were they using others to support their learning? Were they asking others to be sounding boards for their ideas or to be consultants? Were they actively inviting quiet members of the group to contribute? Did individuals seem to be gravitating toward particular students as comfortable partners?

When I began my teaching, in a time when presentational talk (not exploratory talk) was fostered in the language arts curriculum, I doubt that I would have found much merit in these children's talk about *Rotten Ralph* (a naughty cat in a well-loved story):

*Meaghan:* In the *Rotten Ralph* books, he would be rotten at the beginning of the book and then be nice at the end of the book. But in the Leo Lionni books it would be different. Like when Tico got her golden wings, then she shared them with everybody. But Rotten Ralph stayed home and kept on being evil.

*Sloan:* Tico was really nice to all the people she saw, and she gave away all her golden wings to the other people. But Rotten Ralph would just mess up everything. He wouldn't help at all. He would just say, "Too bad, I got all I wanted." How come people liked Rotten Ralph when he was rotten, and they didn't like him when he was nice?

*Max:* Rotten Ralph was like swinging on things inside, like he wasn't supposed to. And when his owner said, "Be a good cat and don't be rotten" . . . the other cats, they wanted him to be rotten and to do rotten things. And he did.

*Mark:* In the first book, he was doing things that were dangerous, like cutting off trees when people were swinging on
them and . . .

*Cameshia:* Sarah had a kind of home party for him when he
came back . . . where did he go? Oh yeah, that school.
When he came back from that [finishing] school. He was
sleeping all day. And now he's home and sleeping all the
time and doing what she wanted . . . and now she wants
him to be rotten again!

*Cory:* Another reason she might have done that—tried to get
Ralph to be rotten again—well, Ari thought of this one. I
think maybe she just didn't like him being rotten but it
was . . . it was even more boring when he was asleep, and
it was sort of like a waste of money to get a pet that was
like that.

I was excited to hear students making reference to our earlier study of
Leo Lionni books, using them as a point of comparison. I was pleased
to hear students building on what others had said. I was impressed by
Cory's attentive listening to the ideas of others, his willingness to
credit others for their ideas, and his pulling together the contributions
of others.

I have learned to value exploratory talk like this, for I know it
supports my students' learning and their social growth. Cory, and
other students like him, help to create safe spaces in which classmates
can feel comfortable putting forth half-baked ideas, rough draft thinking, and tentative hypotheses. Contributions like his invite others to
engage in exploratory talk—to use talk to explore and create new
understandings for themselves and others.

## References

Barnes, D. (1992). *From communication to curriculum* (2nd. ed.). Portsmouth,
NH: Boynton/Cook.

Estes, E. (1994). *The hundred dresses*. New York: Harcourt Brace.

Gantos, J. (1976). *Rotten Ralph*. Wilmington, MA: Houghton Mifflin.

Lionni, L. (1963). *Swimmy*. New York: Knopf.

Lionni, L. (1967). *Frederick*. New York: Knopf.

Lionni, L. (1969). *Alexander and the wind-up mouse*. New York: Knopf.

Lionni, L. (1992). *Tico and the golden wings*. Magnolia, MA: Peter Smith.

Piaget, J. (1977). *The development of thought*. New York: Viking Press.

Short, K., & Harste, J., with Burke, C. (1996). *Creating classrooms for authors and inquirers* (2nd ed.). Portsmouth, NH: Heinemann.

Snyder, Z. K. (1995) *Cat running*. New York: Delacorte Press.

Spinelli, J. (1992). *Maniac Magee*. New York: HarperCollins.

Yashima, T. (1976) *Crow Boy*. New York: Viking.

## Bibliography

**Kathryn Mitchell Pierce**

*Professional resources that have been especially important to me include:*

Barnes, D. (1976). *From communication to curriculum*. Harmondsworth, U.K.: Penguin Education.

Dewey, J. (1963). *Experience and education*. New York: Collier Books.

Rosenblatt, L. (1978). *The reader, the text, the poem*. Carbondale: Southern Illinois University Press.

Short, K., & Burke, C. (1991). *Creating curriculum: Teachers and students as a community of learners*. Portsmouth, NH: Heinemann.

*Children's books that I especially enjoy using with children include:*

Leo Lionni books.

Baillie, A. (1994). *Rebel*. New York: Ticknor and Fields Books for Young Readers.

Clement, R. (1991). *Counting on Frank*. Milwaukee, WI: Gareth Stevens.

Cole, H. (1995). *Jack's garden*. New York: Greenwillow Books.

Estes, E. (1994). *The hundred dresses*. New York: Harcourt Brace.

Garland, S. (1993). *The lotus seed*. San Diego, CA: Harcourt Brace.

Snyder, Z. K. (1994). *Cat running*. New York: Delacorte Press.

# 12 Letters Home

**Rebecca King**
Travis Heights Elementary School, Austin, Texas

Every Friday afternoon, the children in Becky King's K/1/2 multi-age classroom carry a handwritten (photocopied) newsletter home to their parents, telling about some of the past week's events. One of Becky's favorite quotations heads each weekly letter.

Here are the first five letters from one year. They give a good sense of what the beginning of a new school year is like in this classroom, and they remind us of how wonderfully vibrant life—and language—in a classroom community can be.

————

*Learning is a consequence of community.*

*Dixie Goswami*

*August 18, 1995*

*Dear Parents,*

*I was delighted to see my old children and their parents and **very happy** to meet our new children and their parents during our first week together at school. The old children all looked like they had grown about a foot over the summer! We are so pleased to welcome our nine new friends (Wynne, Ben, Steven, Maya, Vanessa, Dante, Richard, Sierra, and Oscar). We spent our first week getting to know each other and getting used to our routines (and getting used to getting up early again!). One of my main goals for our classroom is to help it become a warm, cooperative, and comfortable community—a place where everyone is not only accepted but also respected for his or her unique gifts, a place where everyone feels safe—and free to take risks and to learn and grow together. I was so encouraged and touched this week by the warm welcome the old children gave the new children all week long. They were so kind and patient and helpful! A wonderful community spirit is already developing. Our new children are adjusting so quickly and easily!*

*We have begun studying about pets and will continue for awhile. On Monday, the class made our first big book, in which we drew self-portraits and wrote about our favorite pets. We make this self-portrait big book every year, and it is a class favorite all year long. The children also made a scattergraph of pets they would like to have. We then tallied the results. Some children analyzed the graph and recorded the information they got from it.*

We have read some poems about pets. The children illustrated their first poem for their poetry notebook.

We read nonfiction and fiction books about cats and dogs. We read Eric Carle's **_Have You Seen My Cat?_** We talked about the patterns we discovered in the book. The children worked with partners creating a big book called **_Counting Cat Ears._** The partners worked together making cats out of colored paper. We assembled the book and counted the cat ears by twos. Some children wrote addition equations, and some children wrote multiplication equations to go in the book. It's a lovely book, and the children worked beautifully with their partners.

We read a lot of Clifford books this week and ended the week with Clifford Day. The children made Clifford ears and noses to wear. They worked in groups and made delicious bones to eat. We made our own Clifford class book. We sorted and graphed (and then ate) our red fruit. Everyone looked so cute in their Clifford outfits! Some children made paper Cliffords. Some children painted Clifford at the easel. Some children worked together and made a giant paper Clifford by following written measurement specifications. We had a really fun day!

Attached you will find general information about our classroom, our class schedule, and a parent survey. Please fill out the survey and return it to me on Monday. THANKS.

I will be sending a parent letter home every Friday in your child's bag (Friday is Bag Day), so please be on the lookout for it. Please know that I am available to you at any time to answer questions or discuss concerns. Just let me know, and we'll set up a time. Have a great weekend! Thanks for sharing your children with me!

Becky King

**Important Dates:**

Next Tuesday: Our class will go fishing in the creek. Every year we catch minnows to live in our aquarium. I will send more information home on Monday.

------

**_Teaching that impacts is not head-to-head, but heart-to-heart._**
*Howard G. Hendricks*

August 25, 1995

Dear Parents,

We continued our study of pets this week, concentrating on pets we have in our classroom. On Monday, the children helped me set up our aquarium. We talked about what fish need. Then they put in the gravel and plants. We estimated how much water it would take to fill the tank before we filled it up. When we finished it, it looked beautiful! We tried to make it as much like the creek as possible so the minnows would feel at home.

Tuesday was Fishing Day! We collected our nets and a bucket and walked down to our favorite fishing spot. There wasn't very much water in the creek this year, so the minnows were a lot harder to catch than last year. But everyone had a lot of fun trying (and getting wet), and we caught plenty. The variety of sizes that the children caught was interesting. However, we have noticed that the large minnows eat the tiny ones. The children observed the aquarium and wrote about and/or drew their observations. Some children made little aquarium books that showed the sequence of setting up our tank. We wrote a class story about our fishing experience. It was a really successful, enjoyable day.

On Wednesday, we read some fiction and nonfiction books about guinea pigs. Then everyone met Silky, our class guinea pig. On Thursday, we read about mice. Then everyone met Snowball, our pet mouse. On Friday, we met our two turtles. We are deciding on names for them. We weighed Snowball and found she weighs five tiles. Then we estimated the weights of Silky and our turtles and weighed them. We were astounded at how much Silky weighs.

The children have been working on identifying, extending, and creating patterns: "Once children begin to understand and trust the notion of pattern, they begin to see patterns in other areas: number sentences, reading, art, and music, in short, the world around them." (Mary Baratta-Lorton); "Children who look for patterns become more persistent and flexible problem solvers. They expect a problem to be solvable" (Mary Baratta-Lorton). We will do a lot of work with patterns this year.

We spend a lot of time engaged in activities that promote community building at the first of the year. The children have been doing a lot of work with partners, which helps them get to know new friends. As the children work, I am busy assessing. This helps me make goals for each child. I really appreciate you all taking the time to fill out the parent survey I sent home. It really helps me when I know what your goals are for your child this year. If you haven't had a chance to turn it in to me, I hope you will soon. If you've misplaced it, let me know and I'll get you another. Thanks a lot!

Next week, we'll continue our study about pets. We will be going on a field trip to PETsMART on Thursday morning. We'll ride a school bus there.

I loved seeing both parents and children (and grandparents and siblings) at Back-to-School Night. The children were so excited about showing you their room and their work! They have already taken ownership. The new children seem so comfortable. The old children are so accepting. I feel so happy about that. If you were unable to come, please know that you will have many more opportunities to visit us this year. You're always welcome.

*Thank you for your kind words, your caring and concern, and your support.*

*Have a good weekend!*

*Becky King*

———————

**In a multiage atmosphere, differences become strengths instead of liabilities, and time is a friend.**

**Katy Alioto**

*September 1, 1995*

*Dear Parents,*

As we worked and played together this week, we continued to strengthen our learning community. It already feels like the new children have been with us forever, they have become such a part of our classroom. Politeness and respect, for ourselves and each other, are always a big focus in our room. We pride ourselves on being a polite classroom, so we're spending time at the beginning of the year concentrating on what a polite class looks and sounds like. I believe it is really important for the children to learn to assess their own behavior to determine if they are being the polite persons they want to be.

We continued our study of pets this week. On Monday, we talked about our hermit crabs and how they should be handled. We observed them and weighed them (after predicting their weight). We compared their weight with our other pets' weights. We thought our small one was lost, but it was really just hiding inside a large shell.

We read a wonderful counting book called **Counting Our Calico**. Then the children worked with partners creating our own big book based on this story. The pairs observed our mouse, Snowball. Then they decided on something pertaining to Snowball to make their number page about (e.g., three holes in her tunnel). They painted illustrations. We put it all together to make a delightful big book. We're so proud of it that we're going to put it on our hall bulletin board. I hope you all get a chance to see it.

We read the book **Six Dinner Sid**. Then some children did a problem-solving activity to figure out how many dinners Sid (a cat) ate in one week. I mainly wanted to see what children remembered about various problem-solving strategies from last year. I was amazed. Last year's children whizzed through the problem (tallying, using manipulatives, drawing pictures and diagrams). They also wrote about their mathematical thinking, as communication is also important in math. Some children made a kitten basket game. They used it to act out various math problems.

Wednesday was Rabbit Day in our classroom. The rabbit, Al, who lives in the science lab came to visit us for a few days. The children were really excited! We talked about observing like a scientist. The children observed Al and recorded their observations in words and/or drawings in their observation books. They also followed a recipe and made rabbit salad with buttermilk dressing. We shared it with Al. He loved it!! So did we! It was made with cabbage, carrots, and apples. Nineteen out of twenty-two children chose to have some! We read fiction and nonfiction books about rabbits. We sang a rabbit song and learned a rabbit fingerplay. We made some rabbit books (one was a math book involving skip counting and subtraction).

We observed some finches that are like our classroom finches. We haven't gotten to see our own finches yet because they are still at Jules's house (where they spent the summer). The female recently laid eggs, so they have been too nervous to move. After meeting and observing all our classroom pets, the children made a graph showing which pet they are the most interested in. We used the information from the graph to form pet project groups. They will begin working on their projects next week.

We started Writing Workshop this week. I modeled the writing process of an author by writing a rough draft of a story of my own. We talked about planning out stories first. The children generated topics of things they can write stories about. Then they began writing stories in their draft books. When they finish their rough drafts, they conference with a friend, conference with me, and finally publish their stories in the form of a real book. They get to sit in Author's Chair and read their story to the class. The class then gives them positive feedback. Parents are always invited to Author's Chair time for the year. It is a **wonderful** weekly event! I'm pretty sure it will be on Tuesday mornings at 7:55.

On Thursday we went to PETsMART. We saw a dog being groomed. We saw many, many beautiful and unusual fish. We saw interesting birds and interesting pet supplies. We also got a great tour of the veterinary clinic. We had a picnic lunch at Garrison Park and played on the playground there. It was a lot of fun!

We went to our school library on Wednesday and Friday. Mrs. Stovall showed the children how to check out books. They got to check one out on Friday. We will go to the library every Friday to check out books. Please help your child remember to bring the book back each week, so he or she can check out another. Thanks!

Thank you all for your active participation in your child's reading homework. My goal is for that time to be an **enjoyable** reading time for you and your child. Attached is a letter of suggestions. Please let me know if you ever have any concerns or questions concerning homework (or anything else). All the children have been so responsible about returning books and their folders each day. I really appreciate the involvement and support!

Have a great long weekend!

*Becky King*

**Important Dates:**

**September 4:** *No school.*

**September 15:** *Pet Show. Children with pets can bring them to school for our class pet show on the playpad. Details will be sent home later.*

**Please see the back of this page for a list of things we would like to have donated to our class.*

———————

*In the competitive classroom, some students must benefit at the expense of others, whereas in the truly cooperative classroom everyone achieves a high level of understanding.*

**Robert Berkman**

September 8, 1995

Dear Parents,

We had a short, but busy and very exciting week last week. We continued our study of pets. We have two new beautiful finches now. We have all of our classroom pets in the room now. The children formed interest groups by signing up for the classroom pet that they wanted to learn more about. The groups began by observing their chosen pets, discussing them, and recording their observations with pictures and/or writing. On Thursday, they met with their pet groups again and experimented with various foods to see what their pets like to eat. It was fascinating. I actually saw a hermit crab eat for the first time (a banana!). The children will continue using scientific inquiry skills this week as they continue with their pet projects (i.e., questioning, observing, researching, recording data).

We read a story called **Too Many Cats**. It was about a family that acquired twelve cats. The children worked with partners, drawing various combinations of cats that equaled twelve. We made a chart of their drawings that shows all the combinations they came up with. Some children worked on various problem-solving activities related to the story. When they engage in problem-solving activities, we focus on their various strategies and their communication of mathematical thinking rather than "right answers."

A small group of children created a survey to find out what kinds of pets Travis Heights teachers have at their homes. They are working on collecting the data and recording the results in a graph.

Some children made paper bag pet puppets, and some made pets out of clay. We began our committees this week. We have five committees (art, science, math, reading, and writing). The children are assigned to one of the committees for about a month. The committees meet first thing every morning and do various jobs necessary in maintaining our classroom. Working in their committees involves a lot of cooperation and responsibility. It also gives them a wonderful sense of ownership and contributes to our community spirit. They take their jobs seriously—and sometimes even decide they need to add new jobs to their list.

Friday was the really exciting day! We had some light in our classroom, luckily. We started the day with a very small group of children, but by the afternoon, there were fifteen. We had a really different kind of day that actually turned out to be very peaceful and nice. We went out to play on the fitness court playground because our usual one had too many tree limbs in it. The children worked really hard clearing the fitness court of sticks before using it. Everyone had so many stories to tell about the storm that we decided to make a wall story for the hall. Each child wrote a storm story about their personal experience. Then they painted a picture to go with it. When we have them mounted, we'll hang them on the wall in the hall, along with our graph of whose lights went out. In the afternoon, we were hot and sticky, so we got out the shaving cream and shaving creamed our tables. It was a day that we won't forget!

This will be our last week to study about pets. Next Monday, we'll begin our study of **Gardens**. We'll be planting our fall garden on **Wednesday**, September 20th at **8:00**. We need parents to help us plant. A garden note will be sent home soon.

Becky King

**Important Dates:**

**September 12:** Our first official Author's Chair this year. Parents are invited to come hear children read their published books.

**September 15:** **Pet Show** at 7:55—on playpad

**September 20:** Garden Planting Day at 8:00

**September 27:** Field Trip to Boggy Creek Farms at 9:30. We need parent drivers!

*Please keep sending the twelve-ounce juice cans. Thanks!

———————

*Learning is not an occasional event, to be stimulated, provoked or rein-forced. Learning is what the brain does naturally, continually.*

*Frank Smith*

September 15, 1995

Dear Parents,

We had a busy week as we began culminating our study of pets. On Monday, with life back to normal after the storm, we made and baked animal crackers. First we read the book **Good Night, Gorilla,** to get us in the mood. We read the recipe together. We talked about fractions of a cup and fractions of a teaspoon. The children got into three groups. Each group worked together following the recipe and independently made a batch of dough. (I just stand around and watch.) They selected the animal they wanted to make and rolled out and cut the dough. We made a graph showing the various kinds of animals children chose to make. This graph was a picture graph. We make and interpret lots of different kinds of graphs (real, picture, symbolic) (bar graphs, line graphs, scattergraphs, pie graphs, etc.). I didn't try one, but their animal crackers looked and smelled delicious to me.

The children worked all week on their pet projects. They worked in groups observing, experimenting with, and researching one of our classroom pets. They took notes in their observation books. They decided on important information. Each group will use their information to publish an information booklet about the pet. The booklets will stay in our classroom — near the pets — so that visitors to our room can read them and learn about our class pets. The children have worked very hard on the booklets. They **love** doing both research and observations. Please stop in to admire the informative booklets. We're sure you'll learn something! The children work beautifully in groups. After big group projects like this, they get a chance to fill out self-evaluation sheets as a means of reflection.

We had our first Author's Chair on Tuesday. It went so very well. It's always a very touching event for me — for many reasons. The children are so **proud** of their published books. I'm touched by how comfortable they are taking the risk of sharing them with a big audience. It's so heartwarming to see how accepting, encouraging, and polite the audience is. Their feedback to one another is often very thoughtful and insightful — and **kind.** Author's Chair is every Tuesday morning at **7:55.** It usually lasts fifteen to twenty minutes. Parents are always very welcome. It is important for children to be at school on time that day especially, so that they don't interrupt the readers. Thanks!

We got new pets in our room—mealworms—which we are raising as food for our turtles. The children were fascinated as they observed, drew, measured, read about, and experimented with the mealworms. They even named them.

On Wednesday, a group of four-year-old children from the Open Door Preschool came on a field trip to our classroom. Coco, Dante, Evan, and Max all went to Open Door before coming to Travis Heights. It was such a good experience for both groups. The Open Door mainstreams children with disabilities, so some children with disabilities came on the visit. Our class had a great discussion afterward about the visit and about disabilities and how we felt about the experience. We have been invited to go visit their school sometime in the future.

The children wrote animal cracker math story problems after making the cookies. They continued working on patterns. Many children used hundreds charts to record various skip counting patterns (counting by twos, threes, fours, etc.) and wrote about what they noticed about the different patterns. Some children made pattern headbands, belts, and bracelets to wear. The survey group used their survey data. They graphed and tallied their information and made a display for the hall that shows what kinds of pets Travis Heights teachers have at home.

On Friday we had our PET SHOW! We read Ezra Jack Keats' book, **The Pet Show,** to set the mood. What excitement!!

We decided to have a pet race to find out which of our classroom pets moves the fastest. Some children used blocks to build a racetrack. Everyone predicted which animal would win. We graphed our predictions. The guinea pig, mouse, turtles, and hermit crab were the contestants. The children recorded their observations.

We planted some of our different pet foods to see which ones will grow. The children learned how to measure the pet food so that each pet gets the right amount.

Next week, we'll start studying about gardens. Thank you so much for contributing to our plant fund!! We'll plant our outdoor garden on Wednesday.

*Book orders are due on FRIDAY.

*Children should bring their library books to school by **Friday** every week so they can check out new ones.

*If you haven't joined our PTA, please do so. It really helps our school, and your children benefit so much from your involvement.

Have a great weekend! Thanks for all your help and support.

Becky King

## Bibliography

**Becky King**

*Professional resources that have been especially important to me include:*

Armstrong, T. (1987). *In their own way.* New York: Tarcher.

Calkins, L. M. (1986). *The art of teaching writing.* Portsmouth, NH: Heinemann.

Cambourne, B. (n.d.). *The whole story.* New York: Scholastic.

Cohen, E. P., & Gainer, R. S. (1976). *Art, another language for learning.* New York: Citation Press.

Glover, M. K. (1997). *Making school by hand: developing a meaning-centered curriculum from everyday life.* Urbana, IL: National Council of Teachers of English.

Levy, S. (1996). *Starting from scratch.* Portsmouth, NH: Heinemann.

*Children's books that I especially enjoy using with children include:*

Ehlert, L. (1995). *Snowballs.* San Diego, CA: Harcourt Brace.

Fox, M. (1984). *Winfrid Gordon McDonald Partridge.* Brooklyn, NY: Kane/Miller.

Kesselman, W. (1993). *Emma.* New York: Dell.

Lionni, L. (1961). *On my beach there are many pebbles.* New York: Astor-Honor.

MacCarthy, P. (1990). *Ocean parade: A counting book.* New York: Dial Books for Young Readers.

Reid, M. S. (1995). *The button box.* New York: Puffin Books.

Rylant, C. (1987). *Birthday presents.* New York: Orchard Books.

# III Using Language to Connect with Others

When we ask our university students to describe what the word "language" means to them, the first word many come up with is "communication." And they're right! This is the way we know language most deeply from birth throughout our lives. "Communication" is a word that highlights the social aspects of language. Yes, we use language to create and imagine (Part I) and to explore and understand our world (Part II), but even in these there is always connection with others. Sometimes the connection is with an author whose words we read; sometimes it is with an audience for whom we write; sometimes it is with those close to us with whom we speak. But connection is the thing, and to connect with others is to engage in social behavior. Communication indeed!

Clearly, the students and teachers you have read about so far have all been engaged in communication. In their talk, their reading, their writing, they have been connecting with others. But the articles of this section draw attention to some special social aspects of classroom communities and the communication that occurs within them. Diversity is a major theme. Cora Five's story of two learning-disabled children in her (inclusion) classroom, Mary Krogness's description of life with her (mainly) low SES African American middle schoolers, Dorothy Taylor's discussion of listening to and learning from her ESL students, and Renée Bachman and Julia Fournier's focus on building community in their bilingual classrooms all serve to remind us of how wonderfully diverse classrooms are nowadays. With this increasing diversity comes an ever-wider range of opportunities for connection, and this inevitably means the development of an ever-wider range of ways to communicate for every student. As our students express themselves to classmates, and as they interpret and respond to the expression of classmates, they are connecting through talk and reading and writing and illustrating and dramatizing and. . . . They must understand their classmates and be understood by them. This is communication, and the more socially diverse the membership of that classroom community is, the greater its potential for each member's development of a rich, flexible, and effective language instrument. Each student's language stretches to accomplish the communication work he or she is trying to do, and the more diverse that work, the more flexible the language instrument the student develops to carry it out.

Lynne Strieb takes us beyond the immediate classroom, but again communication—and connection—is the focus. She tells us how she brings her children's families into the educational endeavor, thus extending the classroom community to include these individuals who are so important in her students' lives. Her inclusion of the children's families in the life of her classroom goes well beyond kids putting routine reminders and memos into the backpacks they lug home. The home–school connections she builds are substantive and continuing.

Finally Bill Bigelow draws us (and his students) into a still wider social community, one in which issues of gender and ethnic bias and preservation of the environment must concern us all. Bigelow's students enter this larger social community and consider these important social issues through the materials their classroom affords. In this case, the materials in question include a CD-ROM.

We recognize that when we as teachers select materials for our classrooms (e.g., textbooks, books for our classroom libraries), we consider the "messages" these works convey. Whether the material in question is a history textbook, a biography, or a novel, we would reject a work that portrays particular social groups or individuals inaccurately or disrespectfully or simplistically. Sometimes the messages in printed materials are overt. Often they are not, and we become aware of them when we wonder why a particular detail was included, or when we feel uneasy with the tone of the writing, or when we hear an author's voice that sounds arrogant or condescending. Perhaps we notice important omissions: What is *not* included sometimes speaks as loudly as what *is* included. And so we examine classroom materials carefully, critically, for the social messages we know must be there, for no materials are neutral. Every work speaks from a particular point of view: that of the author.

Bigelow's article reminds us that this is not just true of the words and ideas that students and teachers encounter on the pages of their textbooks; it is also true of the words and ideas they encounter on their computer screens. Bigelow extends critical consideration of classroom texts to the technology that is playing an increasingly important role in classrooms. Better yet, he engages his students in this critical consideration as they examine the orientation of, the images in, the omissions from the CD-ROM, *The Oregon Trail.* As with the other articles in this section, the focus is social, but in this article the connections are with Americans of an earlier era. Yet the connections are *now* as well, for the students' critical examination holds within it the possibility of a new perspective—a different lens—through which to view matters of gender, ethnicity, and environmental awareness today. Inevitably, these connections are created through language as the students read and write, discuss and dramatize.

# 13 Ownership for the Special Needs Child: Individual and Educational Dilemmas

**Cora Lee Five**
Scarsdale Public Schools, Scarsdale, New York

I didn't really understand the importance of ownership until I started observing children with special learning needs. I had heard the term ownership many times as I learned how to teach writing through the process approach. I knew that for the process approach to be truly effective in my classroom, I would need to create an environment that ensured Mary Ellen Giacobbe's (1989) three basics: time, ownership, and response.

In the writing process environment, students are encouraged to "own" their ideas. Respected as individuals, they have choices; they select their own topics for writing, topics that are meaningful to them. The establishment of a community of writers allows students to respond to each others' ideas. As students write and share their work, they begin to realize that they are vulnerable and that response to writers should be supportive and constructive. Response also means that I listen to students to understand their special ways of learning. Teaching becomes a response to learners.

As I evolved as a teacher of writing, I changed my reading program. Time, ownership, and response were again essential ingredients. Each day I made time for reading workshop and for reading aloud to the class. Students selected the books they wanted to read and responded to their books in a variety of ways. Along with choosing meaningful texts to read, they wrote on topics important to them. I tried to ensure that my students could confer and collaborate and still maintain ownership.

Time and response are oriented toward supporting ownership. Time gives room and respect for the student's own pace, while response derives from an attitude that there cannot be a violation of

Reprinted by permission from WHO OWNS LEARNING? QUESTIONS OF AUTONOMY, CHOICE, AND CONTROL edited by Curt Dudley-Marling and Dennis Searle (Heinemann, A Division of Greenwood Publishing Group, Portsmouth, NH, 1995).

any child's mind. While criticism and disagreement stay an active part of the learning process, no one's ideas are demeaned or negated. Criticism is something that the child is encouraged to think about: The child maintains the option to accept or reject the input of others.

I again extended time, ownership, and response to my teaching of math, history, science, and other areas. Gradually, I realized that ownership could not exist in isolation. Time, ownership, and response could not be separated. Ownership develops over time through response.

As I grew as a teacher, I began to recognize the importance of ownership for all of my students, but particularly for those with special learning needs. My studies of these children made me see what ownership meant for them. Ownership came to mean that learners were able to follow their own interests, to take some control over their learning, and consequently to accept and feel greater responsibility for it. In the process of studying two particular children recently, Alex and Mike (Weaver, 1994a, 1994b), I discovered the importance of ownership for me as well. I will discuss Alex and Mike, both of whom were habitually used to renunciation of ownership of their own mental capacities. My focus will be the way in which they were helped to reclaim ownership and the way in which the system colluded against this goal. I will also share how I, too, struggled with ownership within the school system.

## Alex's Background

Alex, who had been placed in my fifth-grade classroom, had been classified by the Committee on Special Education as learning disabled. With a history of learning problems, he had received skills help since first grade. His Individual Educational Programs (IEP) stated that he had difficulty with reading and was tested at a beginning third-grade level at the end of fourth grade. He could not decode well, and his written and oral language were limited. He had problems with spelling and seemed unable to express his ideas. It was noted that Alex needed much time to process information, often asking for directions and for questions to be repeated.

The recommendation was that Alex be taught in one-to-one situations in the classroom. In previous grades, he apparently did not participate in class discussions and was "lost" in a whole class or group setting. He was also to receive help initiating and completing assignments. He was placed in my classroom because an aide would be there for Mike, and it was felt that Alex, too, could receive the benefit of the aide.

Alex's IEP contained a list of isolated skills under each curriculum area. These were the goals and objectives for the year. His IEP also specified that he was scheduled to leave the classroom to work with skills teachers four times a week.

## Mike's Background

In kindergarten, Mike had been classified as learning disabled because of his speech and language problems. He had gone to a special school for children with language disabilities from kindergarten through second grade in classes of six or seven children. When he returned to my school, he was tested and classified as ADHD and given an aide for twenty-five hours a week.

Mike's IEP noted his reading problems. He was reading well below grade level and had difficulty with phonic skills. He also had problems with written and oral language. Though he had many ideas, he was afraid to write because of his spelling mistakes. Handwriting was a problem for him as well. Mike barely knew how to write in cursive and printed most of his written work. His impulsivity and focusing problems interfered with his oral language, and his distractibility caused problems in learning.

Mike's IEP recommended that he, like Alex, be taught in a one-to-one setting. He had difficulty in the past participating in class discussions and could not function well in a large group. He needed help in beginning and completing assignments and was assigned an aide. His IEP also listed specific skills that became the goals and objectives for fifth grade. Mike was scheduled to leave the class five times a week to work with skills and speech teachers.

With both these boys, I saw difficulties in ownership, as expressed in their inability to have interest or direction, to express ideas, and to make decisions.

## Fifth Grade: The Beginning

Looking forward to having Alex and Mike in my class, I was interested to see how a workshop approach, one that ensured ownership, would affect their reading and writing. I had realized through my readings and my previous case studies of students with special learning needs that they learn best when they are actively involved in their own learning, when they are immersed in a subject, when they are reading, writing, speaking, and listening for a variety of meaningful purposes. I also wondered how Alex and Mike would respond to a supportive classroom environment, one that valued ideas and treated students with respect. I knew the importance of creating an environment that gives children ownership—chances to make decisions, to take risks, to follow their interests, and to take responsibility for their learning. Within this environment students come together as communities of learners to work together collaboratively and to learn from one another as they develop hypotheses and as they discuss and share ideas. Would Alex and Mike be able to become part of this community of learners? Would they be able to take risks with me, their peers, their own minds? Would they find the freedom to experiment?

My initial problem occurred during the first week of school when I received skills schedules for Alex and Mike. They were scheduled to leave the room during reading workshop to work in a one-to-one setting on isolated skills. How could they become part of my reading–writing community? When I looked at my special class schedule and added in chorus, band, and instrumental music lessons, I realized that there was no way I could find enough time to reschedule reading. I went to speak to the skills teachers, but their own schedule restrictions made them unable to reschedule the boys. I felt the importance of having the boys be in my room each day when reading workshop began. I wanted them to be part of the mini-lessons; I wanted them to be settled with a book and be surrounded by readers; I wanted them to participate in group shares.

When I suggested that the boys work in small groups in skills instead of in an isolated setting or that the skills teachers work with the boys in the classroom, I ran into the issue of ownership. The skills teachers had *their* programs in *their* special rooms. As the principal tried to help in this matter, I realized that the pressure of state requirements interfered with his ability to grant ownership to other people. The decision was, after examination of the IEP, that Mike would leave the room for skills each day but that Alex would have a skills teacher come into the room to help him in writing and reading for forty minutes one afternoon a week. When I asked about the programs and approaches that the skills teachers would use with these boys, I received little information. It appeared that the three of us would work with the boys in our own way with little communication or connection.

Even though I was glad to have Alex in the room and to have the skills teacher work with him there, I was not happy about Mike's leaving every day, and I was sorry that there was little communication between the specialists and me. We seemed to value our own individual philosophies, approaches, and programs; perhaps we were afraid that communication might expose us, increase our vulnerability, and make us feel inadequate. Perhaps in our busy days there was little time to share our thoughts and observations.

I wondered about the IEP and its list of isolated skills. It seemed to conflict with the philosophy of teaching the whole child in whole contexts. Was the IEP determining what and how the child should be taught? Were the skills teachers required to teach these skills? Was I? Who was responsible for the special needs child's learning? My principal told me that the skills teacher was in charge of the IEP, and I felt confused. The child was in my class, my aide and I worked with him most of the day, I wrote and signed the report cards, yet someone else was in charge of his learning program. Later, the skills teacher told me that Alex, too, had to be removed from the class; he could not be taught skills in the classroom. "It's illegal," she told me. "The state says you have to take them out of the room." Thus began a year of conflict and frustration that made me reflect and take another look at ownership. I considered not only the importance of ownership for the child but also ownership from a different perspective—the ownership of the educational philosophy of the classroom teacher.

## Alex's Story

At the beginning of the year, Alex displayed behavior problems. He shouted out, usually comments that seemed to be irrelevant. Doing little work, he spent much time crawling around on the floor, under desks, and in the coat closet. He spoke in a babyish voice and walked like a toddler. All the children laughed at Alex's antics; they liked him because he pretended to be (or perhaps he thought he was) dumb. His behavior always got him in trouble in every class. Knowing at the beginning of the year that other students thought that he was funny, Alex seemed to enjoy being the class clown. Easily distracted by his peers and the events in the classroom, he had learned to substitute indiscriminate attention for what he really desired—affirmation of himself as a person with ideas.

I knew from past experience that establishing a positive, supportive environment—one that valued ideas—was the basis for developing a community of writers. I spend much time at the beginning of each year modeling conferences and responses that are positive and constructive. Usually, students learn to respond in a similar way through conferences at my round conference table. I was glad that Alex was in my classroom during writing workshop.

During the first month of school, Alex was not involved in writing. I was not surprised because I knew that he had done little writing in fourth grade. Whatever he had written had been with the help of skills teachers. At the beginning of fifth grade, when Alex was not writing, I tried to brainstorm topics with him. He remained silent. Sometimes he answered, "I don't know" in a high-pitched voice and rolled his eyes, causing the other children to laugh. He seemed to enjoy acting dumb and immature; often, he crawled on the floor, examining something he found on the carpet.

At the beginning, Alex would not come to the conference table by himself. I encouraged him, but he seemed to have little interest, a sign of renunciation of ownership. I noticed, however, that Alex listened to the conversations as children shared drafts and explained problems that they were having in writing. Eventually, I coaxed him to come to the table to listen to the other children's topics. Wanting him to become part of our writing community, I hoped that the experience might inspire him. He sat and said little; sometimes he made faces. When he returned to his desk and I looked at him, he told me, "I'm thinking." This was a response that I heard throughout the year as he sat for long periods of time doing what I assumed to be nothing. I was never sure what his words meant, but I respected his response and let him think. This is how ownership works at the beginning.

After a month of sitting at his desk without writing but presumably listening to writing conferences, Alex finally decided to write about his trip to the Grand Canyon. He wrote slowly but did not stop, as he had a lot to tell. Finishing his three-page draft at the end of the week, he read it to me. He decided that he liked it and did not want to change it. The skills teacher was coming in the next day, and I suggested that he read it to her and then proofread it with her. "I know how to put in periods and capital letters," he informed me, attempting to assert himself.

On arrival next day, the skills teacher immediately started helping Alex copy his homework. She began to look for his writing piece even though Alex knew where it was. She searched through his desk until I showed her where the writing folders were kept. When I told her that Alex could get his folder himself, she explained that she wasn't sure he'd be able to find it. I told her that Alex's piece was finished and that I hoped they could proofread it together. As Alex read his Grand Canyon piece, she corrected it, having him change and add words and sentences. Unfortunately a well-intentioned adult, eager to pursue her assigned task of skills teaching, had intervened and taken a first story away from a child. In the process, she had taken the child away from my writing community. When she left, Alex looked at me and said, "I thought my story was finished." I cringed. Was he really saying, "I thought it was my story, I thought I had ownership"? In the pressure to learn skills, this became a repeated experience for Alex and his skills teacher.

When Alex completed his story, he didn't know if he wanted to share it with the class. Although I encouraged him, I let him make the decision. Finally, days later, he decided to read it. Seeming very embarrassed, he rolled his eyes, behaved in a silly way, and waved his cover around for the class to see. At first he read in his babyish voice; then he switched to what I described to him as his "fifth-grade" voice and read very fast. Despite his behavior, the class did not laugh at him (thanks to rules we had established) but responded with many positive comments. He seemed surprised and confused at first. He was used to their laughter, not to their positive response. Shame began to be transformed into pride.

Alex's next writing piece was somewhat easier for him to write. After thinking about topics for a week, he decided to write about his birthday party. He was well into his draft when it was time for the skills teacher's weekly forty-minute visit. She came a few minutes late, in the middle of my mini-lesson on dialogue and how it can add to a story. Before the class and I had finished sharing our ideas on the use of dialogue, the skills teacher told Alex to take out his draft. "We're going to add dialogue to your story," she announced. Alex looked confused. "You heard what Ms. Five said about dialogue," the skills teacher responded. "We're going to add it."

"But nobody said anything," Alex told her.

"I'm sure they did. And if they didn't we'll put it in, anyway," she said.

Alex sat at his desk with a blank face. While I tried to continue working with other children, I was aware of the battle going on at Alex's desk and inside me as well. He was not responding. The skills teacher was doing everything she could to force him to write, especially to learn the mechanics of writing dialogue. Since part of his writing problem, according to his IEP, was how to use correct punctuation, she planned to teach it. Alex remained silent except to tell her over and over again that nobody said anything. I decided to explain my writing program to her after school. I felt that she must understand the importance of ownership for a child like Alex, who was just beginning to express his ideas. But her orientation and goals were different. My explanation was not received well. She was responsible to her job description and told me that Alex needed help in writing. Her job was to help him with writing skills.

Slowly, Alex became a more active learner. During the next few months, he began to write on the days when the skills teacher was not there. He came to the conference table to read parts of his draft; and, when he was not distracted by other children, he seemed to listen to the comments of the group at the table. Sometimes he made minor revisions based on the feedback he received, but he did not respond to classmates' writing. Sometimes he came to the table to listen for a short time and then would wander back to his desk. I felt that Alex was gradually becoming part of the writing community. Perhaps, as he listened to other children responding to one another's writing, he began to realize that writing was not easy for everyone, that all writers were vulnerable, and that their ideas were respected.

Later in the fall, Alex was showing progress. He was better able to select a topic and to write a draft. Without any help from the skills teacher, he wrote a piece and decided that he wanted conversation in it. He came to me to learn where to put quotation marks and when to indent. Alex had realized the need to use the correct skills for his own writing. I was pleased that he took a risk with dialogue, and as a result, wanted to learn. It happened when he was ready, at his own timing. I noticed his changed attitude when he wanted to learn for a meaningful purpose. He was interested, he talked, and he asked questions. After we worked on the beginning of his piece, he experimented with his draft to see if he could put quotation marks around conversation at the end. He was beginning to take charge of his writing.

I also began to notice that Alex adopted a different pattern of behavior when the skills teacher arrived. Becoming stubborn, he would not do as she asked. He sat in silence or answered with "I don't know." The more frustrated she became, the more he refused to do, as if he had experienced some ownership in his writing and did not want to give it up. After she left, he reverted to his babyish behavior and crawled on the floor or disrupted the class with his "class clown" antics. He seemed to find some comfort in acting dumb, or perhaps the fact that she worked with him on his writing made him feel inadequate and humiliated. Perhaps he became angry when he felt that she took away his authority or control over his writing. Defiance can be an early expression of ownership.

The situation was very different when it came to reading. Alex was present without the skills teacher for all of reading workshop and for the stories I read aloud to the class. Although he was free to select the books he wanted to read—books that had meaning for him—at first he had difficulty selecting them. He was not a reader. In the past the skills teacher had given him paragraphs to read, and sometimes aides or his teachers had selected books for him. In my room Alex could choose his own books; but, since he had little experience with making choices, he didn't know how.

In the beginning, I suggested a few books I knew from past years to be favorites: short, high-interest trade books. I gave him book talks and encouraged him to choose one. Eventually, he read one of the books and wrote a letter to me about it in his reading journal. He mentioned a particular part that he liked and included a sentence about a favorite character. After Alex finished his book, he came to me for another. This time he selected two, looked at both of them carefully, and made a choice. He read slowly, continuing to read short books for many weeks. Listening to his classmates' ideas during group shares, he drew mazes on pieces of paper but said very little about his reading.

During my first reading and writing evaluation conference with Alex, he had difficulty evaluating his progress. We looked through his reading folder and reread his journal letters. We also looked through his writing folder and tried to determine his best piece. I gave him lots of time to think about, and respond to, my questions. I wanted to hear his ideas. Alex told me that he had trouble thinking of topics in writing. He was concerned about his spelling and set a goal for himself to improve in this area. His second goal was to write more pieces. He was able to select as his best story the one about the Grand Canyon. This was the first piece he had written after selecting a topic that was meaningful to him. Alex felt that he had improved in reading because, as he wrote in his journal, "I anderstand books moor. and I read moor books."

Alex became involved in the stories I read to the class. Even though he drew as I read, I knew that he was listening because he began to enter into discussions about the book with a word or two, sometimes in his babyish voice, sometimes in his fifth-grade voice.

At the end of December, Alex selected on his own a book with longer chapters. He loved this book and became hooked on reading, going through all the sequels. From that time on, he had no trouble selecting books. The letters in his reading journal became longer, and he began to connect what he read in books to his own experiences. He often ended his letters with questions or predictions, and he enjoyed reading my responses. When Alex had finished all the books in the series, he found *Tales of a Fourth Grade Nothing* (Blume, 1972) and the other books that described Fudge and his adventures. He continued to read slowly but was totally involved in his books.

By February Alex was reading books on colonial America. The class was immersed in this topic through reading, writing, simulations, films, discussions, music, and class trips. Alex was particularly interested in colonial schools and school punishments. He read many trade books on this topic and expressed more of his ideas in his journals and in discussions. During conversations about colonial schools, the other children listened to him, questioned him, and learned from his brief answers. He seemed surprised by their interest and by the fact that he knew so much about the topic.

I began to notice that Alex now used his fifth-grade voice more often and that he had stopped crawling on the floor. Also doing well in math, he discovered that he could help other children and that solving problems with his peers was enjoyable. It seemed as though he was becoming part of the greater community of learners.

Just when I saw Alex's confidence in his abilities increase, the skills teacher decided that Alex needed help in reading. Certain reading skills were prescribed by the IEP, and she wanted to take him out of the room to help him read. I explained that he seemed to have developed greater self-confidence in reading and writing; I thought that removing him from the room for skills in reading might destroy his growing positive image of himself as a reader and learner. Still, because she felt that it was important to follow the IEP, she removed him to help him with reading. I wondered what went on in these sessions. When he returned after forty minutes, he reverted to his baby voice and ran around the room out of control. The skills teacher felt that Alex still had many of his old problems, that he could not decode, that he was slow to process information and slow to respond, that it was difficult for him to write, and that he could not express his ideas. I wondered if she saw any of his strengths. I suspected that he continued to be his stubborn, nonresponding self with her. This was not the same Alex I saw in the classroom.

At this time Alex made another decision. He wanted to pursue his interest in colonial schools by writing a report. He divided his long draft into two chapters based on the response he received in conferences. When his chapters were finished, he drew a colonial school for his cover with detailed illustrations. He even made a replica of a hornbook. Again, I realized that art was an important means of expression for him. When Alex was interested and involved, when the work was meaningful for him, when he felt that he could make choices and decisions, and when he had some control, he stopped his babyish voice and silly behavior and put forth greater effort. He was able to write on his own and even took risks writing in another genre. Reading his report to the class in his normal voice, Alex seemed proud of his final product. He listened carefully as the students told him what they liked and what they had learned. Again, he seemed surprised at their response.

Alex was becoming more involved in the stories I read to the class. He seemed to be thinking about the stories all the time. Once, after I read a chapter from *Tuck Everlasting* (Babbitt, 1975) where the spring in the Fosters' wood was explained, he blurted out later in the day while he was copying his homework, "Oh, that's why they call it *Tuck Everlasting.*" "Why?" I asked. "Because they can't change, they're everlasting," he explained. He was the first one in the class to express his ideas about the meaning of the title. Respecting his opinion and his comment, the class launched into a discussion of that particular title and of titles in general. And Alex was involved in the discussion.

When I had my second reading–writing evaluation conference with Alex at the end of March, I was interested in the changes he expressed. He described his progress in reading by telling me, "I like books much, much more." I was surprised when he told me that he felt writing letters to me in his reading journal helped him as a reader. He explained, "You hear more words. The letters help you understand the book more." Perhaps, even though he wrote brief letters, he was able to reflect in his own way on the books he read. Alex set goals for himself: to read more books, to read different kinds of books, and to read faster. When he talked to me about his writing, he told me that he liked his colonial report the best because he learned a lot about colonial schools; he liked his illustrations, too. He set goals for himself for the remainder of the year. A child who did not take himself seriously as a learner now wanted to improve by adding details to his pieces and by working faster in drafting and copying. It was interesting that spelling had ceased to be a major concern for him. It seemed that meaning had become more important to him than skills.

Continuing to grow as a writer, Alex experimented with similes and began to express his feelings. In his favorite piece about his part in a team sport, he wrote:

> The ball hit me and I went flying across the field like an arrow
> hitting the target. . . . I kicked the ball. It went into the goal and
> we won by 1 point. I felt great about winning the game.

At the end of the year Alex was able to evaluate his writing and reading with greater confidence. He knew that he liked his piece describing how he scored the winning point. "I put a simile in it and I told more about how I felt." He knew that he had improved in reading. He had read more books during the year than he could ever remember reading. Moreover, he planned to read over the summer and to write about some of his trips.

## Mike's Story

At the beginning of the year, Mike, like Alex, was a behavior problem. He ran around the room, shouted out, did little classwork and homework, and constantly played with tape. Disorganized and unable to find school materials, Mike relied on his aide, Marie, to help him with everything.

During the first month of school, Mike did not write on his own. He continued to rush around the room, talking back and forth to his friend. Frequently, he came to me and to Marie to tell us about his various topics. As with Alex, I encouraged him to begin a draft by himself and then to come back to the conference table to share it with me and some classmates. Instead, he brought his paper and pencil to Marie, and I listened in frustration as he tried to write his draft while she, in her eagerness to teach skills, changed it around, adding words and phrases. It seemed that it was no longer his draft, but hers.

Mike was not interested in coming to the conference table. Accustomed to a one-to-one setting, he was content to work with Marie; however, he often circled the conference area on his trips to the pencil sharpener and to Marie's desk. He heard the constructive response that classmates gave one another and in October he began coming to the conference table at my invitation. He played with tape while listening to a draft; then he decided that he had an idea for a new story. I encouraged him to write his draft by himself. "I can't spell the words," he told me. I reassured him that his ideas were most important and that we would work on the spelling together after he finished his draft. Looking doubtful, Mike went back to his seat, wrote for a short time, and then started toward Marie. As soon as I saw him heading for Marie's desk, I asked him to join the conferences at the table instead. After that, he returned to the conference table often to read his draft. As a result of the response he received, he gradually began to add to his story to clarify some parts. I helped him proofread his piece, which he was now eager to read to the class. His excitement about the response he received from his peers motivated him to begin another piece. Still, this second story, although much shorter than the first, remained his favorite for many weeks. I suspect that was because he wrote it himself and expressed his own ideas.

Eventually, Mike began to write without the help of his aide but with the support of his peers. He began to enjoy moving parts of his piece around and changing words as he revised. He made these decisions by himself, ensuring his control over his writing. I felt that he was becoming part of my community of writers as he realized that the writing environment was safe for taking risks with his ideas.

During the next few months, Mike began to come to the conference table on his own. He did not seek out Marie unless he needed help in spelling. When I was reading poetry to the class, he decided to write a poem. He needed many conferences to follow through on his poem because he was concerned about rhyme; but, when he was finished, he was glad that he had tried because "I've never written a poem." I was glad that he felt secure enough to try a new genre.

Unfortunately, Mike did not have the same success in reading. Since he was not in the room at the beginning of reading workshop, he was unable to get settled. He returned from his skills sessions distracted and confused. He relied on his aide to select the book that he read with her each day. When I suggested that he choose a book that he could read when he went to skills and to continue reading it when he returned to the classroom, he was quite agreeable. We found a book that he enjoyed after we read the first few pages together, and he seemed motivated to read it because it was funny. When I discussed this plan with the skills teacher, she told me that the book I had recommended was too difficult for Mike, that the vocabulary was too hard. Mike never came back with the book to read in reading workshop. When he returned to class, he read the book that Marie had selected for him. His journal letters to me were short and written with the help of Marie. Often, he could not remember much about the books he read and therefore could not express his ideas. With specialized help in skills, he repeatedly seemed to lose track of himself.

Mike's first reading–writing evaluation conference revealed that he continued to be concerned about spelling. He set a goal for himself to improve in spelling. He had little to say about reading except that he thought he was reading more books.

Continuing to grow as a writer, Mike was able to select topics and to make decisions about revision. He was not as successful with reading; in that setting he was still unable to choose books or to read them by himself. When he returned from skills, he continued to be disorganized and unable to sustain interest in a book on his own. When I questioned him about the book he was reading in skills, he told me that he could read the book only with the skills teacher. When I asked him if he could read it with Marie, he told me that he could not because he was reading another book with Marie. I asked him if he would like to select a book to read on his own, but he expressed ambivalence about his abilities and his expectations. He felt that the skills teacher and Marie were there to help him with reading and that he had to read with them.

During his second evaluation conference, Mike was still concerned with spelling, although this time in connection with his reading. He felt that if he read more, he would become a better speller. Writing letters in his journal helped him because "you learn to spell better." He thought that he had improved in reading and mentioned that he could recognize similes, which I had taught in mini-lessons on some of the days that he was in reading workshop for the whole period. He thought that he might try some similes in his own writing. Setting goals for himself in writing, Mike said that he would write a story about a trip he had taken to New York. Another goal was to improve in proofreading. Spelling, although of concern to him in reading, was not specifically mentioned when it came to his own writing. Perhaps it was not as important to him as it once was. Expressing his own ideas in his writing seemed to be more meaningful to him than spelling correctly.

Fortunately, Mike became involved in colonial times, too. He followed his interest in colonial farming that had developed as a result of our visit to a colonial manor. Suddenly, I noticed, he began in reading workshop—without Marie—to read books about the farm. I was amazed. He was very excited and wrote to me in his journal about the information he had gathered on colonial farms. His interest increased his desire for more information on farming tools. Going to the library himself, he found a book, which he shared with another boy also interested in this topic; in fact, Mike was able to tell Mark a great deal about farming. Because of his involvement in farming, Mike became a more active participant in history. He wanted to read to the class from the history book and was able to do so with few mistakes. His personal investment in learning about history allowed him to take a risk with reading a more difficult book. His IEP program, though, did not support such choice and control. Its insistence on mandated skills continued to interfere with Mike's claiming ownership. He was not sufficiently independent to enjoy learning skills without feeling that he was being deprived of his own ideas.

In the spring, Mike, like Alex, was taking more risks in writing, too. Besides using words in his pieces that he did not know how to spell, he experimented with words from his speaking and listening vocabulary. It was at this time that Mike switched to writing in script.

I had not forced him. Perhaps he wanted to write in cursive because all his classmates did, or perhaps his personal investment and pride in his own writing prompted his desire to copy his finished pieces in script. I imagine that he was ready and thus made the decision.

At the end of the year, Mike was excited about his writing. He liked the similes that he used and told me, "I use better words and I don't worry about spelling." He felt that he had improved in reading because he was reading longer books. And he was—but most of his reading was done with his aide. It was only when he was personally involved in a topic, when he wanted to pursue his own interests, that he could read on his own.

Both boys left fifth grade feeling successful. They were pleased with their achievement. I was especially interested that they had progressed in writing and that over time they were able to take control of it. Ownership gave them choices. They selected topics, and they made decisions about revision, about sharing their work, and about collaboration. They took risks by writing in different genres and by using similes, dialogue, and vocabulary that they couldn't spell. And they evaluated their work and set their own goals for themselves. Mike was able to leave his aide and to become a writer. He developed ownership in writing because, perhaps, he was in the classroom and became part of the writing community. Alex, too, became a writer and was able to express his ideas despite his "limited language" prognosis at the beginning of the year. He also sensed ownership, which he attempted to preserve when the skills teacher arrived. Alex became not just a reader but an independent reader who chose his own books and responded to them with his own ideas. How would Mike have changed as a reader if he had had greater control over his reading, if he had become part of the community of readers, if he had made choices, if he had believed that he could read on his own, and if his reading had not been composed of the isolated skills established by the IEP?

## My Story—Reflections

My story was one of frustration. In the past I felt that I could follow my own interests and philosophy, establishing an environment that I sensed was best suited to my students and to me. By the middle of the year, I realized the skills teachers' need for ownership—to teach the boys in their own way with little collaboration with me. I had discussed the situation and the issue of ownership—mine and the boys'—many times with my principal and with other administrators. I explained my philosophy and wondered why there could not be greater communication between skills teachers and classroom teachers. Couldn't we work together for the benefit of the boys? Couldn't there be some congruency? How can personal ownership and collaboration be integrated so that cooperation occurs? It seemed the same issue with which Alex and Mike struggled. I had found a solution in the classroom, the creation of a community of learners. Could this be extended to the school as a whole?

Providing few answers, the administrators told me that I had good questions, but explained patiently that I really didn't have ownership in my classroom because I was expected to teach the prescribed fifth-grade curriculum. This came as a surprise to me. I had always thought that I had ownership within the confines of the school's and state's curriculum. I felt defeated. Again, like Alex and Mike, my philosophy (like their ideas, which were so important) was being restricted. I felt all year as the boys were taught different approaches in one-to-one settings that I had no idea what they were learning, what strategies were used, or how I could build on that learning in the classroom.

In the confusion of the conflicts that seemed to surround me for most of the year, I didn't realize until the end that both boys were able to become part of the class community of learners—Alex to a greater extent than Mike, who seemed at times on the fringe except for writing. The ownership they discovered over time through the response they received in writing workshop gradually spread to reading and other areas of the curriculum. They realized that their ideas were valued and respected. Beginning to take themselves and their learning seriously, they started to take risks with their own ideas by participating in discussions and simulations. The personal investment they made in learning led to greater independence. Alex no longer had to be the class clown. He realized that his baby voice could be substituted by a more mature voice. As I struggled to provide a supportive environment—one that responded to them with respect and gave them time to grow at their own rate—I realized that they were able to develop some sense of control or authority over their learning despite the disruptions caused by their IEP schedules. Through this ownership, these special learners discovered that they had a voice.

Alex and Mike taught me about my own need for ownership, something I had taken for granted in the past. In other years I did not feel as hampered or trapped by IEP regulations, the problems of scheduling, and communication between teachers. My year of frustration was not due to pull-out/put-in programs; it had more to do with my philosophy and the setting—the environment I wanted for my special learners. If the environment with the skills teachers was consistent with the environment in the classroom, if there was congruency, if there was collaboration, if we had all worked together for the benefit of the boys, perhaps ownership would not have been an issue for me personally. As the school year ended and I had time to reflect, I was left with two nagging questions: Do children own their own minds? and How do teachers maintain ownership of their philosophy within the classroom and the system? Both of these questions will, no doubt, provide the seeds of reflection in years to come.

## References

Babbitt, N. (1975). *Tuck everlasting.* New York: Farrar, Straus & Giroux.

Blume. J. (1972). *Tales of a fourth grade nothing.* New York: Dutton.

Giacobbe, M. E. (1989). Learning to write and writing to learn in the elementary school. In A. R. Petrosky & D. Bartholomae (eds.), *The teaching of writing: 85th yearbook of the National Society for the Study of Education* (pp. 131–147). Chicago: University of Chicago Press.

Weaver, C. (1994a). *Reading process and practice from socio-psycholinguistics to whole language* (2nd ed., pp. 544–550). Portsmouth, NH: Heinemann.

Weaver, C. (1994b). *Success at last: Helping students with AD(H)D achieve their potential* (pp. 196–220). Portsmouth, NH: Heinemann.

## Bibliography

**Cora Lee Five**

*Professional resources that have been especially important to me include:*

Atwell, N. (1987). *In the middle: Writing, reading, and learning with adolescents.* Upper Montclair, NJ: Boynton/Cook.

Fletcher, R. (1993). *What a writer needs.* Portsmouth, NH: Heinemann.

Graves, D. (1983). *Writing: Teachers and children at work.* Portsmouth, NH: Heinemann Educational Books.

Harste, J. C., Short, K. G., & Burke, C. L. (1996). *Creating classrooms for authors: The reading-writing connection.* 2nd ed. Portsmouth, NH: Heinemann.

Harwayne, S. (1992). *Lasting impressions.* Portsmouth, NH: Heinemann.

Reif, L. (1992). *Seeking diversity: Language arts with adolescents.* Portsmouth, NH: Heinemann Educational Books.

Routman, R. (1994). *Invitations: On the teaching and learning of writing.* Portsmouth, NH: Heinemann.

Routman, R. (1996). *Literacy at the crossroads.* Portsmouth, NH: Heinemann.

Weaver, C. (1994). *Reading process and practice.* 2nd ed. Portsmouth, NH: Heinemann.

**Children's books that I especially enjoy using with children include:**

Babbitt, N. (1975). *Tuck everlasting.* New York: Farrar, Straus & Giroux.

Collier, J., & Collier, C. (1974). *My brother Sam is dead.* New York: Four Winds Press.

Fleischman, P. (1991). *The half-a-moon inn.* New York: Trophy Books, HarperCollins.

Keehn, S. M. (1991). *I am Regina.* New York: Philomel Books.

Paterson, K. (1978). *The great Gilly Hopkins.* New York: Crowell.

# 14 Time on Our Side

**Mary Mercer Krogness**
Teacher, Author, Language Arts Consultant,
Cleveland, Ohio

By choice, I moved from a small and nurturing elementary K–6 school, where I'd taught gifted and talented sixth graders from all over the school district, not *up* but *to* the middle school. I decided to teach students at the opposite end of the academic spectrum: seventh and eighth graders who read at or below the third stanine on the Stanford Achievement Test in reading comprehension and vocabulary and who experienced serious academic problems. They qualified for my language arts/reading class because of their low reading and vocabulary test scores. The idea was to give low- and underachieving students an English class (the regular curriculum) and also a language arts/reading class to support their language skills development.

Although I had a sprinkling of ESL students—mostly Asian students—who were just learning English, most of my students were African American, more of them boys than girls. Many had repeated at least one grade; although some came from strong, stable, nurturing families, many came from unstable homes. Key people (their mothers, fathers, or grandmothers) were dead, out of work, in prison, or had left their families. My kids' home phone numbers (although not everyone had a telephone) changed frequently; they moved often too. Many of my students also shared a negative attitude toward school. In a cartoon (Figure 14.1), Micah creatively conveys the pain that school had caused him and his attitude toward school (Krogness, 1995, p. 10).

Upon my arrival at the middle school (a middle school in name only), I was struck by its hugeness—a low sprawling building with three wings, made mostly of brick and glass, and bursting with close to nine hundred adolescents. The school aimed to be academically rigorous, but to many of our faculty, this meant teacher power and student submission—a readiness to "kick butt," as more than a few of the teachers expressed it. Early in the school year, certain colleagues advised me to bear down on my low- and underachieving kids, who often were the most serious behavior problems in and outside of our school.

**Figure 14.1**  Micah's Cartoon

Having come from an elementary school where teachers generally set their own daily schedules (except for music, art, and physical education), I was struck by an unbending eight-period school day and ringing bells. Our forty-two-minute class periods made me feel like I had to set a metronome and efficiently march through academic work in a clipped, mechanical way. I felt anxious and rushed and jangled, as if I were doing the jitterbug instead of a waltz. (I certainly just dated myself.) Certain students skidded into my class late and then, maybe five minutes before the bell, started preparing to dash, helter-skelter through the long corridors to their next class.

I felt sure that short class periods didn't give my students the necessary time to settle down and become engaged in learning. I wondered how I was going to set a nice, easy tempo in each of my five classes of mainly overage, underachieving seventh and eighth graders who especially needed the precious commodity of uninterrupted time. I knew that when a block of time was on my side, I was able to vary the pace and content of each class, bringing all of the language arts (listening, talking, reading, writing, speaking, viewing, and thinking) together. But a fragmented schedule would make it impossible for us to weave the language arts into a wholesome fabric. Even over the span of a school year, I couldn't see how I—in collaboration with my students—could create a classroom atmosphere that was lively without being chaotic; focused without becoming rigidly task-oriented; purposeful without being didactic; student-centered without being "warm and fuzzy" and academically soft.

I was a seasoned teacher. I had nearly twenty-five years of classroom experience teaching students from a wide range of socioeconomic, racial, cultural, ethnic, and linguistic backgrounds. I had taught in urban Washington, DC, in Columbus, in Cleveland, and in suburban Shaker Heights, Ohio. But I was in a quandary. In this huge, traditional, teacher-centered, curriculum-driven, test-taking junior high school, how would I be able to use my elementary school approach, a philosophy that rested on getting to really know the whole child and his or her family and build community and trust? How could I find out my students' special interests and learning styles, their fears and worries? How would my students and I ever be able to create a rich language laboratory together?

Confronted with these institutionalized constraints and what I perceived to be an entrenched teaching philosophy and narrow perception of academic goals, how could I possibly help my low-achieving students to value themselves? I quickly observed my kids were smart, but they were street smart, not school smart. They did not perform well on standardized tests, do homework, study for tests, do the assigned projects, achieve good grades in school, and behave themselves according to school standards. How could I help them recognize and develop their many untapped talents and multiple intelligences by immersing them in the language arts? How could we translate my kids' street smartness to school smartness, so that school, and eventually society, didn't lose them to the streets?

Although I asked myself these heady questions almost weekly, with missionary zeal and a zest for tackling a mighty challenge, I began setting the stage for success—my students' and my own. I often felt like Sisyphus who struggled to push the huge stone up hill, but no matter how hard he tried, slid backwards. For many years, I'd designed freewheeling, comfortably paced classrooms that had benefitted the majority of my students. But I soon found out that my new students weren't accustomed to taking the academic responsibility and risk that an open forum demands. Over the years they had been subjected to a steady diet of skills sheets, programmed learning kits, and teacher talk. This approach doesn't ask much from students; in fact, it actively discourages them from taking initiative. Most of my students hadn't practiced developing the habit of speaking up in school; instead, they either yelled out or remained silent. Often they behaved outrageously and derailed class activities, acting out their anxiety, frustration, and anger. Other times they sat passively, waiting for me to tell them what to do. They had not had the experience of being generators of ideas in school. I suspect they worried they couldn't make the grade in school, so they had learned not to contribute. Many of my students were simply too preoccupied with worries of their own to be interested in school.

One day Lisa M. yelled out, "You gotta holler at us, Mrs. K." She was telling me in no uncertain terms that she, along with many of my kids, expected me to establish firm limits and standards, and they would function more comfortably and successfully within an obvious structure that had simple and clear expectations. Hollering was not my style, but I knew that somehow I had to build a tighter structure for, and with, my students.

But those short class periods simply didn't give me the necessary time to slowly build their trust, to help them relax, and get them engaged. So, after one school year of trying to accomplish my goals in forty-two minutes, I begged my principal to let me have at least one double, eighty-four-minute period, during which time I would teach both language arts and English. How well I remember my seventh graders grousing and groaning when they found out we were going to be together for two consecutive periods! Eventually they enjoyed beginning our class calmly and building intellectual stamina and staying power as the class continued. They liked coming together as a strong community where individuals could try out their ideas in a safe space, could exercise their imaginations, and could assert their leadership. Let me tell you some classroom stories about how my seventh graders and I set an easy tempo and learned to work together during that eighty-four-minute, back-to-back class. Those longer class periods helped me be the teacher I wanted to be and helped my students become the students I believed they could be.

## Burning Issues

Chi, Marie, Lisa S., Jawan, Jermaine, Jamar, Jung, Joe, Chris, and other seventh graders and I would often start our class by asking questions. Early in the school year, I was the one who asked questions that I hoped would lure the students into talking and debating and raising other questions. "What do you think about teachers banning book bags?" I asked. Nearly every student got into the act—sputtering at first about the adults' disregard for students' dignity and civil rights and the injustice of it all. I pushed them to debate the book bag issue further—first verbalizing both the pros and cons of banning book bags that often were strewn around the corridors and on stairways, and finally writing about this school issue. I capitalized on their natural adolescent tendency to buck authority. In doing so, I accomplished one of my major goals: to get my students generating their own ideas orally. I tried to make student-driven conversations central in our classroom. I wanted to create a noisy classroom—noisy with my students' questions, responses, and their ideas. I found that issues that were compelling to my students—burning issues—helped me to accomplish this goal.

Sometimes literature provided the spark. One day we started class by considering T. J. Avery, a character in Mildred Taylor's (1978) remarkable young adult novel, *Roll of Thunder, Hear My Cry.* This character was sneaky, untrustworthy, and needy. I pushed the students to examine the circumstances of America's history that directly impinged on the black boy's life in the deep South during the 1930s and helped to shape his character. Before we even opened Taylor's novel, which we read and savored together *during* class, we read and talked about the historic events, laws, societal attitudes, and history in which this novel is embedded.

I introduced my students to the *Plessy v. Ferguson* case of 1869, in which the U.S. Supreme Court upheld the right to separate but equal schools for black people. We talked about the effects of Jim Crow laws (separate public drinking fountains and toilets). We considered the Great Depression and its effects. We discussed World War II, Hitler's rise to power in Europe, and his oppression of a whole group of people. A discussion of Hitler's oppression of Jews led naturally to a discussion of America's internment of Japanese Americans during its involvement in World War II. A Japanese American, who with his family had been held in camps in California, came to our class to speak. We read and talked about the landmark decision, *Brown v. The Board of Education, 1954* and the civil rights and women's movements of the 1960s. One burning issue led to another. Then we drew a time line of these important events.

Chris chuckled: "Hey Mrs. K., I thought this was language arts class, not history!" As we built significant background knowledge—what I call a language landscape—for reading Mildred Taylor's novel, we engaged in language in vigorous ways. Together we learned to talk about intellectual matters, and through our important conversations inside our classroom, we built a community. I never, ever sent the good stuff (such as reading *Roll of Thunder*) home. We did the important processes in our classroom laboratory where collective support, knowledge, camaraderie, and conversation were available to all of us. After all, isn't school the most natural place for students and their teacher to think, talk, write, and read together?

## The Power and Politics of Language

We never stopped practicing the art of asking provocative questions during class. I think immediately of Jawan, a big fifteen-year-old but still curious seventh grader. One day he initiated a lively conversation by asking our volunteer, a British woman, a stunning question: "Hey Ms. Bratt, where did y'all get that cool accent?" Like all good questions, Big J.'s inquiry set all of us thinking and asking more good questions. Jawan's question invited Judith Bratt to imitate many different British accents or dialects—the West Midlands (where Judith had been raised), the Welsh dialect, and the dialect most common amongst residents of Newcastle, which Judith called the "Geordie" dialect. In rare form by this time, Judith glided easily into Cockney, typical of London's East End.

Hands were waving. The questions came in a rush: "Where does the language come from?" "Who makes the language?" "Who gets to decide what the 'correct' [standard dialect] English is?" "How come we keep on getting new words?" These intellectual, linguistic, and political questions led us to make several important discoveries: We, the people (not lexicographers or dictionary citators), coin words and change the language to suit our needs, thereby insuring its richness. We discovered that the people who are in power determine the standard dialect. We found out that by using the language and giving it a good workout, we, the people, keep the language alive and well!

This promising, ongoing conversation, which the students found so engaging, prompted me to suggest that we make dictionaries of black expressions coined out on the street: e.g., *dissin', def, homeboy, homegirl*. The students picked up on the suggestion, making their own dictionaries of black expressions (Figure 14.2), which (as they pointed out) are rapidly replaced with new expressions (Krogness, 1995, p. 36). This conversation stirred interest in knowledge and nurturing of a language—any language—within this particular class. So did a heightened awareness of a speaker's (also a writer's) distinctly different audiences and the necessity for that speaker and writer to know both

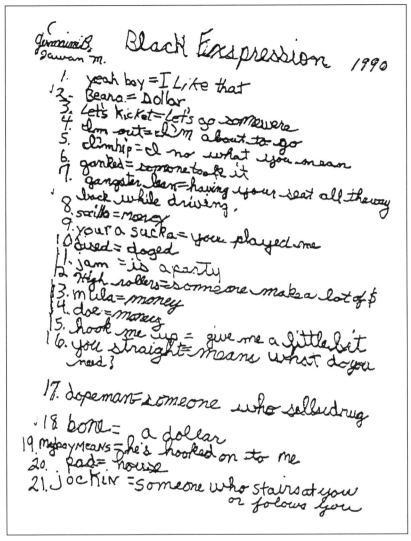

**Figure 14.2** Dictionary of Black Expressions

the standard and nonstandard dialects in order to operate successfully in society. After this discussion about language, my kids better appreciated the value of talking, perhaps to their friends and family, in a nonstandard dialect while speaking in a standard dialect at school and someday in the work place. Implicit was a healthier respect for all language and the speakers of all dialects—standard and nonstandard, especially their own nonstandard dialect.

We pondered Jawan's wonderful question during chunks of several class periods. Surely these conversations accomplished what no work sheet, no programmed reading kit, no teacher-made test could ever have accomplished: We talked to ask questions and explore ideas; we worked together; we built healthy relationships within our classroom. In her 1995 book, *The Power of Their Ideas*, Deborah Meier, the remarkable educator who started Central Park East in East Harlem, defines *teaching* as listening carefully and *learning* as telling. I agree.

### On The Spot: Another Time to Talk

Talk was central to our language laboratory. We continued to get better at generating ideas and questions and responding to each other's views on any number of issues. Daily we talked about what we valued or were trying to figure out or were struggling to master. And I can tell you that we talked about classroom decorum. We had to! In one back-to-back seventh-grade class, we decided to devote ten to twenty minutes each Friday to discussing specific improvements in our behavior and connecting its mighty effect on academic progress.

On The Spot (our name for this weekly Friday forum) was designed to acknowledge students who were taking better charge of their lives: getting to class on time, sitting down quickly without "pickin'" with each other, refraining from making incendiary comments that derailed the class, destroyed a discussion, or even caused a fight to break out. We evaluated behavior (including mine). No one was permitted to point an accusing finger during these informal assessments. We used this time to take stock of what we were learning and what we were able to do better: work together, work in small and large groups more productively and actively, ask better questions, be more active and responsive listeners, initiate ideas more often, focus on language work for longer periods of time, thereby building intellectual muscle or stamina. Jamar's written description of one of our class meetings (Figure 14.3) provides a good example (Krogness, 1995, p. 114).

### Exercising Our Imaginations

We spent a lot of class time exercising our imaginations. (Remember: I never, ever send the good stuff home, but keep it for class.) Elliot Eisner (1985) and E. Paul Torrance (1970), creativity experts, say that students in all grades should have regular opportunities to exercise

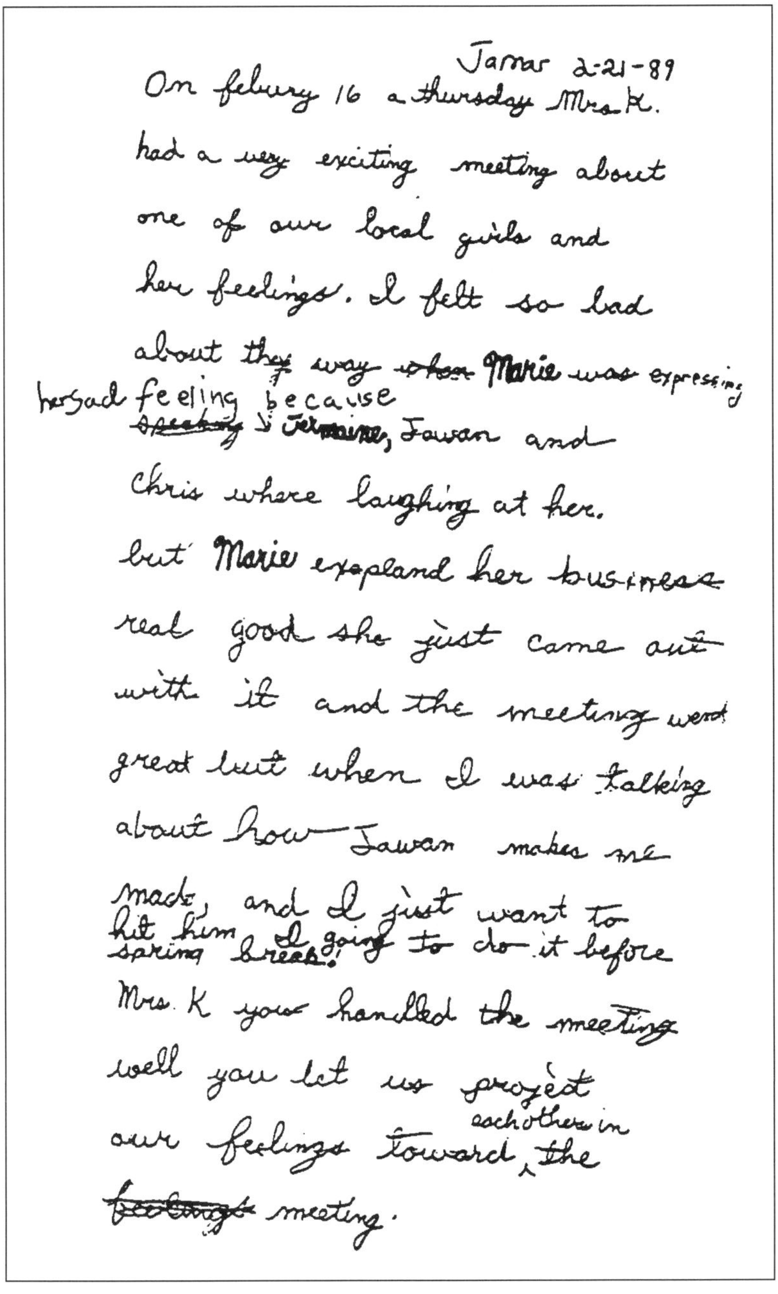

Jamar 2-21-89

On febuary 16 a thursday Mrs K.
had a very exciting meeting about
one of our local girls and
her feelings. I felt so bad
about the way when Marie was expressing
her sad feeling because
speaking & Jermaine, Jawan and
Chris where laughing at her.
but Marie expeland her business
real good she just came out
with it and the meeting went
great but when I was talking
about how Jawan makes me
made, and I just want to
hit him I going to do it before
spring break. Mrs K you handled the meeting
well you let us projèct
                              eachother in
our feelings toward the
feelings meeting.

**Figure 14.3**   Jamar's Response

their imaginations. They also say that the more ideas students generate, the better their ideas become. My classroom experience bears this out.

Picture a large, green, ghoulish plastic foot, a remnant from a Halloween costume. After arranging our chairs in a large circle, theater-in-the-round style, my students and I examined the claw by turning it over, touching it, and looking at its shape and contours. The foot's gnarled, bony appearance gave rise to an almost infinite number of possibilities. "How might you use this monster's claw or foot? What might it become?" I asked my seventh graders. "Don't tell us—get up and *use* it and let us guess. You can either pantomime or do a combo of miming and talking."

My students—even the shy ones—eventually got into the act. The more limber their imaginations (and bodies) became, the more imaginative and fluid their responses to the green claw. One girl wore the claw as an earring while another cradled it tenderly in her arms. One boy sat down and pecked away on the ugly toenails of our prop pretending he was typing a paper, while another turned it over and showed us his Jell-O mold. The students generated maybe thirty ideas in forty minutes! Some ideas were more original than others, but the point—at this moment—was not to evaluate my students' contributions, but to encourage their imaginative engagement. Most students dared to participate more than once; the electricity was palpable and the laughter infectious.

During our more sustained and vigorous creative workouts such as the green claw exercise, my kids were becoming more deft at being prime movers, and during these intense sessions, we would spend whatever time it took to consider what made certain of their ideas exceptionally fresh and imaginative. We used boxes, scarves, and tea bags (each a likely prop because of its potential to become an infinite number of other things) to heat up our brain cells. Eventually everyone found something extraordinary in the ordinary.

## Classroom Drama: A Tool for Teaching; A Tool for Learning

Exercising the imagination was something we did in class quite by design; it was a habit of mind that I wanted my students to practice and value. After limbering our bodies and focusing our attention by doing simple theater games that everyone could easily manage, I seriously engaged my students in doing what the great dramatist/teacher, Dorothy Heathcote (see Heathcote and Bolton, 1995), calls classroom drama, which, I hasten to tell you, is *not* producing a play, doing skits, or acting out characters—that's theater. The classroom drama I'm talking about is improvised drama, based on a human condition, e.g., survival, loss, ethics. A moment in history, a story character's dilemma, or even a current event from the newspaper might serve as the point of departure for an improvised drama.

When students actually become the characters who are struggling to figure out a particular human problem—perhaps losing a parent, surviving a difficult situation, or grappling with an ethical problem—the young people are learning how to deal with universal human difficulties that challenge us all. In bringing their own experiences to an improvisation, students are learning to empathize and gain more authentic understanding of the literary characters they meet in novels, people they're reading about in history, and the current events they find in newspapers. Through improvised drama, young people can actively gain better understanding of their own attitudes and feelings too. Classroom drama is a powerful teaching and learning tool. Here is an example of how I used classroom drama to help one class of seventh graders connect literature with their lives.

I chose the popular fairy tale, *Cinderella,* an ancient story with hundreds of different versions from different cultures, as a point of departure. *Cinderella* is an ancient tale with contemporary meaning: Like Cinderella, so many of our children are members of reconstituted families. It's a universal story because there's not a person alive who hasn't felt like Cinderella did when she sat by the hearth watching her stepsisters get dressed to go to the ball; there's not a person on earth who hasn't felt rejected, abandoned, left out, unappreciated, or devalued by family, friends, or even society.

I told my seventh graders that we were going to look at the old fairy tale from fresh points of view and connect Cinderella's life with our own lives. I told them that we were going to do improvised drama, which meant we would create our own unwritten scripts on the spot. I said we were going to play roles—I would be playing the role of an investigative reporter who asks questions; they *all* would play the role of Cinderella, whom I would interview. Some of the boys looked puzzled—dismayed. But never mind. Quickly and without any more explanation, we began getting into character. I assumed my role of the investigative reporter by asking only one important question: *"When in your life—at home with your families, at school with your teachers and classmates, on the bus, or in the cafeteria with your friends—have you felt like Cinderella when she sat by the hearth?"* Slowly at first, then faster, my students' Cinderella stories welled up and out: stories of being slighted or treated unjustly at home, worrying that a teacher didn't value their work, feeling left out or betrayed by friends, even abandoned because of death or divorce. Issues of race dominated many of my students' stories.

The stories these seventh graders told in our class were passionate and real. Their voices trembled and sometimes they wept because we were getting to the heart of the matter and to matters of the heart. I watched my students' faces and their eyes. They were intensely interested in their own and classmates' stories that by this time were spilling out unself-consciously. When I asked them, finally, to step out of character and revisit the story of *Cinderella*, they were able to connect this piece of literature with their own lives because they now knew Cinderella's heartache firsthand. Jamar said, "Before doing this drama, I thought *Cinderella* was a story only for girls—but every one in here has a Cinderella story to tell!"

A scaffolding or a framework like the one I've just described can be used to advantage with any age group and in various ways. For instance, I asked my students to be the investigative reporters while I played the role of Cinderella's stepmother. When one investigative reporter asked me the inevitable question, "Why are you so mean to Cinderella—don't you like her?" I responded by saying that Cinderella and her father were sticking together and leaving my two daughters and me out. I told the reporters that, quite frankly, Cinderella had been haughty and mean and that my daughters and I hadn't felt welcome. I said I hadn't bargained for a rude stepdaughter and a milquetoast husband! This improvised drama helped participants understand that characters have different points of view. Classroom drama gave my students a vehicle for thinking on their feet, solving problems, and making connections between literature and their own lives. And it offered me a means of making school real and relevant for my students, one of my major goals.

## Poetry's for Everyone!

Poetry has a way of strumming students' emotional chords. My kids—especially the ones with severe decoding problems—took pride and pleasure in chanting the words of poets like Maya Angelou, Nikki Giovanni, Lucille Clifton, and Langston Hughes over and over. They caught the rhythms and sound effects of the poetry after they'd practiced interpreting the poetic lines; they often swayed or danced to a poem's cadence. Rayshon, a boy with serious reading difficulties, said: "Before I started performing poetry, I used to be a terrible reader." And he imitated the halting way he used to read: uh, uh, uh. For Rayshon and most of his classmates, for whom print was overwhelming, poetry—with its short, clean, spare lines—was manageable. When we performed poetry, like Lucille Clifton's "Homage to My Hips," my students' voices became instruments. They slid easily from low to high, from loud to soft. Sometimes they repeated whole lines of a poem or important words. Much like jazz musicians, the small groups of performers (composed of maybe three kids) often punctuated their poetry performances with sound effects and new rhythms.

Poetry was the balm that soothed our souls and excited our imaginations. Side by side, we wrote with our favorite poets, our creative companions, inspiring and instructing us as we tried finding the best words we could and arranging them into pleasing pieces. In the margins of Xeroxed copies of our favorite poems, my kids wrote their own poems. Poems like "Samuel" by Bobbi Katz (1973), a short, sweet poem about a little salamander that "died very quietly during spelling" evoked memories about childhood and loss. The short, sometimes repeated lines of this poem unfailingly moved us and helped us tap our own memory banks; its language and rhythms set us free, first to tell our own stories of loss and worry orally, and then to put pencil to paper using words imaginatively and with voice.

Chi, recently from Vietnam, was just learning English when she wrote this poem next to Bobbi Katz's poem, "Samuel." Here is Chi's poem (Krogness, 1995, p. 206).

This is 8 year ago
Me 5 year old I am to
short I am not
really like go to
school I like new
sweater I like
I have a wash [wish]
but my mother
She not buy
For me she
is buy For
My Sister
Not For
Me every
night I go
to bed I am
crying why
My Mother
love my sister
now I don't like every
Thing, but NOW I like how can't
I speak english very much that
is I am very happy.

Jamar was inspired to write a joyous poem about his Grandma Williams after we read aloud and talked about "Kisses" by Judith Thurman (1976). Here is Jamar's poem about his Grandma Williams (Krogness, 1995, p. 212).

> When I go over my
> grandma Williams,
> She say's come
> here honey bun
> give me some
> sugar.
> I feel like a sweet role [roll]
> all wraped [wrapped] up
> and tightened
> up! but
> when she
> Pokes out
> them lips
> I am traped [trapped]!
> I don't have
> any choice because
> my parents are
> looking over me like
> executioners.

Big Jawan, who put his head down on his desk because he was sure he couldn't write poetry, wrote his poem after I primed the pump a little more by asking him: "Hey J., where do you get kisses?"—a dangerous question to ask a 15-year-old boy!

"I mostly get kisses when I go to church," he said matter-of-factly. "That's the first line of your poem, J.," I quickly acknowledged. A couple more questions from me and Jawan was off and running. My job description meant helping my kids find their poems, stories, plays, and most of all their voices. Here is Jawan's untitled poem about getting kisses at church (Krogness, 1995, p. 213).

> I mostly get kisses
> when I go to
> church—Holy
> Trinity Baptist
> Church at 131st
> Sister Morrison
> give me the water rain
> puddle kiss of the
> Sunday. And when she
> pucker up, it
> *Is* a rainfall.

Within minutes of writing this poem—with its wonderful rush of words, water-rain-puddle-kiss-of-the-Sunday—and reading it to his classmates and me, Jawan wrote a poem about his aunt, Annie Sis, earthy and funny. Here is Jawan's poem about Annie Sis (Krogness, 1995, p. 213).

> I have a aunt
> name Annie
> Sis. She give
> Me a kiss and
> she have a mustache
> When she kisses me it feel
> Like a brush
> bristle and like
> a dog kiss—wet
> and wild.

Oh, how we cheered and savored each other's success.

As I reflect on these stories, I know that many of them could not have happened in forty-two-minute periods. My students and I needed *time* to discuss compelling issues; to explore language together; to reflect on our growth as a learning community; to exercise our imaginations; to plumb the human condition through classroom drama; to experience poetry by reading, writing, and performing it. Time—the blessed commodity of uninterrupted time—was definitely on our side, and our growing commitment to learning proved it.

I certainly didn't fulfill all of my goals with all of my students, but I knew one thing: I had planted seeds. When all is said and done, teachers have to be content with planting seeds, trusting that—in time—they will germinate.

## References

Angelou, M. (1971). *Just give me a cool drink of water 'fore I diiie.* New York: Random House.

Clifton, L. (1969). *Good time poems.* New York: Random House.

Eisner, E. (1985). *Learning and teaching the ways of knowing.* Chicago: NSSE, distributed by the University of Chicago Press.

Giovanni, N. (1985). *Spin a soft black song: Poems for children.* New York: Hill and Wang.

Heathcote, D., & Bolton, G. (1995). *Drama for learning.* Portsmouth, NH: Heinemann.

Hughes, L. (1982). *Listen children: An anthology of black literature.* (D. S. Strickland, ed.). New York: Bantam Books.

Katz, B. (1973). *Upside down and inside out: Poems for all your pockets.* New York: Franklin Watts.

Krogness, M. M. (1995). *Just teach me, Mrs. K.: Talking, reading, and writing with resistant adolescent learners.* Portsmouth, NH: Heinemann.

Meier, D. (1995). *The power of their ideas: Lessons for America from a small school in Harlem.* Boston: Beacon Press.

Taylor, M. (1978). *Roll of thunder, hear my cry.* New York: Bantam.

Thurman, J. (1976). *Flashlight, and other poems.* New York: Atheneum.

Torrance, E. P. (1970). *Encouraging creativity in the classroom.* Dubuque, IA: W.C. Brown.

## Bibliography

**Mary Mercer Krogness**

*Professional resources that have been especially important to me include:*

Ayers, W. (1993). *To teach: Journey of a teacher.* New York: Teachers College Press.

Edelman, M. W. (1992). *The measure of our success.* Boston: Beacon Press.

Heath, S. B. (1983). *Ways with words: Language, life, and words in communities and classrooms.* New York: Cambridge University Press.

Kozol, J. (1992). *Savage inequalities: Children in America's schools.* New York: Harper Perennial.

Meier, D. (1995). *The power of their ideas: Lessons for America from a small school in Harlem.* Boston: Beacon Press.

Rose, M. (1989). *Lives on the boundary.* New York: Penguin Books.


*Children's books that I especially enjoy using with children include:*

Bridgers, S. E. (1976). *Home before dark.* New York: Knopf.

Bridgers, S. E. (1996). *All we know of heaven.* Wilmington, NC: Banks Channel Books.

Cisneros, S. (1991). *The house on Mango Street.* New York: Vintage.

Clavell, J. (1981). *The children's story.* New York: Delacorte.

Cormier, R. (1974). *The chocolate war.* New York: Pantheon.

Curtis, C. P. (1995). *The Watsons go to Birmingham—1963.* New York: Delacorte.

Gallo, D. (1984). *Sixteen: Short stories by outstanding writers for young adults.* New York: Delacorte Press.

Greenfield, E. (1978). *Honey, I love and other love poems.* New York: Crowell.

Guy, R. (1983). *New guys around the block.* New York: Delacorte.

Hopkins, L. B. (1995). *Been to yesterdays: Poems of life.* Honesdale, PA: Word Song/Boyds Mills Press.

Paterson, K. (1977). *Bridge to Terabithia.* New York: Crowell.

Paterson, K. (1978). *The great Gilly Hopkins.* New York: Crowell.

Paterson, K. (1980). *Jacob have I loved.* New York: Crowell.

Taylor, M. (1978). *Roll of thunder, hear my cry.* New York: Bantam Books.

Taylor, M. (1990). *Mississippi bridge.* New York: Dial Books for Young Readers.

Wolff, V. E. (1993). *Make lemonade.* New York: Holt.

Worth, V., with pictures by Babbitt, N. (1986). *Small poems again.* New York: Farrar, Straus & Giroux.

# 15 The Teacher as Listener

**Dorothy M. Taylor**
Fairfax County Public Schools,
Fairfax County, Virginia

On the day of my first formal observation when I was student teaching, Barbara Agor, my supervising professor from the University of Rochester, came to the classroom about midday. I was working with a small group of beginning English as a second language (ESL) elementary school students, mostly Amerasian refugees. I had brought in some flowers known as Queen Anne's lace, a box of food coloring, and some small cups. We reviewed the colors as we put the dye into the cups, talked a little about flowers and their parts, and then placed the flowers into the cups. I explained how the dye would travel through the stem and eventually turn the petals that color. Throughout the lesson, the students were engaged and excited. I was pleased with the lesson. It was content-based, kinetic, visual, basic enough for beginners, yet not insultingly simple.

When Barbara and I sat down to talk after the children had gone home, she had many good things to say about my lesson. We talked about the children and their different personalities and needs. I expressed a few concerns about Tuan. He had arrived near the end of the previous school year and would be repeating first grade. He was a restless little boy and tended to fidget.

"Did you notice how he was humming and singing softly under his breath?" she asked me.

"Uh oh," I thought, "she thinks I should have stopped that."

"Have you considered taking advantage of that musical interest?" she said.

No, I hadn't. I'd been much too focused on my own agenda and on getting good results from the carefully laid-out lesson plans I had prepared at home.

When we think of teaching, we tend to focus on what the teacher is doing to activate the student. But through the years, as I've watched good teachers and have reflected on my own teaching, I've come to realize that one important characteristic that good teachers share is that they listen to their students.

On the surface, listening to children appears to be such an easy skill to develop in the classroom. But when you think about twenty to thirty squirming children, a couple of open windows, a PA system blaring an announcement, someone knocking at your door, and a head filled with must-do items for the day, it seems a little more difficult.

Unfortunately, I don't have any magic solutions for the many distractions that can prevent us from listening to our students. What I would like to share with you, however, are some of the strategies that I have developed for listening to my students and, more importantly, some of the knowledge that I have gathered by listening to my ESL students over the past eighteen years.

## Making Time to Listen

I believe that one of the key factors to developing a listening classroom is organization. Kevin Murphy, who has written a book on effective listening for business, advises managers to "develop a routine and make communication time an integral part of it" (Murphy, 1987, p. 21). I try to let my students know that I am open to listening to them at all times, but in a busy classroom, even I recognize that's an ideal and not a reality. However, I do incorporate a time to listen to my students each and every day. In the elementary grades, I called it "sharing session." Many teachers call it "show and tell." In each case, the idea is the same. Students talk about something of their choosing, and I listen. I include it in my lesson plans; it's the only time of the day when my sole agenda is to listen. It's also my favorite time, and I've discovered I'm not alone. Judith Lindfors, in an article on the good classroom environment, has the following to say about "show and tell":

> [In my second-grade classroom], one of the absolutely predicable daily "get to's" [as opposed to "have to's"], was "show and tell." I confess I never could understand why. What, I wondered, could be so compelling about telling or listening to others tell about an object or event that, from my perspective at least, was often minimally interesting at best. But we had show and tell almost daily, not because I understood why the children liked it, and not because I saw special value in it, but basically because there were twenty-four of them and only one of me. But now I'm glad they outnumbered me, and I see that they were right. The situation was authentic: They wanted to tell each other about the events and objects they lugged in; they wanted to have and to be audiences for one another. And I'm sure there were matters of social status and acceptance and such which were crucial

here that I didn't even begin to recognize. But these are language, too—what language is about, what language is for. So show and tell was authentic for these children, and it was a "get to," *because* it was authentic for them. And besides this, it was the perfect opportunity for them to control, to shape, to design—yes, to creatively construct both what to tell and how. (Lindfors, 1989, p. 46)

During sharing sessions over the years, I've learned what a My Little Pony doll looks like and how many different kinds there are, how a car engine works, the twenty-five different ways to detect counterfeit bills, how to make a moon cake for the Chinese moon festival, that Puerto Ricans in New York City sometimes keep pigs in their basement for slaughter to make various delicacies for Christmas, and that if you buy the two-liter glass of beer at Hooters for five dollars, you can bring it back and get a half price refill. Sharing time is unpredictable, educational, and never boring.

## Listening with our Eyes

Because the verbal contributions that beginning ESL students can make during sharing sessions and at other times are limited, drawing pictures is a good alternative to allow them to express themselves orally. I've served as a substitute teacher in many ESL classrooms, and one of my favorite "sub" activities is to share my life story through pictures and then ask my students to do the same. This task is one in which the most limited English speaker can participate. In the lower grades, on Fridays I used to ask my students to draw a picture of what they planned to do over the weekend, and on Monday we would revisit the pictures to see if that's what they had done. In an excellent resource book on drawing for ESL students, Sharron Bassano and Mary Ann Christison write, "Visual communication is universal and international; there are no limitations of pronunciation, vocabulary, or grammar. Visual language can be perceived and conceived by the literate as well as the preliterate. It may convey facts and ideas in a wider range than any other means of communication" (Bassano & Christison, 1982, p. 1). Just as Barbara Agor attuned me to the fact that a teacher shouldn't just listen to what students say but also to what they hum, my students' drawings have taught me that listening can be done with the eyes as well as the ears.

Unfortunately, it's been through miscommunication that I've learned how important nonverbal cues are when listening to ESL students. Nonverbal cues can run the gamut from voice tone and pitch to dress and posture (Brownwell, 1986). One interesting study on nonverbal communication found that in situations where speakers' facial expressions and vocal messages were inconsistent, listeners paid more attention to the nonverbal facial expressions than to the verbal messages (Bostram, 1990). Eye contact is one area of nonverbal communication that is particularly important. Books designed to teach business people how to listen effectively urge managers and salespeople to make direct eye contact with their employees and clients, not only to pick up unstated nuances of behavior, but to convey a genuine interest in what the person is saying (Reed, 1985; Brownwell, 1986; Robertson, 1994).

Most ESL teachers pride themselves on their ability to communicate nonverbally: For example, they hold up two fingers to express the number two, or they pantomime common activities such as brushing your teeth or washing your face. Likewise, our students quickly become adept at expressing themselves in nonverbal ways. I learned one of my earliest lessons in the importance of making eye contact when I was student teaching. Su-Lin, a sixth-grader from China, had been having some problems with her eyes, and I wanted to write a note about these problems to her aunt with whom she was living. It was the end of the day, and I was short on time because she needed to catch a bus. I asked her if her aunt could read English. She nodded her head yes. I bowed my head to write the note, wrote the date and started the letter, "Dear Mrs. . . ." At that point I realized I didn't know her aunt's last name, so without looking up, I asked Su-Lin her aunt's last name, unintentionally initiating a classic comedy routine as I did so:

> "What's your aunt's last name?"
> "Hu."
> "Your aunt."
> "Hu."
> "Your aunt, what's your aunt's last name?"
> "Last name Hu, H-U," as I finally looked up and saw her writing the letters H-U in the air.

I would have saved myself and Su-Lin a great deal of time and frustration had I made eye contact with her throughout our conversation.

Adult ESL students I have taught have told me that one of the things that irritates them in their conversations with native English speakers is when the native speakers finish their sentences for them, rather than giving them time to come up with the words themselves. One of them developed her own efficient nonverbal way of letting others know that she needs a little time to think of the word. She simply holds up her hand, just as the crossing guards hold up their hands in the "Stop" salute, until she thinks of the word. This is only one of many different ways that ESL students can and do signal their needs non-verbally, and it's our responsibility to remember that watching for these signals is an important part of listening.

## Questions and Listening

Simply giving children the opportunity to talk and listening to them do so is one of the greatest joys I receive from teaching. But it was my friend and fellow researcher, Katharine Samway, who eventually taught me that guiding students by asking them questions is also an important role for the listening teacher. We were working together on a cross-age correspondence research project. Katharine was writing to a group of my fourth- through eighth-grade ESL students and me about our writing, while I was corresponding with the same students and with Katharine in reading dialogue journals. Toward the end of the project we seemed to have more questions than answers, so Katharine suggested that we formally interview the students about the reading–writing connections they were making during our project. I was reluctant. I thought that interviewing students one at a time would take too much time, and I really didn't think they would have anything to say that they hadn't already told us. I was wrong. The students were clearly flattered and proud to be asked to participate in this new stage of the project. We shared our questions with the students prior to the interviews and asked them to look through their reading journals, writing pieces, and correspondence with Katharine as they pondered the questions. During the interviews, their responses were thoughtful and honest. As Katharine put it:

> Sometimes we are fortunate to be in the right place at the right time to hear children spontaneously share insights into the literacy process. As teachers, we have made inferences about how children's reading has influenced what or how they wrote. . . . [But] we cannot rely solely on our hunches. We need to talk directly with students about these issues in order to better understand them as learners. (Samway & Taylor, 1993, p. 7).

The kinds of questions Katharine and I were asking the children were valuable because they were the "good questions [that] provide surprises for both child and teacher" (Graves, 1983, p. 107). When I interviewed the children about their reading and writing experiences, I wasn't listening for the right answer because I didn't *know* the right answer.

Interestingly enough, it was one of the kinds of questions that Graves would call a bad one that gave me an opportunity to watch theory turn into practice one day. In my teacher education program, I had learned that books with recurring patterns, rhythms, and rhymes, such as those used in fairy tales, nursery rhymes, and pattern books, help children build oral language skills. But it was listening to Emily, a first grader from China, one day that convinced me of the veracity of this theory. Emily had basic conversational skills in English, but because she spoke Chinese at home with her parents, she had quite a few gaps in her vocabulary. On this occasion, we were looking at Eric Carle's *The Very Busy Spider*. I pointed to the spider and asked her one of those inane questions that ESL teachers sometimes find themselves asking: "Do you know what that is?" Emily was silent for a while, but I could tell from the way she was wrinkling her brow that she was thinking. Then I noticed her lips were moving. Finally I heard her saying softly under her breath, ". . . along came a . . ." and then, *"spider!"* she cried gleefully. Because somebody had put "Little Miss Muffet" into Emily's head, a spider came out when she needed it. And, because I had the patience and foresight to listen to her, I found out where that spider came from.

Having spent a number of years in the classroom, I know that, when students come to us, they bring a potent mixture of experiences with them. These experiences, in which their use of language and beliefs about it are intermingled, cannot be ignored. As we gain information about our students' language skills by listening to them talk with one another and with us, we can categorize and analyze this information in helpful ways; but we also must remember that learning is a fluid process. One of my friends puts it like this: "Our minds don't stay in one place. Where I am today is not necessarily where I will be tomorrow." Learning about our students means carefully listening to the answers they give us, but it also means listening just as carefully the next day because it's entirely possible that the answers (and even the questions) have changed.

## Listening to Parents

In addition to listening to my students, I have learned to listen carefully to their parents. Parents of all children are an important resource, but I think this is particularly true of the parents of ESL students. Unless we come from the same cultural background as the student or have worked extensively with that ethnic group, we teachers are often ignorant of the belief systems and conditions from which our students are coming.

For a time, I taught ESL in a school that had a large Israeli population. The Hebrew bilingual teacher, an Israeli herself, had told me that Israeli parents expect their children to be given homework, so I had gotten in the habit of sending work for the children to do at home. One morning the mother of Luisa, a second-grade Brazilian student, stopped by to tell me that this homework had become a problem in their household. Luisa spoke no English when she arrived but had made tremendous strides in a short period of time. She was a socially engaging child and had quickly become the darling of her class. Little did her classroom teacher or I know, however, what an exhausting toll this effort was taking on the child. Luisa, her mother told me, would come home from school and immediately go to sleep for two or three hours. Because of their busy professional lives, Luisa's parents often had limited time to spend with Luisa and her ten-year-old brother. My "homework" was cutting into that small amount of relaxed time they had with Luisa, yet Luisa's sense of duty wouldn't permit her to slack up on the homework. How fortunate I was that Luisa's mother felt comfortable enough to explain the situation to me. A talk with Luisa, some lessening of the amount of homework, and explicit permission to delay some work until the weekend quickly resolved the problem.

In addition to struggling with individual family circumstances, parents of ESL students may be having difficulty with English themselves or be feeling culturally and socially isolated. Finding a translator other than the child for parent–teacher conferences is one way of facilitating communication. Some kind of orientation to help parents and children become familiar with the school and its staff is also important. Unfortunately, this lesson again is one I learned through my mistake.

The school guidance counselor had informed me that there was a first grader from Finland who would be needing ESL instruction, so I visited her classroom to get a brief informal assessment of her English. Anna appeared to be comfortable in the first-grade class, but her teacher told me she hadn't spoken. When I showed her some crayons and asked her about their colors, she just smiled at me. I wasn't surprised, since young children often go through a silent period when learning a new language—a time in which they are taking in a great deal of the new language, but not yet producing it.

The next day, I received a phone call from Anna's mother. She introduced herself and explained that Anna had come home yesterday a bit confused by this "nice lady" who kept asking her if she knew her colors. "Of course, I know my colors," Anna told her mother, "I just don't know them in English." Anna's mother and I made arrangements to meet the next day when she brought Anna to school. I met Anna's baby brother, and Anna's mother explained to Anna in Finnish who I was and how I would be helping her to learn English. I think I have been very fortunate in my relationships with parents, but this is definitely one case in which I could have saved Anna and her mother a great deal of confusion by making the effort to introduce myself at the outset. I am grateful to Anna's mother for teaching me that lesson.

## Continuing to Listen

Learning how to listen is a never-ending process, as I learned quite clearly while I was working on this article. I was sitting at my desk when I received a phone call from Atsuko, one of my adult ESL students from Japan.

> "There will be Noh performance," she told me.
> I was silent.
> "June 19," she continued.
> "There will be no performance on June 19," I repeated.
> "Yes," she replied, "probably at Studio Arena, but not for sure."
> "You don't know where it was supposed to be," I said.
> "Right, but I'll call you."
> "What performance?" I asked
> "Noh performance," she replied.
> "There was supposed to be a performance, but now there's no performance," I asked.
> "Huh?" she said.
> "There was supposed to be a performance, but it was canceled?" I asked.
> "It has?" she asked in a surprised voice.
> "I don't know. I thought that's what you were telling me!" I was practically shouting into her ear at that point. "You said no performance, so I'm thinking that the performance, whatever it was, must have been canceled."
> Atsuko laughed. "No," she said. "Noh performance is special kind of Japanese theater. There are dancers. They wear masks and there are people who sing. There's going to be this kind of performance on June 19, I think at Studio Arena, but it's not for sure. Do you understand?"
> I understood.

Our miscommunication involving the Noh performance can be easily analyzed. If I were Japanese or knew more about Japanese culture, I would have known about Noh theater. If Atsuko were a native

English speaker, she would probably have used the article "a" and referred to "a Noh performance," which might have clued me in to the fact that she was telling me about a kind of performance. If we had been talking face-to-face, instead of on the telephone, gestures might have cleared up the confusion. I'm sure that we both learned something about how to communicate more effectively from our exchange. But to me, that's not the most important lesson to be learned from this conversation. The more important lesson is that we continued to listen to each other, even when the message wasn't making sense. We listened until it did make sense.

## Conclusion

I know that listening to my students helps me learn and teach more effectively. But, quite frankly, these are not the reasons that push me to listen to my students. I listen to what they have to say because it's interesting. Last week, one of my students told me the following joke that she had read in a joke book. The gist of the joke went something like this:

> A young man was talking to an older man who had been married for a great number of years. The young man asked the older man, "How have you and your wife managed to get along for so many years?"
>
> "Well," the older man replied, "my wife and I made an agreement early in our marriage that I would make the big decisions and she would make the little decisions."
>
> "And that's worked out well for you?" the young man asked.
>
> "Yes," replied the older man. For example, my wife has made the decision about what jobs I should pursue, what city we should live in, and what house we should buy."
>
> The young man looked at the older man strangely and asked, "And what decisions have you made?"
>
> "Oh, we haven't had any decisions big enough for me to make yet," he replied.

I laughed heartily after she told me the joke. "Did you understand it?" she asked.

"Of course," I replied.

"I'm so happy," she told me, "because I tried to tell this joke to an older American man, but he didn't understand."

"I can't imagine why not," I told her, "it was perfectly understandable to me."

"That's because you're a patient listener," she replied.

I hope so. I know that I try to be, but I know, too, that I'm not always the perfectly patient listener I want to be. But even when I have made what I've referred to here as mistakes in communication, I've learned something. I look back at my eighteen years of teaching in wonder at all the pieces of information I've picked up simply by listening to my students, and I look forward to walking into my classroom tomorrow because I know there will be more. As for the teachers who are just beginning their careers, I envy the years of listening they have ahead of them.

## References

Bassano, S., & Christison, M. A. (1982). *Drawing out.* San Francisco, CA: The Alemany Press.

Bostrom, R. N. (1990). *Listening behavior: Measurement and application.* New York: The Guilford Press.

Brownwell, J. (1986). *Building active listening skills.* Englewood Cliffs, NJ: Prentice-Hall.

Carle, E. (1989). *The very busy spider.* New York: Putnam.

Graves, D. H. (1983).*Writing: Teachers and children at work.* Portsmouth, NH: Heinemann Educational Books.

Lindfors, J. W. (1989). The classroom: A good environment for language learning. In P. Rigg & V. G. Allen (eds.), *When they don't all speak English* (pp. 39–54) Urbana, IL: National Council of Teachers of English.

Murphy, K. J. (1987). *Effective listening.* New York: Bantam Books.

Reed, W. H. (1985). *Positive listening: Learning to hear what people are really saying.* New York: Franklin Watts.

Robertson, A. K. (1994). *Listen for success: A guide to effective listening.* New York: Richard D. Irwin.

Samway, K. D., & Taylor, D. M. (1993). Inviting children to make connections between reading and writing. *TESOL Journal, 2* (3), 7–11.

## Bibliography

**Dorothy M. Taylor**

*Professional resources that have been especially important to me include:*

Atwell, N. (1987). *In the middle: Writing, reading, and learning with adolescents.* Upper Montclair, NJ: Boynton/Cook.

Cazden, C. B. (1988). *Classroom discourse: The language of teaching and learning.* Portsmouth, NH: Heinemann.

Dulay, H., Marina, B., & Krashen, S. (1982). *Language two*. New York: Oxford University Press.

Elbow, P. (1986). *Embracing contraries: Explorations in learning and teaching*. New York: Oxford University Press.

Freire, P., & Macedo, D. (1987). *Literacy: Reading the world and the world*. South Hadley, MA: Bergin & Garvey.

Graves, D. H. (1983). *Writing: Teachers and children at work*. Portsmouth, NH: Heinemann.

***Children's books that I especially enjoy using with children include:***

Carle, E. (1994). *The very hungry caterpillar*. New York: Philomel Books.

George, J. (1972). *Julie of the wolves*. New York: Harper & Row.

Kipling, R. (1912). *Just so stories*. Garden City, NY: Doubleday.

Lionni, L. (1963). *Swimmy*. New York: Pantheon.

Mosel, A. (1968). *Tikki tikki tembo*. New York: Holt, Rinehart & Winston.

Silverstein, S. (1974). *Where the sidewalk ends*. New York: Harper & Row.

Smith, D. B. (1973). *A taste of blackberries*. New York: Crowell.

# 16 Building Common Ground

**Renée Bachman**
Machan Elementary School, Phoenix, Arizona

**Julia Fournier**
Machan Elementary School, Phoenix, Arizona

Julia writes:

*I am a teacher in a bilingual 2/3 multiage-classroom. For the past seventeen years, I have been teaching primary children, and the past eleven of these have been at a large urban school in Phoenix, Arizona. During those eleven years, I have gone from being perceived as a young, idealistic newcomer to an experienced veteran. Each year starts fresh for me, just as it did during my first years. There are still many struggles and challenges, along with the celebrations and rewards. What has made a great difference throughout the years for me and for my colleague, Renée Bachman, is enlarging the space we provide for talk that "matters." Taking time for what matters in the lives of our students helps us be better teachers and in turn promotes better learners.*

## Morning Meeting

The bell rings; announcements start. At the far end of my 2/3 classroom, one of a group of four boys, busy building a parking garage of wood blocks, goes to the scrap paper pile and inspects a colored sheet that has writing on only one side. Satisfied that this will suit his purpose, he goes back to his group and starts making a sign asking others not to touch or disturb the structure and listing the names of those who have contributed to the block construction. At the same time, five other children, who have been playing a board game, begin packing the pieces into the box. Similarly, the other children in the room finish the projects they have been working on and put away their materials. Two children are arranging chairs in a circle in the large open part of the classroom; they are in charge of meeting this week. As the announcements end, one of them calls out a warning to all, "Five minutes to meeting!" There are two other students in charge of attendance, and they begin calling out the names from the oversized roster. They put a clothespin beside the name of each absentee. Lunch money is collected, roll sheets filled out, and messengers hurry off to the office and cafeteria. The two children in charge of Morning Meeting pull out a notebook and sit down; the class "falls in," adults and children settling down to begin.

"Quien quiere compartir?" (Who wants to share?) is the first invitation of the day. Several hands go up. As the recorder of the meeting writes down the names, the facilitator says them aloud and hands go down. The first name is called, and the sharing begins. In theory, all attention is to be on the person talking. If there is a group within the circle that cannot settle down, they might be warned first and then asked to leave. Sometimes those in charge of circle might get a valued object from the science table (e.g., a conch shell) or a favorite doll from the house corner, and tell the group that only the person holding this item may talk. These are considered drastic measures, however, and are initiated only when necessary (preholiday and basketball play-off season are annual trouble times). When the person sharing comes to a natural pause in his or her "share," the meeting facilitator asks the group if there are any questions or comments.

As they chair Morning Meetings, the children develop important listening skills: determining when the person sharing is really finished, or when the sharer has exceeded the proper amount of time, or when the "share" is important enough to warrant extra time. Of course, at the beginning of the year, I do a lot of modeling during Morning Meeting, as do the returning students (a benefit of a multiage classroom). And the job of co-chairing the Morning Meeting does not start on day one of school (as does the job of being messenger or taking attendance), but comes a little later, once the community has been firmly established and the standards for this position have been set through example.

Sharing is followed by News. This part of Morning Meeting is meant to connect the students to the world outside their homes and neighborhoods. As is the case with "sharing," it takes many weeks of example to start getting the kinds of current events that lend themselves to discussions we can all enter into and learn from. Young children will remember only a small piece of a story—an incident too insignificant to conjure up the bigger picture for us. We practice asking "who, what, where, why, and how" questions. It is important that the adults in the classroom listen to or watch the news so that they recognize the event the child is attempting to convey. Young children are often drawn to news stories that deal with violence toward children— abuse, kidnapping, murder. Because such an event has happened to others does not, of course, mean it will happen to them, but it does mean that it *can* happen. Talking about what they can or should do when they are in scary situations makes them feel safer.

One day, a young child, Bobby, relayed a bizarre car chase story that resulted in two people being shot. The assailants were unknown and had not been caught. While we had no doubt that there was some fact in this story, we were unable to connect it to our lives.

"Why did you remember this story?" an older child asked.

"I know why," offered an older boy, Mario. "It's because that's the kind of news that gives you nightmares."

Bobby nodded, as did many of the other children. The world our students live in is much different than the one their teachers grew up in. The circle sometimes acts as a giant hug and lets the children know that it's okay to have the feelings they're having, that there are people who have the same feelings, and that sometimes there are things they *can* do to control the situations in which they find themselves.

An example of why this time to talk about news events is so important became evident after the suicide of Kurt Cobain, the lead singer for the group Nirvana. The children were particularly upset about the implications this suicide had for followers of the band and for "the baby he'll never be a dad to." It takes time for the discussions to come around to what is at the heart of the story. Usually it is the sensationalism that initiates the interest, so some work is needed to get past that. This discussion ended up focusing on the importance of listening and being listened to.

What we are working for in News is some common ground for decision-making. By sharing the news events of the world around us—how we feel about them, how we are affected by them—we begin to understand what values we share . . . and do not share. Although parents are usually the first and foremost teachers when it comes to these life lessons, schools and teachers are important too.

Many times we will follow a particular news event for days, even weeks. Some news events lead us to social issues, others to scientific ones. Some events (e.g., floods, earthquakes, new discoveries) prompt us to look for particular places on our map, or to read from a reference book to check facts, or to call another classroom for clarification. When students express continued fascination for such themes, these can become the springboards for content area studies; and when children see their interests become part of the curriculum, they realize they can control their own learning in meaningful ways (Freire, 1970).

News is followed by Sports, which became a distinct category (separate from News), because the fanaticism of loyal professional sports enthusiasts sometimes grows to overwhelming proportions. We even instituted a "No news, no sports" rule when basketball play-offs were dominating the Morning Meeting time.

The next part of Morning Meeting is Business, when children state the special classes or events we will have that day. It is also the time for announcements: whose birthday it is, what objects have been found or lost, what classroom problems still linger (e.g., children not putting caps on the markers, books that are missing). We end Morning Meeting with something that ensures the participation of the entire group. Sometimes this is The Question of the Day (Would you rather be the most intelligent, most athletic, most attractive, or have the most friends? At what age do you think people should be allowed to start dating?) Sometimes there is a survey question, prepared by children working together to make a graph.

The last thing we do is sing a few of the many songs we have learned together or "pass the pulse": We join hands and, beginning with the person who is in charge of circle, we pass a squeeze from person to person, until the "pulse" has gone completely around the circle. Sometimes a child will suggest that we think about something as we pass the pulse, or that we dedicate the singing of the song to someone. For example, when Fabian's mother was having surgery, he wanted us to sing "Flag of the Sun" by Tish Hinojosa. After the bombing in Oklahoma, the students wanted to think about the families as we passed the pulse. At these times, the rituals take on an almost spiritual tone.

These rituals (Peterson, 1992) become the invisible framework of the day. I do not have to tell the children what comes next or what we will do; we all already know. The predictability of the structure of the day gives children the confidence they need to move around within this structure and to find their own rhythms. The opportunity to hear and be heard in Morning Meeting lessens the need for this at other times of the day. Thus the children are ready to talk about literature, art, and mathematics when it is time to do so, for the immediacy and urgency of personal or world events has been given an important space early in the day. Morning Meeting also helps establish the habit of treating other people fairly and with respect (Delattre & Russell, 1993).

## Concern Circle

Visitors to our school might notice the absence of posted rules on the walls of the classroom and the absence of names on the board (with accompanying checks). If they were able to stay awhile and listen, they might also notice the virtual nonexistence of tattling, the high level of "on task" behavior, and the seriousness and self-motivation of the children as they work.

Most visitors come to our school to observe a particular aspect of the curriculum, such as literature study, writing notebooks, or our project approach to content area study. Some people come to see how an entire program works (e.g., multiage, bilingual, Head Start Transition). But by the end of the day, they have questions not only about the approach they came to study, but also about the children's behavior—the ways our students treat one other, respond to conflict, and appear fairly autonomous as they make their way through the school day. Concern Circle fosters these behaviors.

Concern Circle is a group meeting time (right after lunch) to talk about problems. At first my teaching partner and I had to continually remind the students to wait until our meeting after lunch to work out their problems. Most of the children were accustomed to telling the teacher immediately when something happened and then standing back and waiting for justice to be served. But with Concern Circle, the bottom line is, "If the problem is important enough to take up class time, then you should be able to remember it until group meeting."

Another challenge is helping the children learn that, during Concern Circle meetings, they need to speak directly to each other. It is amazing how many students would prefer to speak through the teacher. When the students start to tell me their problem with so-and-so, I look at them and ask, "Was the problem with me?" or "Why are you telling me?" It is a real skill to be able to look your peer in the eye and say, "I have a problem with the way you keep walking by me and stepping on my foot," or "I didn't like it when you called me stupid."

Now, with multiage, it's easy to model the expected behaviors for Concern Circle. On the first day of school, when a newcomer comes to tattle, an "older" will just tell him he needs to wait until Concern Circle, and when it comes, I make sure olders go first to model the way people with problems talk directly to each other.

Though these group meeting times have changed somewhat over the years, the most important elements have remained constant: Wait until Concern Circle time, talk to each other, write each complaint down in a notebook designated for this purpose, give warnings first and then logical consequences as necessary. Most problems are very simple misunderstandings that have gotten blown out of proportion. When given the opportunity for discussion, the children typically settle these problems with an apology and handshake.

The importance of writing down every complaint cannot be emphasized enough. The students need to know that there is a record of each problem and that they will be held accountable. When there is controversy over whether warnings have been given or over "repeat offender status," we need only to check the notebook.

At the beginning of each Concern Circle, I turn off the lights to give a serious tone to the room, I bring out the notebook, and I ask, "Is there anyone who had a problem today that they couldn't solve on their own?" Hands go up. I call out the names as I write them down, and the hands go down. Once the names are noted, the children state the person or persons they had a problem with, and one by one the concerns are brought to the table. There can be no sudden memories of problems once the names have been recorded.

The children's discussion during Concern Circle is embedded in the shared understanding—developed from the beginning of the year—that everyone needs to feel safe at school, both physically and emotionally. Failure to consider this for oneself or for others results in a problem. This shared understanding provides a framework for talk during Concern Circle about treating others the way you yourself want to be treated. We try to devise logical consequences for the problems discussed in Concern Circle meetings.

Although serious problems like fights occur from time to time, I find that providing this daily time to talk prevents most misunderstandings from getting to that point. Students are given the time to work things out, and they come to know the child they have problems with better so that fights don't have to occur. Some of the problems the children and I have dealt with stand out vividly in memory. One such memory involves Carrie, a very aggressive child who came to our class in November. Her way of making herself known to the community was by calling names and hitting. By the end of the first week, Carrie had managed to offend every child in the class, either by hitting or name-calling. As a new student, she had been given quite a bit of extra consideration, but the group had finally had enough. During Concern Circle six children stated the problems they were having with Carrie— behaviors she had already been warned about.

"Carrie, you called me stupid."

"Carrie, you pushed me in line."

"Carrie, you marked in my notebook."

Carrie stared back at the children with a hard, fixed look, refusing to respond. By the time the sixth child had issued his complaint, Carrie broke down.

"It's just that no one in this class likes me!"

The class stared in disbelief as Carrie cried, her hands covering her face. Rudy waited until Carrie lifted her face. Looking into her eyes, he spoke.

"We like you, Carrie; you just don't know how to be a friend to us."

The conversation that followed marked Carrie's real entry into the class. She did not need punishments; she needed time to make her way in, to discover the boundaries and limitations of her new environment, and to be accepted by her peers.

One time Tanya, a child of mixed race, experienced unprecedented name-calling and racial insults. What began as a somewhat playful name-calling contest, ended with tears. Although there had been no overt racial incidents prior to this, Tanya felt discriminated against. We focused on the name-calling. Going around the room, we vocalized every name we had ever been called that we disliked. Then we went around again, each of us telling what we would like to be called. Tanya began by saying, "I just want to be called by my name, Tanya."

With serious offenses such as stealing, we often need purposeful, guided reflection. Students can become self-righteous when another person has been identified as a thief or liar. During these times, it is important to recognize that everyone has stolen something at some time. On different occasions, we have gone around the circle describing a time when we have stolen and why we did it. We then work to understand why someone in the class might be stealing, instead of condemning him or her for something we have all done ourselves.

One incident especially stands out in my memory. Jesse, a student in our class, had spent two months convincing us and himself that he was no longer a thief. We had finally learned to trust Jesse again, after having been victimized by him time after time. At the end of October, the classroom was bustling, getting ready for our Halloween celebration. A child reminded me not to forget the goodies our nursing home buddies had sent over the week before. I reached for the bucket containing the treat bags, only to find it half full. I counted the bags and sure enough, fourteen of the twenty-nine bags were missing. With genuine disbelief, I asked the class, "Who would have taken our treats?" No one had any idea. We opened one treat bag to determine the contents. A pumpkin pen, a bat eraser, and a few candies were the items common to each bag. One student remarked that he had seen Marco with a pumpkin pen like the one we were holding up. Marco immediately turned to Jesse, naming him as the boy who had given him the pen. All eyes now turned toward Jesse who denied having had anything to do with the treat bags, saying an aunt had given him the pen.

At that moment another child pointed to the clock, reminding me it was time for P.E. My face was red with anger, and my eyes were swelling with disappointment. I told Jesse I wasn't ready to believe that he had stolen from us again. I had him wait in the classroom so I could talk with him after I took the rest of the students to P.E.

After depositing the class with the P.E. teacher, I walked to the classroom of Jesse's younger sister.

"Ever seen one of these before?" I asked.

"Oh yeah. Jesse was giving those out at our day care."

On my way back to pick up Jesse, I just couldn't think of what to do. I was too upset. We had all worked so hard.

"Are there any left?" I asked him, when I got back.

Jesse began to protest his innocence. I stopped him.

"I've talked to your sister."

Jesse hung his head and shook it. I sat in silence, trying to think about how we would handle this, the class and I. I knew the kids would feel as hurt as I did. Jesse sat in silence.

"What would you do if you were me?" I asked Jesse.

He shrugged his shoulders.

When I picked up the kids from P.E., I still didn't have a plan.

"Did he do it? Did he do it?" the kids asked.

"Let's talk about it in Concern Circle, an emergency meeting," I suggested.

The chairs were already set up in a circle when we returned to the room. Jesse was seated in one of them. The lights were out. The rest of the class filled in the seats. I picked up the bucket, half full of treat bags, and placed it in front of Jesse.

"Pass them out," I told him.

Jesse looked at me and got up. When he got to the sixteenth child, he had nothing to give her.

"There aren't anymore," said Jesse.

No one spoke.

"Tell us what happened," I said.

"I took the pens to my day care and gave them to the kids there."

Children started expressing anger and disbelief all together. Most of the comments were negative ones toward Jesse. Jesse walked around the rest of the circle with the remaining kids looking inside the empty bucket. I quieted them down and asked who wanted to share how they felt. Many hands went up. The first to share were the people without the treat bags. They were upset. It was unfair, they said, that their treats had been given to someone else. It was also unfair that the other kids got to have treats when they didn't.

Finally, one of the children who had a treat raised his hand.

"I don't want my treats if everyone can't have them," he said.

Others expressed the same feeling. One by one, the students went up and dropped their treats back into the bucket. I was feeling so proud of the students and how they were treating each other. I kept watching Jesse. I felt he was learning a lesson about stealing, and also about giving and fairness. I took a big breath, anticipating the end of the session.

"Wait a minute," said Bobby, one of the youngest children. "If he passed them out this way [in reverse direction], then we would get the treats."

"Is that what you want Jesse to do?" I asked.

Bobby nodded. Jesse got up and passed out the treats again, only this time in reverse order. This time Bobby was the first to raise his hand to say he did not want his if all the children did not receive one. I had been afraid that Bobby had asked for the treats to be passed out again in reverse order because he wanted to keep the candy. Instead, I realized he had just wanted the opportunity to show how he felt both when he *did* get candy and when he *didn't*. I learned once again to trust the students and the experience they had had in working problems out together.

## Final Reflections

The underlying principles that have guided my way of thinking about working with children have remained constant over the years: to give children practice in identifying and working out their problems together, to give students the chance to listen to others and to be heard by them too, to work toward autonomy in the classroom, and to develop respect and caring for self and others. Living these principles day after day, we connect ourselves to the world around us and find our place in time. What we do today matters and affects what will happen tomorrow. We cannot care about people until we know them. We come to know them through work and play and talk. Through interactions like those that occur in Morning Meeting and Concern Circle, the children and I come to understand, to value, to care about, and to trust others by recognizing ourselves in them. When we see ourselves in the people around us, the world is a safer place, and when the world is safer, we can take more risks and become true learners.

Renée writes:

> *I am a teacher in a bilingual 4/5 multiage classroom. I have been teaching in the elementary public schools for eleven years, and for the past six years I have been teaching in a large inner-city school in Phoenix, Arizona. I have taught in many classroom settings, and in all of them talk has played an important role. With each passing year, however, the place for meaningful dialogue in the classroom has grown for me and for my colleague, Julia Fournier, broadening and deepening, and working its way into the core of our curriculum. Making time for meaningful dialogue gives our children insight into the world around them and allows them to see themselves as active participants in their own education.*

---

> *Go to the people. Learn from them. Love them. Start with what they know. Build with what they have. But the best of leaders when the job is done, when the task is accomplished, the people will all say we have done it ourselves.*

> Lao Tzu, 604 BC

## Morning Circle

Morning math ends. While the children in my 4/5 classroom put their math notebooks away and grab their language folders, a child turns on the compact disc player. A familiar song begins as the children gather in a circle on the floor, singing:

> The streets are empty at daybreak, the paper lays on the lawn,
> With yesterday's news repeated, though we know yesterday's
>    gone
> But there's a lesson for learning and if we listen we'll see
> Then tomorrow's paper may be good to unfold
> And all that's left to believe.
> Now the kids in their paper sailor hats
> March 'round the living room floor
> The seams are folded on the scene of some unending war
> Well it could go on unnoticed and the children must play
> Does the past make a difference in the news we hear today
> Anyway?

> "Yesterday's Paper," Tish Hinojosa, 1994

Morning Circle takes place right after morning announcements and is one of our established rituals. In Morning Circle, we form the foundation of our community (Peterson, 1992). Each morning we open the circle with a song or two. The songs reflect issues, themes, and topics we feel strongly about. Tish Hinojosa's songs have become very popular in the classroom: "Love is on Our Side," "Yesterday's Paper," "Noche Sin Estrellas," "Cada Niño," "There's Something in the Rain," "The Frida Kahlo Waltz," "Bandera del Sol." Other songs that have been important to us are "Blowing in the Wind," "Zombie," and "Tick Tock." Our singing together has special meaning in our classroom community, for the songs we learn and sing together are the building blocks of our foundation. They provide common ground on which to build. Through common experiences and knowledge, all members of the community—students and teachers alike—can identify and connect with the themes, ideas, and messages in these songs. It is typical for a piece of literature or current event to be compared or related to a song we have sung.

After singing, we jump right into sharing. The child in charge of the circle that day begins by holding up a boomerang to make sure all eyes are on the speaker. We chose the boomerang as our symbol to remind us that all things are interconnected because a boomerang goes around and comes back to the person who threw it. The person who holds the boomerang has the floor and is able to share personal stories or current events. When others have questions or comments, the person with the boomerang calls on them. Before passing the boomerang to another child, the speaker ends by telling how he or she is feeling that day. If a child has nothing to share, that person tells only how he or she is feeling. A child saying he or she feels sad creates a natural situation for classmates to show their concern by asking why the person feels that way.

This time of the day is crucial, as it gives all the children the opportunity to share what is important in their lives and to be validated for how they feel. Our shared rituals during Morning Circle foster the children's developing awareness of the importance of each of us as an individual. These rituals also help the children develop real sensitivity to the feelings of others. If children know they can share their personal stories and feelings every day, they begin to feel a sense of family and caring. This daily sharing also seems to lessen the amount of unproductive talk during work time.

On designated days, directly after share time, we discuss poetry, observations, or specific homework activities. This part of Morning Circle is run much like share time. We pass the boomerang around again, giving everyone the opportunity to contribute to the conversation. Children know that during these discussions, it is okay to "jump right in" with an idea or connection. Children learn real-life conversation skills, such as knowing when to add a thought without interrupting or changing the subject:

> With the boomerang resting on her lap, Celia starts off energetically, "My aunt and my cousin's house has metal and a plastic tarp, and when it rains it sounds like money in your pocket. I

like the way the poem started off: 'Throw coins like rain.'" Celia pauses, then adds, "I write a lot about my grandpa. I read it six times, and it made me think of my poems and I made connections with them."

Lesslie interjects, "It reminds me of you, Celia, because of your poem, 'It Seems Like Yesterday.'"

Cerrin continues, "Mine is kind of related to what you are saying. It made me think of 'She Doesn't Live Here Anymore.' It reminds me of when my grandma went to the hospital . . . but I still have her . . . in my way."

The conversation in Circle on this particular cloudy morning in March was in response to a descriptive poem I had assigned as homework the night before. The poem is about the poet's memories of his grandfather. Since it had been raining that week, I selected this poem for homework because the poet likened the sound of the coins that the grandfather threw on top of the house to the sound of rain.

The sharing of interpretations and perspectives not only allows us to study the poetry, it also helps us learn about one another and enables us to see each other through a different lens, to possibly recognize something about another person that we hadn't recognized before. Caring for the other person's thoughts and feelings in conversation contributes to the learning community. Our reflections on poetry, literature, and specific themes provide opportunities to examine ethical and moral issues. These reflections are essential in building common ground.

Morning Circle quietly leads into a twenty-minute individual writing time. We often begin this writing time with a reflection on a word that may have emerged in that day's conversation in Morning Circle. One morning before a field trip to the Heard Museum, the discussion focused on Native Americans, so we decided to reflect on the words "Native Americans." Here are some of the children's thoughts: colorful, creative, sense of humor, drawing, pottery, sembra, casa, polumas, agua, tierra, montañas, rocas, paja, indios, beads, animal meat, lodo, maiz, pintar, Indian, brown, feel, tribes, adobe, buffalo, art, and water. After the children all have a chance to share, I pull the ideas together, trying to make some connections. In this particular reflection on "Native Americans," I pulled all the words together into three categories: words that had something to do with art, with survival, and with physical or mental characteristics.[1]

Children leave the circle with many thoughts that naturally guide them in their writing. These powerful discussions inspire the children to write about meaningful and authentic themes. Sometimes children draw on the themes we've discussed to write stories to share; other times they use the themes in their poetry or more private writing. Many children are reminded of their own stories through the sharing of news and personal experiences. Children no longer say, "I don't have anything to write about," or ask, "What should I write?" At the end of the twenty-minute writing period, we share some of the pieces that were written that day. Through the sharing, the children learn from one another, gaining insight into different writing styles and techniques.

## Concern Circle

The way that conflict is resolved in the classroom has to match the "way we are" all day long. We must have a time to discuss, share feelings, give different perspectives, and develop our own thinking. We have to come together, establish a ritual, and dedicate time to resolving conflicts that the children cannot solve on their own, as this example shows:

> The lights are turned off and the children file into the classroom, forming a semi-quiet circle on the floor. Cecilia, the person in charge of the circle, asks, "Hay asuntos?" ("Are there any concerns?") Five or six hands go up. Cecilia writes down the children's names and then asks each child individually who the concern is with. Susana is first. She turns and makes eye contact with David.
>
> "David, I don't think it's fair that you come to school in a bad mood, like today, and take it out on Ms. Bachman and all of us. It puts everyone in a bad mood."
>
> (Silence.)
>
> Patricia interjects, "Yeah, it's not fair that you get mad at us when we didn't even do anything."
>
> (More silence.)
>
> Cecilia steps in. "Do you have anything you'd like to say about that, David?" David shakes his head. "Does anyone have any ideas that might help David with this concern?" Some hands go up. "Lorena?"
>
> "I think you should leave it at home. Try to forget about whatever is bugging you."
>
> "Gustavo?"
>
> "I think it is hard to just forget what is bugging you, so if you can't do that, you can talk to someone."
>
> I enter the discussion. "Who are some people you can talk to when you have a problem?"
>
> Gustavo answers, "Your friends, your brother, your teacher."
>
> Other children add more ideas to the list. I remind Cecilia to jot all these people down so we can post the list.

Cecilia asks, "Are there any other ideas? Chris?"

"You can do exercise. When I am mad or upset, I like to play basketball."

Cecilia ends by restating the ideas and asks David if he would be willing to try some of these suggestions. David says he will. Cecilia asks Susana if she thinks the concern is resolved, and she agrees.

This process continues until all the concerns are addressed. We like to end with affirmations and compliments. The children become very good at recognizing people for their kindnesses and their abilities.

In our Concern Circles at the beginning of the year, we discuss what people need to live happy, healthy lives. The children make authentic connections to people's needs through literature, personal stories, and events and issues they have discussed in Morning Circles. We identify our needs as a community, and we discuss the principles that support the fulfillment of those needs. We begin to form a list of our "wants" (this is the term we use in lieu of "rules"). As a class, we come to an agreement about what we *want* from each other and what we *want* to do for each other. In essence, these are our behavioral expectations and standards. Since the children set these standards, they feel an ownership of them. Often when children address each other in Concern Circle, they quote directly from our list of wants in expressing their concern.

The teaching situation I am in is perfect for the use of peer modeling because I have a multiage classroom with returning students. For the first few days at the beginning of the year, we do a lot of role-playing in Concern Circle. We set up common problem situations, and the returning students model how they would resolve the conflict. Then we have a discussion. We have a lot of fun during these role-plays, and role-playing continues throughout the year when we feel it is appropriate. Through our role-play and discussion, we are building a structure not only for resolving conflicts, but also for communication in general—how to listen and respond to one another. The procedures for Concern Circle apply to other interactions as well:

1. Look at and speak in a normal voice to the person you are addressing.

2. Tell the person what he or she did and how it made you feel.

3. The person being addressed has the opportunity to tell his or her side or try to resolve the problem.

4. Tell the person what you want from him or her from now on or what you think the consequence should be.

The children involved in the conflict are not the only participants in the discussion. Often other children join, considering ways to prevent this kind of conflict or additional ways to resolve it. Children are encouraged to make connections with prior events and even world events. These concerns are real-life issues. Our discussions help us build conflict resolution strategies, ways of cooperation, and an understanding of others' viewpoints.

Frequently the conflict is resolved with mutual understanding and an apology, but when the problem is a recurring one, the children discuss logical consequences. The person at fault will many times choose one of the consequences the children have suggested or come up with his or her own. We often discuss the issue of choice, stressing that everyone sometimes makes bad choices, but the idea is to learn and grow from those mistakes so you can make better choices in the future. Though I try to respect the expectations and choices of students, sometimes I must intervene and instruct the children directly. The role of teacher as the authority is sometimes necessary in all educational settings. And "authority is good within the classroom but authoritarianism is not" (Freire & Horton, 1990).

Often the allocated time runs out before all the concerns are resolved. When this happens, I remind the children to try and solve the concerns for themselves before Concern Circle tomorrow. In order for the children to make conflict resolution part of their daily lives inside and outside the classroom, they must try the process on their own. This, in turn, will help them become self-governing members of society. It is empowering for children to make decisions about issues and problems that are central to their own lives.

## The Classroom Context

Concern Circle would not be so effective if we did not each year work to build common ground in our classroom community. The way we work, play, and talk together is the basis for our success as a community of learners. Rituals are very important in our community building, especially rituals that recognize and affirm individuals. When a classmate or adult moves away or leaves our classroom, we have a "farewell ceremony." We make cards and present them in a special circle time. When a student teacher in our classroom ended her semester with us, the children made cards, wrote poetry, and even made special gifts for her. We took turns reading our cards aloud and expressing our feelings. Some children began to cry, and others struggled not to. I noticed two boys in particular who became antsy and began to wiggle around and poke friends around them. Then one boy said out loud, "Look! David is crying." We had to stop our ritual for a moment and talk about respecting others' feelings. Then we went back to our farewell ceremony.

However, I recognized that this issue of crying in public was important and merited further discussion and reflection. I decided to send home a "recollection" for homework that night. The assignment was for the children to remember a time when they cried and to describe the event fully, telling what happened, how they felt, and how the people around them reacted and responded.

The next day we broke up into two groups to share our recollections. I had asked another teacher to come in and chair one of the small groups. Generally during a recollection, all students are given the opportunity to share their stories, and every voice is heard. After each person has shared, the chairperson pulls together common themes and makes connections among events. On this particular day, both groups discussed the connections and then came together in a large group to share these connections. Both groups had made very similar connections. We noticed that there were three categories to our recollections of crying: physical pain, hurt feelings, and sadness from the loss of an important person or pet. We also noticed that crying was more acceptable in some situations than in others. We noted differences in regard to boys and girls. It was acceptable for a boy to cry when he broke his arm or was feeling great physical pain, but it was not acceptable for him to cry when his feelings were hurt or someone died or went away. For the girls, crying was more acceptable in all situations. We also noticed differences in people's reactions to crying. In situations that involved physical accidents, the people around were there to comfort and help, but in situations that involved hurt feelings, people sometimes joined in the name-calling or chose to say nothing. In grieving situations, people around us were less likely to approach us and seemed to not know what to do. As we talked, we came to understand more fully that we all have the need to cry and we all experience similar emotions in times of sadness. We also learned that our society has sometimes created unfair expectations of behavior based on gender. The discussions were rich and enlightening in that we saw similarities in one another that went beyond age, gender, and culture.

## Final Reflections

School is so often thought of solely as a place of academic learning—reading, writing, and arithmetic. We must not, however, forget the most valuable resource: *relationships*. Our interconnectedness is important because learning is such a social experience. Freire notes the importance of

> loving people, believing in the people, but not in a naive way. [Does this mean] to accept that all these things the people do are good just because people are people? No, the people also commit mistakes. I don't know many things, but it's necessary to believe in the people. It's necessary to laugh with the people because if we don't do that, we cannot learn from the people, and in not learning from the people we cannot teach them. (Horton & Freire, 1990, p. 247)

## Note

1. This technique comes from our work with Patricia Carini, who is a consultant to various schools and teachers' groups around the country. Reflections enable the participants to see a word or theme more fully. Different perspectives and connections offer added insight and understanding of the word.

## References

Delattre, E., & Russell, W. (1993). Schooling, moral principles, and the formation of character. *Boston University Journal of Education, 175*(2), 24–43.

Freire, P. (1970). *Pedagogy of the oppressed.* New York: Continuum.

Hinojosa, T. (1994). "Yesterday's Paper." From *Destiny's Gate,* Warner Bros. 9 45566-2.

Horton, M., & Freire, P. (1990). *We make the road by walking: Conversations on educational and social change.* Philadelphia: Temple University Press.

Peterson, R. (1992). *Life in a crowded place: Making a learning community.* Portsmouth, NH: Heinemann.

## Bibliography

### Renée Bachman

*Professional resources that have been especially important to me include:*

Dyson, A. H. (1998). Staying free to dance with children: The dangers of sanctifying activities in the language arts curriculum. *English Education, 18*(3), 135–46.

Heard, G. (1989). *For the good of the earth and sun.* Portsmouth, NH: Heinemann.

Horton, M., & Freire, P. (1990). *We make the road by walking: Conversations on education and social change.* Philadelphia: Temple University Press.

*Children's books that I especially enjoy using with children include:*

Uribe, M. (1987). *El primer pajaro de Piko Niko.* Barcelona: Editorial Juventad.

Uribe, V. (1992). *Tres buches de agua salada.* Barcelona: Editorial Norma.

### Julia M. Fournier

*Professional resources that have been especially important to me include:*

Carini, P. (1993). *Images and immeasurables.* North Bennington, VT: Prospect Center.

Freire, P. (1995). *Pedagogy of the oppressed.* New York: Continuum.

Green, M. (1978). *Landscapes of learning.* New York: Teachers College Press.

Kohl, H. (1994). *I won't learn from you: And other thoughts on creative maladjustments.* New York: New Press.

Smith, F. (1986). *Insult to intelligence: The bureaucratic invasion of our classrooms.* New York: Arbor House.

Wells, G. (1986). *The meaning makers: Children learning language and using language to learn.* Portsmouth, NH: Heinemann.

*Children's books that I especially enjoy using with children include:*

Berenguer, C. (1992). *El rey mocho.* Caracas: Ediciones Ekare.

Carlin, J. (1996). *La cama de mama.* Volcano, CA: Volcano Press.

Farias, J. (1988). *El hijo del jardinero.* Madrid: Anaya.

Velthuijs, M. (1991). *Frog in love.* Atlanta, GA: Anthea.

# 17 Communicating with Parents: One Teacher's Story

**Lynne Yermanock Strieb**
Greenfield School, Philadelphia, PA

In June of 1997, I will have completed my twenty-seventh consecutive year of teaching in public schools in Philadelphia. During those twenty-seven years, I have worked hard to include parents in all aspects of my teaching. In 1963 I taught for a year as a long-term substitute in a school where parents were not invited into classrooms. They did some fund-raising for the school (especially the Wednesday pretzel sales during student recess time) and were invited to help with class trips. That was all. Even then, being new and untrained (I'd done graduate work in history of art, but was drawn to teaching after a visit to a friend's kindergarten classroom), I felt that something was wrong with that. This was considered a tough urban school. I wondered why there was such a break between home and school, why the people who had spent so much time with these children (their first teachers, i.e., their parents) were not recognized for the wonderful job they'd done. I was inexperienced, the children were often difficult for me to work with, and many of the parents were unable to read; but there were wonderful, untapped resources in that community of very poor people. The principal and other teachers discouraged me from having parents work alongside me in the classroom. Some of the reasons: They didn't trust parents; they felt it might be bad for that child to have his or her parent working in the same class; they thought the parents weren't educated enough. I was so overwhelmed teaching thirty-five kindergarten children in the morning and a different thirty-five in the afternoon (I didn't even know how to hold a book so that everyone could see it) that I couldn't begin to ask parents for help, though that was probably exactly what I needed. I left teaching at the end of that year, pregnant with our first child, ready to begin a certification and master's program in elementary education.

When my oldest child was four, he attended a parent cooperative nursery, part of the public school system. We parents were required to work in the classroom one morning a week, though alternative home projects were accepted from parents who were unable to participate in that way. We were also expected to attend one evening meeting a month for focused discussions on child development, discipline, curriculum—almost anything having to do with children at school and at home. The group included parents of different races and social classes. Peggy (Perlmutter) Stone was the wonderful teacher who showed me, in so many ways, how parents could contribute to their children's learning, right alongside the teacher. She was a wonderful model for working with children, and I still use many of her words and ways in my teaching. For the next three years (and two children later, before I was able to return to teaching full time), I worked alongside Peggy Stone with other parents, helping and contributing to the life of my own children's classrooms. I promised myself that when I became a teacher, I would try to value the parents of the children I taught, just as Peggy had valued me.

When I started teaching again, I quickly realized that it wasn't enough to expect parents to join me in the classroom. Many were working outside their homes and could not come in. Some had little children to care for at home and couldn't afford baby-sitters. Some were afraid of schools, having had very bad experiences as school children, and they didn't want to join me. Some were not sure that they had anything to contribute. And some were against the idea of parents helping in the classrooms: "You're the teacher. That's your job."

During most of my years of teaching, I have kept my class for two years. I have received them in first grade and kept them through second grade. My teaching has never been traditional. My classroom has many of the materials one often finds in kindergarten classrooms: blocks, math games, art materials, science materials, costumes, a puppet theater. Desks are not in rows or U's, like those in most classrooms in Philadelphia, but are blocked into tables. Each day, the children have a block of time when they choose from among the many materials and activities in the room. Since 1970, I have had some version of what is now called Writers' Workshop, and children write every day. Though in the beginning of my teaching I taught from a basal, I quickly realized that when children chose books from what has become my vast classroom library (thousands of books, color coded either by subject or level of difficulty), and when they were encouraged to read with friends, they got the practice they needed, practice which they often did not get at home. The classroom was often active and noisy, and to a parent, it might look like the children were "only" playing during a large part of the day. I felt that I should do something about what parents might think and say, and I wanted to do it before they got upset. I believed that sending home something written that explained what was going on in the room would begin to allay their worries that I was not teaching their children; that their children were "only" playing. It was then, in 1972, that I began sending a newsletter home regularly.

There are many reasons for communicating with parents in a variety of ways and for encouraging them to work in the classroom alongside me. The benefits for me are great: Their contributions enrich me and the children. I can communicate what I am doing, what the children are doing, and what they are learning. That makes my job easier. When I explain what's going on, or when the parents see it by being in the room, there are fewer misunderstandings. I also have an expanded view of my job: It's not only to educate children, but it's also to educate their parents.

The parents also benefit. From the written communications I send home and from their experience in the classroom, parents learn different ways of working with their own children. They get good ideas. When they sense my willingness to have them in the room or to converse with them, they feel free to ask questions in a positive way. They know that they, their cultures, and their contributions are valued. They see schools as open to them rather than as barriers or fortresses against them.

The benefits to the children are many: Like their parents, they begin to see home and school as continuous. They feel pride when their parents are recognized for what they know and can do, no matter how small the contribution, no matter whether it is made at home (and sent in) or at school. They get to work with a variety of adults, sometimes from a variety of cultures or social class backgrounds.

In looking through my records from September 1994 through November 1996, I have discovered four major ways in which parents and I communicate:

1. Parents work in my classroom;
2. Parents make suggestions, give ideas, contribute;
3. I communicate with parents in writing;
4. I address parent concerns.

## 1. Parents Work in My Classroom

Parents have worked in my classroom in a variety of ways (other than the usual help with parties and celebrations and going on trips, which are, of course, very important and without which it would be impossible to do those things). Here is a quote from my September 1996 newsletter, *The 205 News* (see Appendix for two newsletters):

> *The 205 News,* **September 1996**—We also are delighted that Teacher Kathryn (Keelor) will be working with the children on Mondays and Thursdays. A retired executive at Bell Atlantic, she has been volunteering with me since the spring of 1993. We are *so* fortunate!
>
> *NOW,* why don't *YOU* come to help in the classroom? For all my years of teaching, some of the most important contributions to the children (besides raising them from birth) have been made by parents. I started out as a parent in a school district Parent Cooperative Nursery and then worked in my children's kindergarten. Here are some of the things parents have done through my years of teaching: heard children read; read to children; played reading and math games with children; helped them to sew; talked to them about their work; taught letters, words, songs in languages other than English; brought babies to observe for science and social studies lessons (in fact, Theo Byrne,* who is in our class right now, was one of those babies brought in by his mom); cooked; talked about their own work and interests. *I'm sure you will be able to think of many more things, including going on class trips.*

Over the years, parents have also joined us to teach me and the children. One parent knew a lot about using computers, set mine up, then talked to us about computers and how they can be used. Another played the guitar and joined us for our weekly sing. A third parent was born and raised in Costa Rica and read to the children in Spanish, while I read the same book in English; another spoke Serbo-Croatian and taught us the alphabet and some songs. Chinese parents have taught us about festivals and have told us about what school was like for them when they were in first and second grade. They have taught us how to cook spring rolls and how to eat with chopsticks.

Each year I invite a parent with a newborn baby to visit the class on a regular basis. The children keep a journal about the baby in which they write their predictions and their observations.

> *The 205 News,* **October 1996**—On Monday, October 28, Dr. Carter, Melinda's mom, brought her baby Paul to visit our class-

---

*Children's and parents' names have been changed.

room. We are starting a program called Educating Children for Parenting. This program was started at Germantown Friends School by Sally Scattergood and is now used in school districts across the country. One part of the program is to have infants and their parents visit the classroom every 6 to 8 weeks for the children to observe both baby and mother. We will write our descriptions and will pay attention to the changes in the baby and what the parent does to keep the baby safe, healthy, and happy. The thematic units are: wants and needs, change, communication, learning, and differences and similarities. All of the material is consistent with the school district curriculum. I hope Paul will be able to visit through our two years together. I also invite other parents to bring their babies for visits. That way we can learn what's the same and what's different about children. We will learn a lot!

I have invited parents in to talk about their work or about something that they are interested in (since not all parents are employed). The following excerpts from my newsletter describe some of those visits.

*The 205 News,* **March 1996**—I want to dedicate the rest of this *205 News* to the wonderful parents who have visited the class and talked to the children about their work. The last time I invited parents to do this was in 1980–1981, and it was very good then. My husband tells me I must write about it, so this is my first draft.

What I have loved more than anything is the wonderful thought those of you who have visited have given to what might interest the children. I *know* that anything parents have to say about their work is interesting to the children (even though the parents are afraid that what they do might be boring.)

Dr. McCall, Sally's dad, was the first parent to visit. He is a pathologist who specializes in diseases of bones. He brought rubber gloves, which the children wore when they touched the human heart and the calf's heart, and the healthy lungs, the smoker's, and the cancer-ridden lungs. He brought a slide viewer through which we saw slides of bone cells. When the children wrote about the visit in their math–science journals, many of them said, "I will never smoke, because it makes your lungs black and disgusting." It *was* dramatic to hold a human heart in our hands!

Donald's dad, Mr. James, works at two jobs. He is a truck driver for a construction company, but what he most loves doing is his other work: being a barber–hair stylist. He brought most of the tools he works with (brushes, scissors, combs, and electric clippers), setting them up neatly in front of the room. He showed how each tool works and talked about the importance of good hygiene. He demonstrated good hygiene when he did his grand finale, which was to give his son a haircut right in the classroom. He also taught us about the differences in the way straight, curly, and wavy hair grows. He told us that it doesn't matter what kind of hair you have, the tools used to cut and style it are always the same. . . .

We are looking forward to visits from an ophthalmologist's assistant, a social worker who places foster children, a medical film maker, a commercial interior designer, a person who works with computers, a carpenter, a crossing guard, some architects, a doctor, a microbiologist, a supermarket worker, a nurse, and someone who is currently searching for a job. I'm hoping for a visit from a mom who leads a fight against drugs and works with an award-winning drill team. Is there a homemaker in the house? AND WHAT ABOUT YOU?

Questioning is very important in my class, in learning, and in life. With questions, children take what is taught and make it their own. To me, questions are much more important than answers. So with each of the parents, the children have had lots of time to ask questions. And the parents have been wonderfully thoughtful and clear with their answers.

*The 205 News,* **June 1996**—Rayna Smith's dad is a carpenter for his day job. But the job he loves to do is to paint signs. While he was talking about his work, he designed and painted a large sign for an imaginary party. As he painted, he told us what he was doing. He showed us the tools he uses: different kinds of brushes, paint, pencil. He told us why he drew a picture here and letters there. When he was finished, we had a large, colorful sign hanging in our room for a few days. It was clear to the children how important it is to make letters large and bright when you make a sign.

Lily Green's mom, Leah, is a doctor. She talked about her work and then got the children to diagnose two illnesses. She pretended she was the patient. She told the children her symptoms; they asked questions to narrow down their guesses, and then they figured out that she had a sore throat that might be a strep infection. They then predicted the treatment. She also pretended to be an older woman complaining of getting out of breath when she walked up steps, and of feeling very tired. As she talked, she related more symptoms. The children thought she might have lung cancer or something wrong with her heart. Someone asked a really good question, and they all realized that it was her heart. Dr. Sorokin said that your children were doing "differential diagnoses!" like real doctors. Because they are such good questioners, they did a great job (though I'm not yet ready to be treated by one of them). . . .

Mark's dad is a Grounds maintenance crew chief in Philadelphia's Fairmount Park. He got the children to explain what those words mean. Mr. Johnson brought a helmet, gloves, goggles, earphones, boots, brightly colored vests, and other equipment, and he dressed Mark and Yolanda in his work uniform. He showed us pictures of different kinds of grass cutters, from smallest to largest. He told us that before he was a crew chief, he was supposed to be cleaning the fish ladders on the Schuykill River and fell in. He had a safety harness, so he wasn't swept away by the water. He told us about all the animals that live in the park. He described the hard work he did during the blizzard, and we thanked him for cleaning all that snow. At the end, he used his walkie-talkie to tell his co-worker that he was ready to meet him outside. He gave us a poster of an antique motorcycle.

This brief summary doesn't do justice to the presentations of these parents, and I can't thank them enough. I wish there had been time to hear from everyone, and you can be sure that the next time I do this, I'll start earlier.

We have many parties and celebrations. Parents are invited to participate in the festivities and also to help. The Authors' Breakfast is a very special celebration and most families send at least one member. Here are two entries from my personal teaching journal that describe one Authors' Breakfast.

**Journal, May 2, 1995**—I explain to the children that we will have an Authors' Breakfast, to honor all the authors in rooms 204 and 205. I tell them it's not a real breakfast, though there will be plenty to eat and drink; that parents are invited to hear them read one of their books to a small group that will include their parents; that we'll have to clean the room, move the desks and chairs to make space for the many people who will be there, and that there will be food, which the parents donate, in both rooms.

**Journal, May 3, 1995**—The Authors' Breakfast was wonderful! My idea, Eve's [my teaching partner's] push to organize—it really worked well. There was certainly too much food and juice.

We moved the desks out of the center and around the room. The food was put on tables in the back of 205 and along the bookcase in 204. We put chairs in semicircular sets of five for adults, and a list of children in the middle of each semicircle. The children knew they would be sitting with their parents. The parents were seated by the time the children came in at the beginning of the day.

I stood in the library in the middle of the room and told about the origin of the Authors' Breakfast: When I taught at another school, the principal insisted that we have an Authors' Tea, at which children read things they have written. Even though I didn't like that principal, I liked the idea. At Greenfield I changed it to an Authors' Breakfast because more parents are able to come at the beginning of the day rather than later in the day. Then I told what would happen: each child will read one story; hold your clapping until the end but that they could applaud in sign language or like a crab or they could finger clap.

All of us—children, parents, and I—had a wonderful time.

## 2. Parents Make Suggestions, Give Ideas, Contribute

The following excerpts from my journal hint at the range of parent contributions to my classroom.

**Journal, September 15, 1994**—Mark brought in a book about butterflies. He reminded me again to read it, and I finally had a chance to read it. He can be so difficult, but when I read the book—which helped us, since our butterfly will soon emerge from the chrysalis—he beamed with pride. I must remember to ask his mom to have Mark bring more books to school.

**Journal, May 8, 1995**—A parent, Amy's mom, gave me a poem about the seasons, that she wrote. I copied it and put it into the children's reading homework books so they could read it and learn it. I wrote the seasons and asked them to find words that describe each season in the poem. We will read the poem and discuss it in class tomorrow.

**Journal, October 11, 1995**—We had a wonderful discussion about weather, inspired by *The Weekly Reader*. There was lots of information about satellites, hurricanes, tornadoes, storms, that fascinates kids. Bonnie was central to the talk about hurricanes because some members of her family live in St. Thomas, the Virgin Islands, which was devastated by the recent hurricane. She will be bringing pictures that her grandfather took when he was there.

**Journal, November 22, 1995**—Matthew Drayton's mom began to talk with me about something that happened on our last trip. She'd asked me if I'm going to give out a list of book reports the children will have to do like the other second-grade teachers. The form explained the different genres and told the date and form of each month's book reports. . . . I am ambivalent about children having to do book reports as the sole way of remembering the books they read (often the case), but I didn't think it was a terrible idea. I told her that I would try to assign a few book reports after report card conferences. Mrs. Drayton said, "I hope you don't think I think the children are not learning. I know they are learning, believe me, and I love the way you've done the insect projects." [Children did research on insects and other animals and taught the class what they had learned.]

I apologized for not sending home the videotapes of her child teaching the class about mosquitoes, but promised to do that soon so that she could see just how much they learned. She said, "We got involved in a project my older daughter was working on, and we wanted her to learn how to do it right, with index cards (what about computers?), so we found out that it took hours of our own time. So I began to wonder, 'What about the children who don't have parents who can help them with these projects? How will they ever learn how to do research if they don't learn to do it in school?' I think that what you're doing is really important." I thanked her for telling me all of that, and told her how much comments like hers meant to me.

**Journal, March 11, 1996**—Jane [a parent] read *The Daisy Chain*, a short story by a friend of hers, about flowers that cooperate in order to give life back to a dying lily. It was a story about the importance of cooperation, and Jane led the discussion with the children. I did not love the story because its premise was preposterous: talking flowers, flowers brought back from being dead, flowers learning from one another. Though I didn't like the story, I felt that the lessons about interdependence and cooperation embedded in it were important ones. I also felt that because a parent offered to read the story, and because she's been wanting so badly to do it, it would be fine. I can't always let that happen, but I saw no harm in this.

**Journal, June 6, 1996**—Kindergarten parents have been visiting first-grade classes to see if they want their children to be with me for two years. One parent was a little unpleasant. He kept talking to me about being a single parent. I told him how hard that must be. Then he looked around the room, especially at the "underwater world" that my teaching partner Eve, the children, parent volunteers, and I had created. He said he loves scuba diving and knows a lot about it. He asked if I'd played the recording of whales communicating to the children. I said, "I've heard it, but I didn't think to do that." He was both surprised and critical. I said, "That's one of the things parents can do for me—they give me great ideas."

## 3. I Communicate with Parents in Writing

Much of my writing to parents is telling them how to help their children. I try to be as specific as possible and to give them words they can use. Each night, children take home a book in a manila envelope to read with or to their parents or to read independently. On the first night the book is taken home, the book envelope has the following letter attached to the front (modified slightly from Routman, 1994, p. 200). Parents have often commented about how helpful those suggestions have been.

### Letter, September 12, 1994

Dear Parents,
To produce independent readers who monitor and correct themselves as they read, try the following before you say "sound it out":

- Give your child "wait time" of 5 to 10 seconds. Don't say anything. See what he or she tries to do to help him- or herself.

- "What would make sense there?"
- "What do you think that word could be?"
- "Use the picture to help you figure out what it could be."
- "Go back to the beginning of the sentence and try that again."
- "Skip back over it and read to the end of the sentence. Now what do you think it is?"
- "Put in a word that would make sense there."
- "You read that word before on another page. See if you can find it."
- "Look at how that word begins. Start it out and keep reading."
- "The person who wrote this story wants it to make sense to you when you read it. Try to use words that make it make sense."
- Tell your child the word.

When your child is having difficulty and trying to work out the trouble spots, comments such as the following are suggested:

- "Good for you. I like the way you tried to work that out."
- "That was a good try. Yes, that word would make sense there."
- "I like the way you looked at the picture to help yourself."
- "I like the way you went back to the beginning of the sentence and tried that again. That's what good readers do."
- "You are becoming a good reader. I'm proud of you."

We often have whole-class discussions, and as the children speak, I type their words into my laptop. I print the discussion at home and then put it into their reading homework books for them to read as homework. The children enjoy reading their own and each others' words, and the next day in school, we read the discussion as a play. At the beginning of the children's first year with me, the instructions to parents are fairly specific:

**Homework, September 8, 1994**

What I Like to Do

On the first day of school, I asked the children to tell the class something they like to do. Your children should try to read this by themselves, but if they need help, that's fine. Ask the children to find their own names themselves and to read what they said. Then they should read about what other children like to do. If children are not yet able to read their passages, make sure they point to the words as you read them.

*Yolanda:* I like to play at home. I like to play house.

*Leonard:* I like to play ball. I like to play catch.

*Matthew D.:* I like to play with my dog. She's a Labrador. Her name's Missy. She doesn't bite me. . . .

### Homework, September 9, 1994
#### Caterpillar

My friend gave me two Monarch caterpillars. On the first day of school, the children observed and described them, just the way scientists do. Some of the children asked questions. We will continue to observe, describe and write about the monarchs. Again, help your child to read this. Start with what your child said. Let your child's request for help be your guide. Remember, your child should point to the words if she or he is just learning. Many of your children can already read. (But, of course, you probably know that.)

*Yolanda:* Does it eat the plants?

*Leonard:* It has white and black.

*Matthew D.:* It's fat and ugly.

*Sally:* It has black, white, yellow, and it's cute. . . .

### Homework, September 14, 1994
#### I Can Read

I read *When Will I Read?* by Miriam Cohen, to the children. We talked about learning to read. I told them that some children learn to read when they are only three years old. Some children don't learn to read until they are ten. But most people learn to read. In 205, some children already know how to read, while other children are beginning to learn. We never say, "I can't read." We say, "I'm learning to read." I asked the children if they can read anything at home: signs, labels, cereal boxes, other boxes, books. Here is what they said:

*Matthew M.:* I can read "Corn Pops."

*Leonard:* I can read "stop."

*Sally:* I can read books. My favorite is *The Lion, the Witch and the Wardrobe.* My father is reading it to me.

*Matthew D.:* I can read "Russian." It's the name of a book.

*Daniel:* I can read the book *Fievel.*

*Laura:* I can read my mom's name.

*Paul:* I can read the word "yes."

*Lily:* I can read the book *Here Comes the Strike-Out.*

*Diana:* I can read the word "no."

*Alan:* I can read the word "power."

*Rachel:* I can read the word "purple."

*Thomas:* I can read a book called *Sir Small and the Dragon.*

*Emir:* I can read "stop."

*Dierdre:* I can read the name "Dierdre."

*Michelle:* I can read "Cheerios."

*Mark:* I can read "Ninja Turtle."

*Amy:* I can read "no" and "Amy."

*Laren:* I can read *Curious George Flies a Kite.*

*Rayna:* I can read the word "balloons."

*Hee:* I can read "flowers" and "apple" and "baby."

I also like to keep parents informed of what's going on in the room in other ways. A good example is sending home videos of children teaching the class after they've done research. Second grade children who were interested in doing independent research learned about an insect or other animal, taught the class, and answered their questions. I videotaped the children teaching, and sent the tapes home for the parents to see. I did this because often, when children write reports or do projects at home, the parents take control. I wanted these projects to be the children's own work, but I also wanted to show the parents what their children were capable of doing by themselves and what a child's project looks like.

> **Journal, October 1995**—Paul and Alan were the first two children to "teach" the class about insects or spiders. They chose scorpions. Paul's mom, who happened to be in school that day, said that she's never seen him so excited about anything in school as he was about this. He insisted that she take him to the library to get information. She photocopied something for him, which he then used in school. The two did a really wonderful job of reading, pointing to their clay models, answering questions. I'll have to look at the videotape to try to find out what the questions were, but I know they had to do with eating and prey. A technology problem: The video picks up sound all around it equally. Thus, it could hear my loud voice over the kids' soft voices. I'm not happy about the way I sound on the tape and don't love that the parents will hear it.

Another way that I let parents know what is going on in the room is through the homework. Much of the homework involves the children practicing things I've taught, but sometimes it is class discussion homework, and the parents learn from the introductions.

**Homework, November 2, 1995**

Some Suggestions for Remembering the Books We Read

The children will be doing book reports, and I will address that shortly. What we were talking about yesterday was more informal. While most children had ideas, not everyone did. These were wonderful suggestions, and I'm going to put them on a poster. I do want the children to have a purpose for recording what they read, and not merely to please me. The children and I will talk about this some more and I'd appreciate your suggestions, too—something the kids can do fairly quickly and often, not a home project, like book reports.

*Daniel:* You could ask us to write a book report. We could write about the long ones, the ones that are hard to remember.

*Lily:* Think about the long books you've read recently and write a little part down. Like if you read *The Three Bears* you could write about when Goldilocks came and ate the bears' porridge.

*Leonard:* You could write the title on a piece of paper.

*Emir:* You could write some of the story.

*Harriet:* Make up a story.

*Donald:* Write the title. . . .

**Homework, Monday, November 27, 1995**

Yesterday we had visits from many grandparents, and we enjoyed them. They were in school for Project Time and helped their grandchildren with their various projects. They also saw how we teach place value by having the children write numbers 1 to 1,000. It happened that Laura reached 1,000 and we all got to celebrate her [achievement] with the grandparents. I wonder if our class seemed strange to them. Encourage your children to talk with their grandparents about what their elementary schooling was like. I wish we'd had time to do that. (I think I'll make that homework soon.) We sat in a circle and talked about what we like about at least one of our grandparents. There wasn't enough time to talk about all of them, though some children tried. When your child reads this, she or he should read at least five of them. For some children, reading all of them is a little difficult. Enjoy!

*Thomas:* I like when my grandparents sometimes come for dinner.

*Nikia:* I sew with my grandmom. I learned to sew from Sally's mom, but now my grandmom is helping me.

*Matthew M.:* I like going to Nana's. We go to the park at the school. (Matthew had pictures of himself playing with his Nana's dogs.)

*Bonnie:* I like to bake cookies with my grandmom's twin and her.

*Daniel:* I like when my grandfather plays sports like football and baseball with me.

*Alan:* My grandmom gives me lots of toys—15 toys. Some we leave at her house and some we take home.

*Gregory:* I like this sweater my grandmom knitted for me.

*Amy:* My grandmom takes me to the mall, and sometimes she gets me things.

*Rashaun:* I get to help my grandmom make pancakes.

*Sally:* My grandmom takes me golfing. I use a kid's golf club.

*Hee:* I like when my grandmom shows me how to get to the garden.

*Emir:* I like when my grandmom buys me fries or a shirt on my birthday. My other grandmom gave me chips and hugs.

*Harriet:* My grandmom and me go on picnics. . . .

I'm so sorry that the children couldn't talk about *all* their grandparents, but it would be nice if you could share what your child said with the grandparent they mentioned. And if your child's grandparents are not living, please tell your child some stories about them.

The newsletter has been my most regular and informative form of written communication. In each newsletter I make sure that I thank each volunteer:

*The 205 News,* **October 1996**—Here comes a *great big thank you* to all of the parents who have helped with the children. I hope I haven't missed anyone!

These parents joined us on **trips**: [list of names of the nine parents who joined us.] Bob Brown invited us to have lunch in the amphitheater of his law office in the Curtis Building. Not only did we have a wonderful, quiet lunch in luxurious swivel chairs, but Mr. Brown also directed us to the beautiful Tiffany glass mosaic in the building lobby.

These parents have helped **in the classroom**: [list of names and what they did] help with homework, work with children at Project Time, at reading and writing, accompany singing with a guitar.

As for Halloween, *many* people helped and made it a really fun day. Thanks to [list].

Many parents have sent things for us to use or helped their children to bring things from home: Alicia's dad sent us a huge roll of brown paper, which we are using for our bodies and will use for murals; the Gregoriou family also gave us their Chinese hamsters for the school year; Janice's mom sent 1996 date books for each child; Jack brought a book about learning to tie your shoes and a box with laces so that children who don't know how, could learn; Ned brought in his Body Game; Theo brought a praying mantis; Melinda brought a garden spider; Carlos's mom lent me some books to help me select CDs; Timothy has brought in many books about animals, especially dinosaurs, which he shares with the children; Ron brought in a wonderful tape of *Chicka Chicka Boom Boom* and some stickers for everyone; Theodore brought a book about a caterpillar/butterfly; and we've had many birthday cupcakes.

We've had many offers of help: Mrs. Castillo and Mr. Zavala have offered to help us with Spanish; Ms. Lane, a medical student, has offered to teach us about our bodies; Dr. Carter, a dentist, has offered to teach us about our teeth; Mr. Shenken has offered to help us with our computers.

I also try to inform parents about curriculum in each newsletter.

*The 205 News*, **February, 1996**—*African-American History Month* The children and I talked about why a month has been set aside in many schools to celebrate African American history. We began by talking about the past—what it is, what things happened in the past. We made our time line, and we will probably continue with that work. We talked about Martin Luther King and his accomplishments. We talked about slavery when we read *Aunt Harriet's Underground Railroad in the Sky* and I read *Frederick Douglass Fights for Freedom* to them. We also talked about the importance of reading and writing as necessary for freedom. We sang "Harriet Tubman" and "If You Miss Me at the Back of the Bus" at a small second grade assembly.

At the end of second grade, I send home all of the writing I've held in children's folders for two years. I attach the following letter to the envelope that holds the writing:

**(Letter to Parents) June 26th, 1996**

Dear Parents,

In this envelope are copies of almost all (but not quite all) of your child's writing for the past two years. It includes her or his drawing–writing book, writing book, published books, math–science journal and baby book. (I'm copying research projects and will return them before the end of the year.)

I hope you will treasure all of this as the beginning of a long process of becoming a writer. Enjoy the content; accept with humor the developing spelling, standard grammar, and punctuation. By now, your child is seven or eight. Your child is not finished learning about writing. This is not the end of your child's education, it's just the beginning.

I am always astonished when I watch a baby like Charity or Paula grow into spoken language. How can it happen so quickly? Well, I feel the same excitement and wonder as I watch children become writers. I hope that, despite what many adults call "mistakes" but what I call "developing skill," you will see the power of their writing. Focus on the strengths—on what the child *can* do; withhold judgment until the end, twelfth grade (I'm still learning and improving); remember that they will continue to learn about spelling, standard grammar, and punctuation. One thing is certain: These children are not so afraid of making mistakes that they are afraid to write (though some of them started that way in first grade.)

This not the last time they will learn about writing. They are just beginning! What a wonderful beginning! And remember: the more you read, the better you write.

Warmly,
Lynne Strieb

## 4. I Address Parent Concerns:

It's important to me that parents feel comfortable telling me when they are concerned about their children's learning experiences. Addressing their concerns can be challenging.

**Journal, September 20, 1994**—Bonnie's dad came in. He told me that some of the kids in the class can already read. He asks, "How can we help her to learn to read?" I explained to him that I've been sending reading homework every night either in the homework books and/or the book envelope. I assured him that if he does what the homework asks him to do, Bonnie will quickly learn to read. I told him, "I see her beginning to read already."

Harriet's mom was in. She told me Harriet knows the letters because they own *Hooked on Phonics*, a commercially available reading program whose advertisements on television and radio frighten parents into not trusting schools to teach their kids to read. I say, "Well, maybe she knows the sounds, but she also needs to learn the letter names." I don't think she knows either—at least she hasn't shown me that she does. I see a little girl who is very nervous about learning to read. I urged her mother to read to her, to read rhyming (predictable) books, and to have Harriet join her in reading.

**Journal, May 2, 1995**—[Rashaun's mom requested that he be removed from the class of the first grade teacher who has taught him for the past eight months. He was placed in my room two weeks ago. It was hard getting him to relax enough to be willing to read to me because he was afraid of making mistakes. He just said, "I can't do it."]

Rashaun's mom said today, "I see a change already." I told her I do too. I told her he talked back and argued with me sometimes, and didn't listen to directions on the first day. But then I told her what he told Emir yesterday "Be quiet, or you'll miss Project Time." I told her my room is a good place for him. It's because every kid has a fair chance every day (or almost). She asked me for a harder book for him to read. I told her today I'd send one home, though the easier books are good because it's how he starts to see himself as a reader and he's succeeding. She told me, "He was memorizing the one he had." I told her "Memorizing is great! That's how reading starts." But I made sure to send home a slightly harder book.

**Journal, Tuesday, March 5, 1996**—Talk with Rashaun's mom. We notice his fighting over everything and his terrific demand for attention. I was really proud of the ending of the conversation because I said I would make a time each day for him to talk to me. He struggles with writing. She agreed to help him write a list of experiences he could write about—the astronaut, the black history summer school, meeting a black author, trips they've taken—and put it in the back of his homework book. I felt good about the talk because I found a way to hear him talk rather than ignore him, as I have been wanting to do. It was positive.

Using my journal entries and tri-weekly anecdotal records, I tell here the story of addressing the concerns of one child's parents during his first term in first grade.

**Journal, October 21, 1996**—I had a talk with Ned's mom today. She began by telling me that Ned (age 6 years, 10 months) is very verbal and so he tells her everything. He has complained of being bored in school and is feeling he is not being challenged. I was surprised about this and immediately felt that I must be doing something wrong (isn't that *always* my first reaction). I was surprised because, in all my years of teaching, no parent has ever complained that his or her child has been bored in my class. I told her that I would think about this, and we set up a meeting for November 4, during which we would talk about this matter. Meanwhile, I promised to pay attention to Ned to try to discover what the issue about boredom is really about.

**Journal, October 30, 1996**—I spoke directly with Ned about his being bored. I asked him if he was bored at Project Time (a time when the children choose from a variety of activities and materials). He said he wasn't. I asked him when he is bored, and he said that he doesn't like Quiet Reading Time, the time of day when children choose books and can read either by themselves or with other children. Ned is a beginning reader. I have noticed that although he can read, he chooses books that are about animals, his major interest. Though we have many and they are all color coded, so that he can tell which are about underwater creatures, which are about mammals, insects and spiders, prehistoric animals, reptiles and amphibians, birds, humans, etc., he and his friends usually choose those with interesting pictures and text which is beyond his growing ability. They love talking about those pictures and are never bored with the detail. It is when I insist that he read easier fiction that he seems unhappy. He also said that writing time is boring. There, I notice that he usually writes one sentence, draws quickly, then waits for a long time to have a conference with me on conference day. Waiting *is* boring.

**Journal, November 4, 1996**—I met with Ned's parents this afternoon. They told me a little more about this issue of boredom. Ned loves learning things, especially about animals. He loves collecting information and can remember what he has heard. He insists that his parents read books to him filled with information. He also has a computer with a CD-Rom at home and enjoys using that for learning about animals. Ned was quite upset that his parents had told me he was bored. He knew it because I used that word with him. His mom said he felt betrayed. I apologized. I told his parents that I know, from class discussions, that he is filled with information and lots of detail, and has acquired knowledge that will probably continue to interest him throughout his life. I told them that it makes me happy when a child is so deeply interested in something, either a material or subject matter. I also told them that I can't compete with the attention he gets at home, since there are 29 children in the class. I can't spend Quiet Reading Time reading to him and the others, because that is the time I must hear children read. And as for the CDs, with only one computer and twenty-nine children, he won't get a turn very often. I told them that my major goal for most of the children right now is to get them to become independent readers so that they can read the more difficult books in the subject matter that interests them. I was sending home easy fiction and the easiest nonfiction about animals that I have. Ned was resisting reading at home. He wasn't interested in the fiction, and he couldn't get the information from the nonfiction quickly enough, so he was insisting that his parents read to him. I reminded them of what I'd said at the Parents' Meeting at the beginning of the year: that the only way to become a better reader is by reading. I told them that somehow they would have to find a compromise in which Ned would read a little and they would read a little.

I also told them that I'd asked Ned to try to write more than one sentence at writing time so that he would spend most of his time writing rather than waiting.

**Anecdotal records, November 13, 1996**—After talking with Ned's parents, I have been insisting that he read some easy fiction. I know they are much happier with his reading to them at home, because he had been taking home books that only they could read. He loves information books and soon will be able to read some of the easier nonfiction himself. Loves facts. He read *The King's Wish,* though he wanted to give it up. He was able to retell it quite well. When he first read the part about the king test, he had to read it about five times before he could explain it. He has just finished reading *The Big Jump* and told the class about it. Good at retelling. . . .

Good meeting with his parents. Talked about why he might be bored. I say he's not doing enough work; furthermore, he is used to being entertained, and now I'm asking him to "entertain" himself for part of the day.

**Daily Record, December 3, 1996**—Ned's mom has told the counselor that he is bored. A meeting is planned for December 16 with the counselor, the parents, the Instructional Support Teacher, and me. I'm not happy about this. Maybe they should just take him out of my room.

**Anecdotal records, December 4, 1996**—Early on, after my meeting with Ned's parents, I found him some easy nonfiction books about whales, sharks and manatees. He told me he'd been reading them with his parents, but then he slipped into very easy readers like *The Snow Book,* and *Go Dog, Go.* He has so much trouble settling into reading and finding a book that interests him. He also seems to want to look at interesting animal picture books, but that doesn't give him the practice he needs in reading. After his parents complained to the counselor that Ned is bored, I went to him and asked him how to make school more interesting to him. He again told me that Project Time is great but that he would like Quiet Reading Time to be different. He said first that he is interested in learning about all creatures. I told him there are millions, and that would be too hard and that he has to choose one. He said he was interested in mammals. I said that would be a beginning. I gave him permission to go through all the books on mammals, to put back the ones he's not interested in, to keep the ones he is interested in, in a pile. Then we'll go through the ones that interest him. I want him to be able to do all the work himself, so the difficulty of some of the books will limit his choices. It doesn't do any good if his parents or another adult or a CD continue to do the work for him. I am going to be pretty insistent about that. Anyway, he had a great time today, and I was very satisfied. He was really happy.

**Report Card Comments, December 1996, language portion**
First Report—As you know, Ned loves books about insects, animals, and other creatures. He can sit for a very long time looking at pictures, finding details to talk about with other children. I am working hard at finding books with this subject matter in which he can read the words, too. Recently I asked him how

Quiet Reading Time could be more interesting to him, and he told me he'd like to learn about creatures. Though he couldn't think of one he'd like to learn about, he did narrow it down to mammals. He sat for three Quiet Reading sessions, sorting all the mammal books into two piles: those with animals he wants to learn about, and those he wasn't interested in. His concentration was remarkable. We then sat together and further sorted the books into content that was similar (rodents, felines, etc.) I told Ned that I'm happy to have him read about animals but that he has to choose books with words he can actually read by himself. His choice was a book about pouched animals, and he is on his way. Both of us have learned lots already, and I will make time for him to share what he's learned with the class. He still could use lots of time reading some fiction, like *The King's Wish* and *The Big Jump*—fairly easy readers which would give him lots of practice—but he seems resistant to reading fiction. He has also enjoyed learning the poems. He has a good sight vocabulary and sometimes uses phonics (though he also loses the meaning if he spends too much time sounding out words.)

Ned's writing was filled with one-sentence stories about his fighting with imaginary creatures like dragons, monsters, and sea ghosts. His drawings were wonderfully detailed. He reversed many letters, which he has stopped doing. He then wrote quite a long story about a trip he took to New York, which he "published." Now he is writing everything he knows about African animals, which I will also encourage him to publish. He is beginning to use the word book for spelling, and I am encouraging him to try to hear beginning blends in words that have them ("st", "sp", "str", etc.)

As I read through this essay, which includes documents from September 1994 to December 1996, I have begun to remember things I've done in previous years: working to please angry parents (not many), teaching parents bookbinding and many math games, holding regular meetings for parents, as we did in the Parent Cooperative Nursery. I did things differently when I taught children of nonreading parents, children whose home language was not English, children whose parents did not have paid work outside their homes. I have so many stories to tell. And I know there are things I'll change when I work with parents in the future. That's what I love about teaching. My learning never ends. As soon as a year has ended, I'm thinking about what will happen next.

I close with the letter I sent in June 1996 to parents whose children I'd taught for two years:

Dear Parents,

First of all, I want to thank you for the very beautiful and thoughtful gifts you gave me. The pin is lovely, and each time I wear it I will think of the wonderful children and parents of the 1994–1996 group at Greenfield School. I also look forward to buying a CD or a program for next year's class with the gift certificate. Learning how to use the school's Mac is always a challenge to me!

When I began teaching at the J. B. Kelly School in 1972, the principal agreed that I could keep my class for two years, and except for my last two years there (fourteen years out of sixteen years), that's what I did. Working with a class for two years now has a name—"looping"—and it is being encouraged in schools all over the city.

As I look back over the past two years with your children, I think of very special things: children learning to read; children unable to put a book down; children who were afraid to try now beginning to take chances with reading, with math, and with answering questions; the wonderful way those who were able to, did "research" and then taught the rest of us. When I began with this class, I told the children as I always tell children, "Some people learn to read at three, some don't learn until they're ten, but most learn between the ages of five and eight." Well, everyone learned to read, though some more quickly and some more slowly. That is the biggest thrill.

Besides the drama of helping kids to read, to love books, and to know how to use them to learn information, I love keeping them for two years because I can learn what they are interested in and "feed" those interests. That's why we have all those materials. In addition, we don't have to "cover" a topic and then drop it. Two years lets a class return to interesting things. Some teachers say, "We did that last year. We can't do it again this year." I believe that it's never exactly the same because *you've* changed by the time you learn something a second (or third or fourth) time. Three things stand out for me:

First, I think of each individual child. No matter how difficult a child, that child has strengths that I have tried to recognize and build on. That is the foundation for the way I teach. And they have such wonderful senses of humor!

Second, after the remarkable and caring discussions we had about recess, the children tried hard to be more inclusive and considerate toward one another (for the most part).

Third, the *wonderful* parents stand out. Whenever people ask me about Greenfield, I say, "It's amazing to teach in a school where all the parents want their children to be." That has shown in all of your help and support for me and all the children. I have indeed been fortunate.

Thank you for a wonderful two years. Please keep in touch. I'll miss all of you.

Warmly,
Lynne Strieb

## References

Cohen, M. (1993). *When will I read?* New York: Bantam.

Routman, R. (1994). *Invitations: Changing as teachers and learners K–12.* Portsmouth, NH: Heinemann.

## Bibliography

**Lynne Yermanock Strieb**

*Professional resources that have been especially important to me include:*

Carini, P. (1979). *The art of seeing and the visibility of the person* [Monograph] North Dakota Study Group, University of North Dakota Press.

Duckworth, E. (1987). *The having of wonderful ideas and other essays on teaching.* New York: Teachers College Press.

Hawkins, D. (1970). *I, thou, it, on living trees.* In *The ESS Reader.* Newton, MA: The Elementary Science Study of Education Development Center, Inc. (pp. 45–51.).

Hawkins, F. (1986). *The logic of action.* Boulder: Colorado Associated University Press.

Himley, M. (1991). *Shared territory: Understanding children's writing as works.* New York: Oxford University Press.

Kohl, H. (1967). *36 children.* New York: New American Library.

Rose, M. (1989). *Lives on the boundary.* New York: Free Press.

Weber, L. (1997). *Looking back and thinking forward: Reexaminations of teaching and schooling.* New York: Teachers College Press.

*Children's books that I especially enjoy using with children include:*

Jarrell, R. (1964). *The bat poet.* New York: Macmillan.

Jarrell, R. (1965). *Animal family.* New York: Pantheon Books.

Storr, C. (1995). *Clever Polly and the stupid wolf* (audio book). Hampton, NH: Chivers Audio Books.

# Appendix

---

MONDAY, SEPTEMBER 6, 1996 — THE 205 NEWS — GREENFIELD SCHOOL — STAN SHECKMAN, PRINCIPAL

*Be sure to see the supply list on page 2. Supplies due Monday.*

## WELCOME! to 205

I'll introduce myself briefly. My name is Lynne Strieb (say "Streeb") This will be my twenty-eighth year of teaching. I have taught kindergarten, first and second grade. I have also taught four-year-olds in England as a Fulbright Exchange Teacher. I have three married sons, and one three-year-old grand-daughter. My husband teaches physics at LaSalle University.

Please watch for this newsletter at least one a month. I have been sending class news home for at least 22 years. I welcome your comments and suggestions. The newsletter will include news of classroom activities, important announcements, recognition of parent involvement, some of my observations of the children and the ways in which I think about teaching and education in general, and other items of interest.

**ALL NOTES, INCLUDING NEWS-LETTERS WILL BE SENT HOME IN A POCKET FOLDER. PLEASE CHECK YOUR CHILD'S** BOOKBAG EACH NIGHT FOR THE FOLDER. PLEASE SIGN NOTES AS QUICKLY AS POSSIBLE.

We welcome Miss Sarah McNally, a Fulbright Exchange Teacher from London, England, in room 204. The second graders from her class and our children have already begun to work together. And I have already learned a lot from her. Miss Adler is getting adjusted to life and to Miss McNally's school in London.

We also are delighted that Teacher Kathryn (Keelor) will be working with the children on Mondays and Thursdays. A retired executive at Bell Atlantic, she has been volunteering with me since the spring of 1993. We are SO fortunate!

In the next newsletter I will tell you about the University of Pennsylvania undergraduate student who will be fulfilling one of her requirements for her elementary education coursework; and about other volunteers.

**NOW** - Why don't YOU come to help in the classroom? For all my years of teaching, some of the most important contributions to the children (besides raising them from birth) have been made by parents. I started out as a parent in a School District Parent Cooperative Nursery and then worked in my children's kindergarten. Here are some of the things parents have done through my years of teaching: heard children read; read to children, played reading and math games with children, helped them to sew, talked to them about their work, taught letters, words, songs in languages other than English; brought babies to observe for science and social studies lessons (in fact, Alex O'Neil, who is in our class right now, was one of those babies brought in by his mom); cooked, talked about their own work and interests. **I'm sure you will be able to think of many more things, including going on class trips.**

It is a School District rule that you stop in the office and sign in before you come to the classroom.

**HAPPY SEPTEMBER BIRTHDAYS**
Charlotte   Jessica   Ashley Z.
Daniel   Alex O.   (over)

*Watch for Scholastic Book Orders. Watch for permission slips for library trips and other walks. Coming in the next newsletter- class rules, reading, math, about Erin Heffernan, our University of Pennsylvania student*

---

*Page 2*

**TO CONTACT ME:**
1. Write a note in the homework book and tell your child to show it to me.
2. Send a note in the pocket folder (tell your child to show it to me.)
3. Call school (299-4666) and leave a message. I'll return your call.

We already have trips planned in September. On September 24th, from about 11:30 until 2:00 we will go to the City Institute Library and have lunch in Rittenhouse Square. On September 27th, we will have a lesson on housing and clothing in various world cultures, at the Baloh Institute. Details will follow with permission slips.

School starts at 8:30 sharp until further notice. Your child will miss reading, and writing if she or he is late.

It is School District policy to require a note explaining the reason for a child's absence. If there is no note, I am required to code the absence "unexcused - parental neglect". I certainly don't want to have to do that.

I am very impressed with the children's writing. I have never had so many children able to write by themselves on the first day of school. That's a tribute to you and to the kindergarten teachers!

**Please** keep your eyes open for insects and spiders. I am especially interested in praying mantises and large yellow and black garden spiders. I know how to keep them alive in the classroom, even after the first frost, when they usually die. Slugs and snails are interesting, too. If you know how to start a wormery, I'd love your help.

### SUPPLIES LIST

Your child needs:
3 black and white, hard cover, <u>sewn</u> homework books. Make sure they are not glued. The black ones are the best quality. No spiral bound or loose leaf books. (For regular homework, reading homework, and writing in class.)

2 pocket folders, one for notes

2 sharpened pencils, daily (wooden casing, not mechanical)

1 eraser

1 small box of crayons

1 package of water color magic markers

scissors (metal are much better than plastic)

a pencil case or small box

1 ruler marked with inches and centimeters (I will collect and distribute these as needed)

1 small bottle of white glue (to be shared)

These supplies may be purchased during this weekend or from the school store on Monday. Your child needs them before the end of the day Monday.

FRIDAY, NOVEMBER 15, 1996      **THE 205 NEWS**      GREENFIELD SCHOOL      LYNNE STRIEB, TEACHER / STAN SHECKMAN, PRINCIPAL

## HAPPY OCTOBER BIRTHDAYS TO
Annie Weinstein
Samantha Beik

Here comes a

**GREAT BIG THANK YOU** to all of the parents who have helped with the children. I hope I haven't missed anyone!

These parents joined us on **trips:** Judy Anastassiades, Wendy Gosfield, Thomas Jackson, Yalta Reed, Mr. Royster, Mary Scott (Briana's grandmother), Miko Tannen, Dustine Hockenberry (Ramon's mom), Connie Weinstein. Jim Kahn invited us to have lunch in the amphitheater of his law office in the Curtis Building. Not only did we have a wonderful, quiet lunch in luxurious swivel chairs, but Mr. Kahn also directed us to the beautiful Tiffany glass mosaic in the building lobby.

These parents have helped **in the classroom:** Connie Weinstein, Wendy Gosfield (Project Time, homework) Yalta Reed, Juanita Royster, (reading, writing, Project Time), Dr. Bea Hibbs (Jared's mom - accompanied singing of 204 and 205 with her guitar).

Many parents have sent things for us to use or helped their children to bring things from home: Andrea's dad sent us a huge roll of brown paper which we are using for our bodies and will use for murals; the Anastassiades family also gave us their Chinese hamsters for

the school year; Jessica Fox's mom sent 1996 date books for each child; James brought a book about learning to tie your shoes and a box with laces so that children who don't know how, could learn; Jared and James brought in their Body Games; Alex brought a praying mantis; Samantha brought a garden spider; Ramon's mom lent me some books to help me select CDs; Devlin has brought in many books about animals, especially dinosaurs, which he shares with the children; Nate brought in a wonderful tape of **Chicka Chicka Boom Boom** and some stickers for everyone; Alexander brought a book about a caterpillar/butterfly; and we've had many birthday cupcakes.

We've had many offers of help: Mrs. Castillo and Mr. Zavala have offered to help us with Spanish; Ms. Lyons (Ashley Z.'s mom) a medical student, has offered to teach us about our bodies; Dr. Beik, a dentist, has offered to teach us about our teeth; Mr. Tannen has offered to help us with our computers.

All of you have been supportive and helpful with getting notes in on time, helping your children with homework, getting your children to school on time, sending in absence notes. giving your child money for trips and supplies.

**BOTH THE CHILDREN AND I THANK YOU FROM THE BOTTOM OF OUR HEARTS. AND THANKS TO TEACHER KATHRYN. WE ARE SO FORTUNATE!**

Erin Heffernan a University of Pennsylvania undergraduate, works in our classroom one and a half days each week. She has been teaching small-group lessons in reading, and has been supervising children in writing and reading.

**THE BABY**
On Monday, October 28, Patty Beik, Samantha's mom, brought her baby Peter to visit our classroom. We are starting a program called Educating Children for Parenting. This program was begun at Germantown Friends School by Sally Scattergood, and is now used in school districts across the country. One part of the program is to have the same infant and a parent visit the classroom every 6 to 8 weeks for the children to observe both baby and mother.

Before the visit, we discussed how to make the baby and the mother safe and comfortable. As the baby sat in his mother's arms or lay on the floor, we observed and described him. The children had a chance to ask questions. We talked about what a baby needs. After the visit, the children wrote something the baby did and something the mother did. As time goes on, we will pay attention to the changes in the baby and what the parent does to keep the baby safe, healthy and happy.

Other thematic units are: change, communication, learning, and differences and similarities. All of the material is consistent with the School District curriculum. I hope Peter will be able to visit through our two years together. I also invite parents of other babies bring them to visit with us. That way we can learn what's the same and what's different about children. We will learn a lot.

*There will be a walk to City Institute Library Tuesday afternoon. We will leave at noon.*

(over)

---

**READING** - We have spent the first two months of school getting excited about books. The range of readers in the class is great, with a few children already able to read difficult "chapter books", (novels), others able to read some easy readers, while others are beginning to read.

I have done reading instruction in a variety of ways. **First**, when the children write daily in their writing books, they are practicing (and often learning) phonics, since I ask them to "sound out" the words. We now also have a phonics/spelling book for everyone.

**Second**, we have spent class time reading the poems and discussions I have sent home for home-work. Those are good for the beginning readers because as they memorize the words, they point and recognize the correspondence between what they are saying and the words that are written on the page. It's GOOD to memorize. Historically, many people have learned to read by first memorizing. We have also read books like **Bony Legs** and **When Will I Read?** and **Chicka Chicka Boom Boom and Pierre**, which have increased their reading vocabulary. We read **The Weekly Reader** and I write messages to the children on the board.

**Third**, children spend about 20 - 30 minutes reading, either alone or with one or two other people. Many who were on the brink of reading have eased effortlessly into it by working with other children. They have surprised themselves (and probably you) when they discovered that they could read. As you know, that discovery spurs them on to greater concentration on and excitement about, books.

**Fourth**, for those who are beginning, we have more formal reading instruction with flash cards and teacher direction. So far, they

have worked on rhyming words (word families) and vocabulary from **Animal Friends** and other basal readers that we have in the room.

**Fifth**, in addition to having the whole class read books together, I read stories to the children as often as possible.

This program will change as he year goes on. Your comments about their reading at the back of their reading homework books have been very helpful. Soon the children will begin to keep their own reading records.

As I said at the Open House, "The best way to become a good reader is by reading." Your child should be reading at home for at least ten minutes each night. That reading could be my homework, but by now, most of them should also read (or pretend to read) part of a book by themselves. It doesn't have to be the whole book at one sitting if that's too much  Take a few days with the book and don't forget to use the bookmark. Please don't spend hours on "sounding out" words or drilling  endlessly, since that could get boring and make a child dislike reading. If your child is a beginner, reading to her or him, occasionally asking her or him to read a sentence or two is a good way to get started. Let him or her read to an older brother or sister who is PATIENT and won't tease because she is a beginner. And even after your children can read, continue to read to them.

 Use flashcards. Play rhyming games (I'm thinking of a word that rhymes with 'day' and it's something you like to do; I'm thinking of a word that rhymes with 'day' and you do it with money when you buy something); play "I Spy" with initial or ending consonants. Try to read

advertisements in the food section of the newspaper. Read what's on labels. There are so many words around us!

Watch for three class-made books to come home for you and your children to read. Please have your child take care of them. All the children contributed to them (unless they were absent.) The books are: **What I Will Be For Halloween, I Can Read**, and **On Halloween Night**. Enjoy those books. The children are quite proud of them.

Remember - our trip to the Art Museum is Wednesday, November 20.

On the Tuesday before Thanksgiving, we will be having a celebration at 1:00 in the afternoon to which you are all invited. We will probably need  help before then. Meanwhile, **THANKS AGAIN** for everything you do for us. Come visit us soon. (Please stop at the office first.)

**IN THE NEXT NEWSLETTER:**
November Birthdays
Math in 205
Writing
Please let me know what else you'd like to know. Any questions? Send them to me.
I'll respond.

*Let me know if you will meet us at the Art Museum, please.*

# 18 On the Road to Cultural Bias: A Critique of *The Oregon Trail* CD-ROM

**Bill Bigelow**
Teacher, Franklin High School, Portland, Oregon
Editor, *Rethinking Schools*

The critics all agree: *The Oregon Trail* (1993) is one of the greatest educational computer games ever produced. *Prides' Guide to Educational Software* awarded it five stars for being "a wholesome, absorbing historical simulation," and "multi-ethnic," to boot (Pride & Pride, 1992, p. 419). The new version, *The Oregon Trail II* (1994), is the "best history simulation we've seen to date," according to Warren Buckleitner, editor of *Children's Software Review Newsletter* (The Oregon Trail II, 1994). Susan Schilling, a key developer of *The Oregon Trail II* and recently hired by Star Wars filmmaker George Lucas to head Lucas Learning Ltd., promises new interactive CD-ROMs targeted at children six to fifteen years old and concentrated in math and language arts (Armstrong, 1996).

Because interactive CD-ROMs like *The Oregon Trail* are encyclopedic in the amount of information they offer, and because they allow students a seemingly endless number of choices, the new software may appear educationally progressive. CD-ROMs seem tailor-made for the classrooms of tomorrow. They are hands-on and "student-centered." They are generally interdisciplinary—for example, *The Oregon Trail II* blends reading, writing, history, geography, math, science, and health. And they are useful in multiage classrooms because they allow students of various knowledge levels to "play" and learn. But like the walls of a maze, the choices built into interactive CD-ROMs also channel participants in very definite directions. The CD-ROMs are programmed by

Reprinted from *Language Arts* 74 (February 1997): 84–93. Used by permission.

people—people with particular cultural biases—and children who play the new computer games encounter the biases of the programmers (Bowers, 1988). Just as we would not invite a stranger into our classrooms and then leave the room, we as teachers need to become aware of the political perspectives of CD-ROMs and to equip our students to "read" them critically.

At one level, this article is a critical review of *The Oregon Trail* CD-ROMs. I ask what knowledge is highlighted, what is hidden, and what values are imparted as students play the games. But I also reflect on the nature of the new electronic curricula, and suggest some questions teachers can ask before choosing to use these materials with their students. Finally, I offer some classroom activities that might begin to develop students' critical computer literacy.

## Playing the Game

In both *The Oregon Trail* and *The Oregon Trail II,* students become members of families and wagon trains crossing the Plains in the 1840s or 1850s on the way to the Oregon Territory. A player's objective, according to the game guidebook, is to safely reach the Oregon Territory with one's family, thereby "increasing one's options for economic success" (*The Oregon Trail II,* 1994).

The enormous number of choices offered in any one session—what to buy for the journey; the kind of wagon to take; whether to use horses, oxen, or mules; the size of the wagon train with which to travel; whom to "talk" to along the way; when and where to hunt; when to rest; and how fast to travel—is a kind of gentle seduction to students. It invites them to "try on this worldview and see how it fits." In an interactive CD-ROM, students don't merely identify with a particular character, they actually adopt his or her frame of reference and act as if they were that character (Provenzo, 1991). In *The Oregon Trail,* a player quickly bonds with the "pioneer" maneuvering through the "wilderness."

In preparation for this article, I played *The Oregon Trail II* until my eyes became blurry. I can see its attraction to teachers. One can't play the game without learning a lot about the geography between Missouri and Oregon. (However, I hope I never have to ford another virtual river again.) Reading the trail guide as one plays teaches much about the ailments confronted on the Oregon Trail and some of the treatments. Students can learn a tremendous amount about the details of life for the trekkers to Oregon, including the kinds of wagons required, the supplies needed, the vegetation encountered along the route, and so forth. And the game has a certain multicultural and gender-fair veneer that, however limited, contrasts favorably with the white male-dominated texts of yesteryear. But as much as the game teaches, it *mis*-teaches more. In fundamental respects, *The Oregon Trail* is sexist, racist, culturally insensitive, and contemptuous of the earth. It imparts bad values and wrong history.

## They Look Like Women, But . . .

To its credit, *The Oregon Trail II* includes large numbers of women. Although I didn't count, women appear to make up roughly half the people students encounter as they play. But this surface equity is misleading. Women may be present, but gender is not acknowledged as an issue in *The Oregon Trail*. For example, in the opening sequences, the game requires students to select a profession, any special skills they will possess, the kind of wagon to take, and the city from which to depart. Class is recognized as an issue—bankers begin with more money than saddle makers, for example—but not gender or race. A player cannot choose to be a female or African American.

Without acknowledging it, *The Oregon Trail* maneuvers students into thinking and acting as if they were all males. The game highlights a male lifestyle and poses problems that historically fell within the male domain, such as whether and where to hunt, which route to take, whether and what to trade, and whether to caulk a wagon or ford a river. However, as I began to read feminist scholarship on the Oregon Trail (e.g., Faragher & Stansell, 1992; Kesselman, 1976; Schlissel, 1992), I realized that women and men experienced the Trail differently. It's clear from reading women's diaries of the period that women played little or no role in deciding whether to embark on the trip, where to camp, which routes to take, and the like. In real life, women's decisions revolved around how to maintain a semblance of community under great stress, how "to preserve the home in transit" (Faragher & Stansell, 1992, p. 190). Women decided where to look for firewood or buffalo chips, how and what to cook using hot rocks, how to care for the children, and how to resolve conflicts between travelers, especially between the men.

These were real-life decisions, but, with the exception of treating illness, they're missing from *The Oregon Trail*. Students are rarely required to think about the intricacies of preserving "the home in transit" for two thousand miles. An *Oregon Trail II* information box on the screen informs a player when "morale" is high or low, but other than making better male-oriented decisions, what's a player to do? *The Oregon Trail* offers no opportunities to encounter the choices of the Trail as women of the time would have encountered them and to make decisions that might enhance community and thus "morale." As Lillian Schlissel (1992) concludes in her study, *Women's Diaries of the Westward Journey*:

> If ever there was a time when men and women turned their psychic energies toward opposite visions, the overland journey was that time. Sitting side by side on a wagon seat, a man and a woman felt different needs as they stared at the endless road that led into the New Country. (p. 15)

Similarly, *The Oregon Trail* fails to represent the *texture* of community life on the Trail. Students confront a seemingly endless stream of problems posed by *The Oregon Trail* programmers, but rarely encounter the details of life, especially that of women's lives. By contrast, in an article in the book, *America's Working Women*, Amy Kesselman (1976) includes this passage from the diary of one female trekker, Catherine Haun, in 1849:

> We women folk visited from wagon to wagon or congenial friends spent an hour walking ever westward, and talking over our home life "back in the states" telling of the loved ones left behind; voicing our hopes for the future in the far west and even whispering, a little friendly gossip of pioneer life. High teas were not popular but tatting, knitting, crocheting, exchanging receipts for cooking beans or dried apples or swopping food for the sake of variety kept us in practice of feminine occupations and diversions. (p. 71 )

The male orientation of *The Oregon Trail* is brought into sharp relief in the game's handling of Independence Day commemoration. Students-as-pioneers are asked if they wish to "Celebrate the Fourth!" If so, they click on this option and hear loud "Yahoos" and guns firing. Compare this image to the communal preparations described in Enoch Conyers's 1852 diary:

> A little further on is a group of young ladies seated on the grass talking over the problem of manufacturing "Old Glory" to wave over our festivities. The question arose as to where we are to obtain the material for the flag. One lady brought forth a sheet. This gave the ladies an idea. Quick as thought another brought a skirt for the red stripes. . . . Another lady ran to her tent and brought forth a blue jacket, saying: "Here, take this; it will do for the field." Needles and thread were soon secured and the ladies

went at their task with a will, one lady remarking that "Necessity is the mother of invention," and the answer came back, "Yes, and the ladies of our company are equal to the task." (Hill, 1989, p. 58)

The contrast of the "Yahoos" and gunfire of *The Oregon Trail* to the collective female exhilaration described in the diary excerpt is striking. This contrast alerted me to something so obvious that it took me a while to recognize. In *The Oregon Trail* people don't talk to *each other*, they all talk to you, the player. Everyone in *The Oregon Trail*-constructed world directs her or his conversation to you, underscoring the simulation's individualistic ideology that all the world exists for *you*, the controller of the mouse. An *Oregon Trail* more alert to feminist insights and women's experiences would highlight relationships between people, would focus on how the experience affects our feelings for each other, and would feature how women worked with one another to create and maintain a community, as women's diary entries clearly reveal.

As I indicated, large numbers of women appear throughout *The Oregon Trail* simulation, and they often give good advice, perhaps better advice than the men we encounter. But *The Oregon Trail*'s abundance of women, and its apparent effort to be gender-fair, masks an essential problem: The choice-structure of the simulation privileges men's experience and virtually erases women's experience.

## African Americans as Tokens

From the game's beginning, when a player starts off in Independence or St. Joseph's, Missouri, African Americans dot *The Oregon Trail* landscape. By and large, however, they are no more than black-colored white people. Although Missouri was a slave state throughout the Oregon Trail period, I never encountered the term "slavery" while playing the game. I found race explicitly acknowledged in only one exchange, when I "talked" to an African American woman along the trail. She said: "I'm Isabella. I'm traveling with the Raleighs and their people. My job is to keep after the cows and watch the children. My husband Fred is the ox-driver—best there is." I wondered if they were free or enslaved, and if we are to assume the Raleighs are white. I asked to know more, and Isabella said: "I was born in Delaware. My father used to tell me stories of Africa and promised one day we'd find ourselves going home. But I don't know if I'm getting closer or farther away with all this walking." The end. Like Missouri, Delaware was a slave state in antebellum days, but this is not shared with students.

Isabella offers provocative details, but they hide more than they reveal about her identity and culture.

*The Oregon Trail*'s treatment of African Americans reflects a superficial multiculturalism. Black people are present, but their lives aren't. Attending to matters of race requires more than including lots of black faces or having little girls "talk black": "I think it's time we be moving on now." (This little girl reappears from time to time to repeat these same words. A man who looks Mexican, likewise, shows up frequently to say, with a heavy accent: "Time is a-wasting. Let's head out!")

Although one's life prospects and world view in the 1840s and 1850s—as today—were dramatically shaped by one's race, this factor is invisible in *The Oregon Trail*. *The Oregon Trail* players know their occupations but not their racial identities, even though these identities were vital to the decisions the Oregon Trail travelers made before leaving on their journeys and along the way.

For example, many of the constitutions of societies that sponsored wagon trains specifically excluded blacks from making the trip west. Nonetheless, as Elizabeth McLagan (1980) points out in her history of blacks in Oregon, *A Peculiar Paradise*, blacks did travel the Oregon Trail, some as slaves, some as servants, and even some, such as George Bush, as well-to-do pioneers. Race may not have seemed important to *The Oregon Trail* programmers, but race mattered a great deal to Bush: Along the Trail, he confided to another emigrant that if he experienced too much prejudice in Oregon, he would travel south to California or New Mexico and seek the protection of the Mexican government (McLagan, 1980).

And Bush had reason to be apprehensive: African Americans arriving in Oregon Territory during the 1840s and 1850s were greeted by laws barring them from residency. Two black exclusion laws were passed in the Oregon Territory in the 1840s, and a clause in the Oregon state constitution barring black residency was ratified in 1857 by a margin of eight to one—a clause, incidentally, not repealed until 1926.

Upon completion of one of any simulated Oregon Trail journeys, I clicked to see how my life turned out: "In 1855, Bill built a home on 463 acres of land in the Rogue River Valley of Oregon," experienced only "moderate success" and later moved to Medford, "establishing a small business that proved more stable and satisfying." Although *The Oregon Trail* simulation never acknowledges it, "Bill" must have been white because in 1850 the U.S. Congress passed the Oregon Donation Land Act granting 640 acres to free white males and their wives. It is unlikely that a black man, and much less a black woman, would have been granted land in 1855 or have been allowed to start a business in Medford some years later.

Why were whites so insistent that blacks not live in Oregon? The preamble of one black exclusion bill explained that "situated as the people of Oregon are, in the midst of an Indian population, it would be highly dangerous to allow free negroes and mulattoes to reside in the territory or to intermix with the Indians, instilling in their minds feelings of hostility against the white race . . ." (McLagan, 1980, p. 26). And Samuel Thurston, a delegate to Congress from the Oregon Territory, explained in 1850 why blacks should not be entitled to homestead in Oregon:

> The negroes associate with the Indians and intermarry, and, if their free ingress is encouraged or allowed, there would a relationship spring up between them and the different tribes, and a mixed race would ensue inimical to the whites; and the Indians being led on by the negro who is better acquainted with the customs, language, and manners of the whites, than the Indian, these savages would become much more formidable than they otherwise would, and long and bloody wars would be the fruits of the commingling of the races. It is the principle of self preservation that justifies the action of the Oregon legislature. (McLagan, 1980, pp. 30–31)

Thurston's argument carried the day. But *The Oregon Trail* programmers have framed the issues so that race seems irrelevant. Thus, once students-as-pioneers arrive in Oregon, most of them will live happily ever after—never considering the impact that race would have on living conditions.

## Just Passing Through?

The Oregon Trail programmers are careful not to portray Indians as the "enemy" of westward trekkers. However, the simulation's superficial sympathy for Native groups masks a profound insensitivity to Indian cultures and to the earth that sustained these cultures. The simulation guidebook lists numerous Indian nations by name—and respectfully *calls* them "nations." Then *The Oregon Trail* guidebook explains that emigrants' fear of Indians is "greatly exaggerated."

> Some travelers have been known to cross the entire breadth of the continent from the Missouri River to the Sierra Nevadas without ever laying eye on an Indian, except perhaps for occasional brief sightings from a distance. This is all well and good, for it is probably best for all parties concerned for emigrants and

Indians to avoid contact with each other. Such meetings are often the source of misunderstandings, sometimes with regrettable consequences.

Emigrants often spread disease, according to the guidebook, which made the Indians "distrust and dislike" them. The guidebook further warns *The Oregon Trail* players not to over-hunt game in any one place, as "few things will incur the wrath of the Indian peoples more than an overstayed welcome accompanied by the egregious waste of the natural resources upon which they depend."

The ideology embedded in *The Oregon Trail* and *The Oregon Trail II* is selfish and goal-driven: Emigrants should care about indigenous people only insofar as they need to avoid "misunderstanding" and incurring the wrath of potentially hostile natives. *The Oregon Trail* promotes an anthropocentric earth-as-natural resource outlook. Nature is a *thing* to be consumed or overcome as people traverse the country in search of success in a faraway land. The simulation's structure coerces children into identifying with white settlers and dismissing nonwhite others. It also contributes to the broader curricular racialization of identity that students absorb—learning who constitutes the normalized "we" and who is excluded.

*The Oregon Trail* players need not take into account the lives of others unless it's necessary to do so in order to accomplish their personal objectives. Thus, the cultures of Plains Indians are backgrounded. The game marginalizes their view of the earth. Contrast, for example, the Indians' term "mother earth" with *The Oregon Trail* term "natural resource." The metaphor of earth as mother suggests humans in a reciprocal relationship with a natural world that is alive, that nourishes us, and that sustains us. On the other hand, a resource is a thing to be used. It exists *for* us, outside of us, and we have no obligations in return.

The consequences of the Oregon Trail for the Plains Indians, the Indians of the Northwest, and for the earth were devastating. In fairness to *The Oregon Trail*, students may hear some of the details of this upheaval as they play. For example, on one trip I encountered a "Pawnee Village." Had I paid attention to the warning in the guidebook to "avoid contact" I would have ignored it and continued on my trip. But I entered and "talked" to the people I encountered there. A Pawnee woman said: "Why do you bother me? I don't want to trade. The things that we get from the white travelers don't make up for all that we lose." I clicked to hear more. "We didn't know the whooping cough, measles, or the smallpox until your people brought them to us. Our medicine cannot cure these strange diseases, and our children are dying." I clicked on "Do you have any advice?" Angrily, she said, "No. I just want you to leave us alone." The implication is that if I just "leave [them] alone" and continue on the trail I can pursue my dream without hurting the Indians.

However, this interpretation hides the fact that the Oregon Trail itself, not just contact with the so-called pioneers, devastated Indian cultures and the ecology of which those cultures were an integral part. Johansen and Maestas's (1979) description of the Lakota language for talking about these pioneers helps us see how they were regarded by the Indians:

> [The Lakota] used a metaphor to describe the newcomers. It was *Wasi'chu,* which means "takes the fat," or "greedy person." Within the modern Indian movement, *Wasi'chu* has come to mean those corporations and individuals, with their governmental accomplices, which continue to covet Indian lives, land, and resources for private profit. *Wasi'chu* does not describe a race; it describes a state of mind. (p. 6)

The *Wasi'chu* cut down all the cottonwood trees found along the rich bottom lands of plains rivers—trees that "offered crucial protection during winter blizzards as well as concealing a village's smoke from its enemies. In lean seasons, horses fed on its bark, which was surprisingly nourishing" (Davidson & Lytle, 1992, p. 114).

The Oregon Trail created serious wood shortages, which even the *Wasi'chu* acknowledged. "By the Mormon guide we here expected to find the last timber," wrote overlander A. W. Harlan in describing the Platte River, "but all had been used up by others ahead of us so we must go about 200 miles without any provisions cooked up." A few weeks later, in sight of the Black Hills, Harlan wrote: "[W]e have passed many cottonwood stumps but no timber . . ." (Davidson & Lytle, 1992, p. 115).

*Wasi'chu* rifles also killed tremendous numbers of buffalo that Plains Indians depended upon for survival. One traveler in the 1850s wrote that, "The valley of the Platte for 200 miles presents the aspect of the vicinity of a slaughter yard, dotted all over with skeletons of buffaloes" (Davidson & Lytle, 1992, p. 117). Very soon after the beginning of the Oregon Trail, the buffalo learned to avoid the Trail, their herds migrating both south and north. Edward Lazarus (1991) points out in *Black Hills/White Justice: The Sioux Nation versus the United States—1775 to the Present* that "the Oregon Trail did more than move the buffalo; it destroyed the hunting pattern of the Sioux, forcing them to follow the herds to the fringes of their domain and to expose themselves to the raids of their enemies" (p. 14).

However, wrapped in their cocoons of self-interest, *The Oregon Trail* players push on, oblivious to the mayhem and misery they cause in their westward drive. This is surely an unintended, and yet intrinsic, part of the game's message: Pursue your goal as an autonomous individual, ignore the social and ecological consequences: "look out for number one."

## No Violence Here

*The Oregon Trail* never suggests to its simulated pioneers that they should seek permission of Indian nations to travel through their territory. And from this key omission flow other omissions. The simulation doesn't inform players that, because of the disruptions wrought by the daily intrusions of the westward migration, Plains Indians regularly demanded tribute from the trekkers. As John Unruh, Jr. (1993), writes in *The Plains Across:*

> The natives explicitly emphasized that the throngs of overlanders were killing and scaring away buffalo and other wild game, overgrazing prairie grasses, exhausting the small quantity of available timber, and depleting water resources. The tribute payments . . . were demanded mainly by the Sac and Fox, Kickapoo, Pawnee, and Sioux Indians—the tribes closest to the Missouri River frontier and therefore those feeling most keenly the pressures of white men increasingly impinging upon their domains. (p. 169)

*Wasi'chu* travelers resented this Indian-imposed taxation and their resentment frequently turned to hostility and violence, especially in the later years of the Trail. The Pawnee were "hateful wretches," wrote Dr. Thomas Wolfe in 1852, for demanding a twenty-five cent toll at a bridge across Shell Creek near the North Platte River (Unruh, 1993, p. 171). Shell Creek and other crossings became flashpoints that escalated into violent skirmishes resulting in the deaths of settlers and Indians.

Despite the increasing violence along the Oregon Trail, one choice *The Oregon Trail* programmers don't offer students-as-trekkers is the choice to harm Indians. Doubtlessly MECC, the publisher of *The Oregon Trail*, is not anxious to promote racism toward Native peoples. However, because simulation players can't hurt or even speak ill of Indians, the game fails to alert students that white hostility was one feature of the westward migration. The omission is significant because the sanitized nonviolent *Oregon Trail* fails to equip students to reflect on the origins of conflicts between whites and Indians. Nor does it offer students any insights into the racial antagonism that fueled this violence. In all my play of *The Oregon Trail*, I can't recall any blatant racism directed at Indians; but as Unruh (1993) points out:

> The callous attitude of cultural and racial superiority so many overlanders exemplified was of considerable significance in producing the volatile milieu in which more and more tragedies occurred. (p. 186)

## The End of the Trail

> Soon there will come from the rising sun a different kind of man from any you have yet seen, who will bring with them a book and will teach you everything, after that the world will fall to pieces.
>
> Spokan Prophet, 1790 (Limerick, l987, p. 39)

A person can spend two or three hours—or more—playing one game of *The Oregon Trail* before finally reaching Oregon Territory. Upon arrival, a player is awarded points and told how his or her life in Oregon turned out. Yet the game fails to raise vital questions about one's right to be there in the first place and what happened to the people who were there first.

In its section on the "Destination," the guidebook offers students its wisdom on how they should view life in a new land. It's a passage that underscores the messages students absorb while engaged in the simulation. These comforting words of advice and social vision are worth quoting at length:

> Once you reach the end of your journey, you should go to the nearest large town to establish your land claim. If there are no large towns in the area, simply find an unclaimed tract of land and settle down. . . . As they say, possession is nine-tenths of the law, and if you have settled and worked land that hasn't yet been claimed by anyone else, you should have little or no trouble legally establishing your claim at a later time. As more and more Americans move into the region, more cities and towns will spring up, further increasing one's options for economic success. Rest assured in the facts that men and women who are willing to work hard will find their labors richly rewarded, and that you, by going west, are helping to spread American civilization from ocean to ocean across this great continent, building a glorious future for generations to come! (*The Oregon Trail II*, 1994)

The Lakota scholar and activist Vine Deloria, Jr. (1977), in his book, *Indians of the Pacific Northwest*, offers a less sanguine perspective than that included in the CD-ROM guidebook. People coming in on the Oregon Trail "simply arrived on the scene and started building. If there were Indians or previous settlers on the spot they were promptly run off under one pretext or another. Lawlessness and thievery dominated the area" (p. 53). From 1850 on, using provisions of the Oregon Donation Act, thousands of "settlers" invaded "with impunity."

As Deloria points out, there were some in Congress who were aware that they were encouraging settlers to steal Indian land, and so Congress passed the Indian Treaty Act requiring the United States to get formal agreements from Indian tribes. Anson Dart, appointed to secure land concessions, pursued this objective in a despicable fashion. For example, he refused to have the treaties translated into the Indians' languages, instead favoring "Chinook jargon," a nonlanguage of fewer than three hundred words good for trading, giving orders, and little else. Dart's mandate was to move all the Indians east of the Cascades, but he decided some tribes, like the Tillamooks and Chinooks, should keep small amounts of land as cheap labor reserves:

> Almost without exception, I have found [the Indians] anxious to work at employment at common labor and willing too, to work at prices much below that demanded by the whites. The Indians make all the rails used in fencing, and at this time do the boating upon the rivers: In consideration, therefore, of the usefulness as labourers in the settlements, it was believed to be far better for the Country that they should not be removed from the settled portion [sic] of Oregon if it were possible to do so. (Deloria, 1977, p. 51)

Meanwhile, in southwestern Oregon white vigilantes didn't wait for treaty niceties to be consummated. Between 1852 and 1856 self-proclaimed Volunteers attacked Indians for alleged misdeeds or simply because they were Indians. In August of 1853, one Martin Angel rode into the Rogue River Valley gold mining town of Jacksonville shouting, "Nits breed lice. We have been killing Indians in the valley all day," and "Exterminate the whole race" (Beckham, 1991, p. 43). Minutes later a mob of about eight hundred white men hanged a seven-year-old Indian boy. In October 1855, a group of whites massacred twenty-three Indian men, women, and children. This incident began the Rogue Indian war, which lasted until June 1856 (Beckham, 1991). Recall that this is the same region and the same year in one *Oregon Trail* session where "Bill" built a home and experienced "moderate success," but, thanks to *The Oregon Trail* programmers, he learned nothing of the social conflicts swirling around him.

Nor did Bill learn that, even as a white person, he could protest the outrages committed against the Rogue River Valley Indians, as did one anonymous "Volunteer" in a passionate 1853 letter to the *Oregon Statesman* newspaper:

> A few years since the whole valley was theirs [the Indians'] alone. No white man's foot had ever trod it. They believed it theirs forever. But the gold digger come, with his pan and his pick and shovel, and hundreds followed. And they saw in astonishment their streams muddied, towns built, their valley fenced and taken. And where their squaws dug camus, their winter food, and their children were wont to gambol, they saw dug and plowed, and their own food sown by the hand of nature, rooted out forever, and the ground it occupied appropriated to the rearing of vegetables for the white man. Perhaps no malice yet entered the Indian breast. But when he was weary of hunting in the mountains without success, and was hungry, and approached the white man's tent for bread; where instead of bread he received curses and kicks, ye treaty kicking men— ye Indian exterminators think of these things.
>
> —*A Soldier* (Applegate & O'Donnell, 1994, p. 34)

*The Oregon Trail* hides the nature of the Euro-American invasion in at least two ways. In the first place, it simply fails to inform simulation participants what happened between settlers and Indians. To *The Oregon Trail* player, it doesn't feel like an invasion; it doesn't feel wrong. After one of my arrivals, in 1848, "Life in the new land turned out to be happy and successful for Bill, who always cherished bittersweet but proud memories of the months spent on the Oregon Trail." (This struck me as a rather odd account given that I had lost all three of my children on the trip.) The only person that matters is the simulation player. I was never told whether life turned out equally "happy and successful" for the Klamaths, Yakimas, Cayuses, Nez Percés, Wallawallas, and all the others who occupied this land generations before the *Wasi'chu* arrived. The second way the nature of the white invasion is hidden has to do with the structure of the simulation. For a couple hours or more, the player endures substantial doses of frustration, tedium, and difficulty. By the time the Willamette or Rogue River Valleys come up on the screen we, the simulated trekkers, feel we *deserve* the land, that our labors in transit should be "richly rewarded" with the best land we can find.

## Data Deception and Thoughts on What to Do about It

In the Beatles' song, all you need is love; in *The Oregon Trail*, all you need are data. *The Oregon Trail* offers students gobs of information: snake bite remedies, river locations and depths, wagon specifications, ferry costs, and daily climate reports. Loaded with facts, it feels comprehensive. Loaded with people voicing contrasting opinions, it feels balanced. Loaded with choices, it feels democratic. But the simulation begins from no moral or ethical standpoint beyond individual material success; it contains no vision of social or ecological justice, and, hence, promotes a full litany of sexist, racist, and imperialist perspectives, as well as exploitive perspectives of the earth. And simultaneously, it hides these biases. The combination is insidious and makes interactive CD-ROMs like this one more difficult to critique than traditional textbooks or films. The forced identification of player with simulation protagonist leaves the student no option but to follow the ideological map laid out by the programmers.

Nonetheless, my critique is not a call to boycott the new "edutainment" resources. But we need to remember that these CD-ROMs are not teacher substitutes. The teacher's role in analyzing and presenting these devices in a broader ethical context is absolutely vital. Thus, teachers across the country must begin a dialogue toward developing a critical computer literacy. We need to figure out ways to equip students with the ability to recognize and evaluate the deep moral and political messages imparted by these CD-ROMs as they maneuver among the various computer software programs.

Before choosing to use CD-ROMs that involve people and places, like *The Oregon Trail*—or, for example, its newer siblings *The Yukon Trail, The Amazon Trail,* and *Africa Trail*—teachers should consider the following questions.

- **Which social groups are students not invited to identify with in the simulation?** For example, Native Americans, African Americans, women, and Hispanics/Latinos are superficially represented in *The Oregon Trail,* but the "stuff" of their lives is missing.

- **How might these social groups frame problems differently than the simulation?** As we saw in the foregoing critique of *The Oregon Trail,* women tended to focus more on maintaining community than on hunting. Native Americans had a profoundly different relationship to the earth than did the Euro-American "tamers of the wilderness."

- **What decisions do simulation participants make that may have consequences for social groups not highlighted in the simulation? And what are these consequences?** Although the very existence of the Oregon Trail contributed to the decimation of Plains and Northwest Indians, simulation participants are never asked to consider the broader effects of their decision-making. What may be an ethical individual choice may be unethical when multiplied several hundred thousand times. In this respect, CD-ROM choice-making both reflects and reinforces conventional notions of freedom that justify disastrous social and ecological practices.

- **What decisions do simulation participants make that may have consequences for the earth and nonhuman life?** Similarly, a simulation participant's choice to cut down trees for firewood may be rational for that individual, but may also have deleterious effects on the ecological balance of a particular bio-region.

- **If the simulation is time-specific, as in the case of *The Oregon Trail*, what were the social and environmental consequences for the time period following the time represented in the simulation?** The wars between Indians and the U.S. Cavalry in the latter decades of the nineteenth century are inexplicable without the Oregon Trail as prologue.

- **Can we name the ideological orientation of a particular CD-ROM?** The question is included here simply to remind us that all computer materials—indeed, all curricula— have an ideology. Our first step is to become aware of that ideology.

These questions are hardly exhaustive, but may suggest a useful direction to begin thinking about CD-ROMs as they become increasingly available and begin to cover more and more subjects.

Finally, let me use the example of *The Oregon Trail* to introduce some ways teachers can begin to foster a critical computer literacy. Once we have identified some of the social groups that are substantially missing in a CD-ROM activity like *The Oregon Trail*, we can try to locate excerpts from diaries, speeches, or other communications of members of these groups. We can then engage students in role play where, as a class, students face a number of Oregon Trail problems. For example, class members could portray women on the Oregon Trail and decide how they would attempt to maintain a community in transit. Or they might role play a possible discussion of Oglala people as they confront the increasingly disruptive presence of *Wasi'chu* crossing their lands. Students might be asked to list all the ways African Americans would experience the Oregon Trail differently than Euro-Americans—from the planning of the trip to the trip itself. (It's unlikely, for example, that every white person on the streets of Independence, Missouri, said a friendly "Howdy," to the blacks he encountered, as each of them does to the implied but unacknowledged white male *Oregon Trail* simulation player.) Students also could assume a particular racial, cultural, or gender identity, and note whether the choices or experiences described in the simulation make sense from the standpoint of a member of their group. For example, would a typical African American in Missouri in 1850 be allowed to choose from which city to begin the trek west?

As we share with students the social and ecological costs of the Oregon Trail, we could ask them to write critical letters to each of the "pioneers" they portrayed in the simulation. Some could represent Rogue River Valley Indians, Shoshoni people, or even Mother Earth. For instance, how does Mother Earth respond to the casual felling of every cottonwood tree along the Platte River? A Native American elder or activist could be invited into the classroom to speak about the concerns important to his or her people and about the history of white-Indian relations.

We could encourage students to think about the politics of naming in the simulation. They could suggest alternative names for the Oregon Trail itself. For example, the historian of the American West, Frederick Merk (1978), aptly calls the Oregon Trail a "path of empire." Writer Dan Georgakas (1973) names it a "march of death." Other names might be "invasion of the West," or "The twenty-year trespass." Just as with Columbus's "discovery" of America, naming shapes understanding, and we need classroom activities to uncover this process.

Students could write and illustrate children's books describing the Oregon Trail from the standpoint of women, African Americans, Native Americans, or the earth.

After doing activities like these, students could "play" *The Oregon Trail* again. What do they see this time that they didn't see before? Whose worldview is highlighted and whose is hidden? If they choose, they might present their findings to other classes or to teachers who may be considering the use of CD-ROMs.

*The Oregon Trail* is no more morally obnoxious than other CD-ROMs or curricular materials with similar ideological biases. My aim here is broader than merely shaking a scolding finger at MECC, publisher of *The Oregon Trail* series. I've tried to demonstrate why teachers and students must develop a critical computer literacy. Some of the new CD-ROMs seem more socially aware than the blatantly culturally insensitive materials that still fill school libraries and book rooms. And the flashy new computer packages also invoke terms long sacred to educators: student empowerment, individual choice, creativity, and high interest. It's vital that we remember that coincident with the arrival of these new educational toys is a deepening social and ecological crisis. Global and national inequality between haves and have-nots is increasing. Violence of all kinds is endemic. And the earth is being consumed at a ferocious pace. Computer programs are not politically neutral in the big moral contests of our time. Inevitably, they take sides. Thus, a critical computer literacy, one with a social and ecological conscience, is more than just a good idea—it's a basic skill.

## References

Applegate, S., & O'Donnell, T. (1994). *Talking on paper: An anthology of Oregon letters and diaries.* Corvallis, OR: Oregon State University Press.

Armstrong, D. (1996, February 23). Lucas getting into education via CD-ROM. *The San Francisco Examiner,* pp. El–E2.

Beckham, S. D. (1991). Federal–Indian relations. In *The First Oregonians* (pp. 39–54). Portland, OR: Oregon Council for the Humanities.

Bowers, C. A. (1988). *The cultural dimensions of educational computing: Understanding the non-neutrality of technology.* New York: Teachers College Press.

Davidson, J. W., & Lytle, M. H. (1992). *After the fact: The art of historical detection.* New York: McGraw-Hill.

Deloria, V., Jr. (1977). *Indians of the Pacific Northwest.* Garden City, NY: Doubleday.

Faragher, J., & Stansell, C. (1992). Women and their families on the overland trail to California and Oregon. 1842–1867. In F. Binder & D. Reimer (Eds.), *The way we lived: Essays and documents in American social history, Vol. I* (pp. 188–195). Lexington, MA: Heath.

Georgakas, D. (1973). *Red shadows: The history of Native Americans from 1600 to 1900, from the desert to the Pacific Coast.* Garden City, NY: Zenith.

Chill, W. E. (1989). *The Oregon Trail: Yesterday and today.* Caldwell, ID: Caxton Printers.

Johansen, B., & Maestas, R. (1979). *Wasi'chu: The continuing Indian wars.* New York: Monthly Review.

Kesselman, A. (1976). Diaries and reminiscences of women on the Oregon Trail: A study in consciousness. In R. Baxandall, L. Gordon, & S. Reverby (eds.), *America's working women: A documentary history—1600 to the present* (pp. 69–72). New York: Vintage.

Lazarus, E. (1991). *Black Hills/white justice: The Sioux Nation versus the United States—1775 to the present.* New York: HarperCollins.

Limerick, P. N. (1987). *The legacy of conquest: The unbroken past of the American west.* New York: W. W. Norton.

McLagan, E. (l980). *A peculiar paradise: A history of blacks in Oregon, 1788–1940.* Portland, OR: The Georgian Press.

Merk, F. (1978). *History of the westward movement.* New York: Knopf.

*The Oregon Trail* [Computer software]. (1993). Minneapolis: Minnesota Educational Computer Company.

*The Oregon Trail II* [Computer software]. (1994). Minneapolis: Minnesota Educational Computer Company.

Pride, B., & Pride, M. (1992). *Prides' guide to educational software.* Wheaton. IL: Crossway Books.

Provenzo, E. F., Jr. (1991). *Video kids: Making sense of Nintendo.* Cambridge, MA: Harvard University Press.

Schlissel. L. (1992). *Women's diaries of the westward journey.* New York: Schocken.

Unruh, J. D., Jr. (1993). *The plains across: The overland emigrants and the trans-Mississippi west, 1840–1860.* Urbana, IL: University of Illinois Press.

## Bibliography

### Bill Bigelow

*Professional resources that have been especially important to me include:*

Freire, P. (1972). *Pedagogy of the oppressed.* New York: Herder and Herder.

Gates, B. (1979). *Changing learning, changing lives: A high school women's studies curriculum from the group school.* Old Westbury, NY: Feminist Press.

Shor, I. & Freire, P. (1987). *A pedagogy for liberation.* South Hadley, MA: Bergin and Garvey.

Takaki, R. (1993). *A different mirror: A history of multicultural America.* Boston: Little, Brown.

Zinn, H. (1980). *A people's history of the United States.* New York: Harper & Row.


*Children's books that I especially enjoy using with children include:*

Bigelow, W., and Diamond, N. (eds.). (1988). *The power in our hands: A curriculum on the history of work and workers in the United States.* New York: Monthly Review Press.

Bigelow W., and Peterson, B. (eds.). (1991). *Rethinking Columbus.* Milwaukee, WI: Rethinking Schools in Collaboration with the Network of Educators on Central America.

Bigelow W., et al. (eds.). (1994). *Rethinking our classrooms: Teaching for equity and justice.* Milwaukee, WI: Rethinking Schools.

Greer, C., & Kohl, H. (1995). *Call to character: A family treasury.* New York: HarperCollins.

King, L. (ed.) (1994). *Hear my voice: A multicultural anthology of literature from the United States.* Menlo Park, CA: Addison-Wesley.

# IV As You Begin . . .

In this final section, Abby Foss describes her first year of teaching, and Fred Burton, an elementary school principal, tells you about some surprises that may await you.

We wish you good luck and good languaging in your teaching–learning journey.

# 19 Leaving My Thumbprint: The Journey of a First-Year Teacher

**Abigail Foss**
Graduate student, University of Arizona, Tuscon, Arizona

*"Will she be nice?" he asked. "Like Maggie?"*
*"Sarah will be nice," I told him.*
*"How far away is Maine?" he asked.*
*"You know how far. Far away, by the sea."*
*"Will Sarah bring some sea?" he asked.*
*"No, you cannot bring the sea."*

from *Sarah, Plain and Tall,*
Patricia MacLachlan

Like Sarah, I traveled from Maine to a far away place in search of another family and home. Right after graduating from college in New England, I visited Arizona for the first time. Recently, over three thousand miles of fragile telephone wire, I had informally accepted a teaching job at a school located in a landscape as dry and vast as the geography of my childhood was wet and compassed. My family thought I was impulsive. I arrived in Arizona during the week of a great heat wave; at 117 degrees, feeling a little like a piece of cooked lasagna, I wondered if I had not been a bit rash in my decision-making.

I grew up on an island in Maine, marking the passage of my life by the waltz of the tides and graceful nodding of the seasons. While many of the kids who shuffled hesitantly into my classroom on our first day of school would spend their childhoods searching in the desert and wearing shorts every day of the year, as a young girl, I spent my days playing at the beach, sailing around Casco Bay, and sweating in my pink-flowered snowsuit. Before I could decode written words, I read the rocks that embraced my ocean:

I never had a hard time
reading the rocks.
                              Sure-footed
I
     would
             leap
                   from
                              rock
                               to
                              rock
like a quiet cat
undaunted by the
     demanding
                 licks of the waves.
My pig-tailed path
over
the
valleys      and      peaks
of those
stone monsters
was easy
and
clear.

Personal Journal, July, 1995

When I first read the book, *Miss Rumphius,* by Maine author Barbara
Cooney, the path of my life became clear. I realized that the ocean is my
home, that I must seek out adventures in faraway places, and that I have
to bring some kind of beauty to the world—to leave my thumbprint.

So, with the salty spray of the sea and a biting wintry wind at my
heels, I tumbled autumn leaf-like into a new life and my first year of
teaching. Nothing could have prepared me for the magic and miracles
or the misery.

In the beginning, I believed that I could be, and expected myself
to be, the best teacher my kids would ever have. Perfect. In full bloom.
From the start, I had read quite a bit of theory and seen a lot of practice, some that I emulated, most of which I opposed. Walking into my
new classroom, which felt and smelled as if it belonged to someone
else, I was overwhelmed and yet inspired. Although I did not know
where to start, I knew my vision and the kind of place I wanted to create for my children and myself. I believed I could do it—before my
children arrived. I had little idea how much those twenty growing
learners and teachers would fill our classroom and my life.

In the two weeks prior to the start of school, I struggled to find
my place and begin to define myself as a teacher. I was intent upon

making an indelible impression on my first classroom, which would extend to a tiny thumbprint on the lives of my children. When I was three or four years old, I took a permanent orange marker the color of pumpkin pulp and wrote my name on the snowy keys of the family piano. Around that time, I also used a pair of scissors to carve an invented spelling of my name into the surface of my family's wooden endtable. Somehow the orange marker wore off through the years of piano lessons, but the carving still remains, though worn and dulled. With the passion and urgency that I possessed as a child, I seized my new job. I would not settle for just any Authors' Chair or its incorrect placement; my room was going to be the most cozy, inviting, and stimulating classroom on the planet on the first day of school if it killed me! I was dedicated; I was devoted; I was deluded.

The room was a metaphor for the way I looked at being a teacher. At that point, I did not notice or understand the process or the journey. I could not have known the way it would all change when those twenty children shyly crept into our room, or the way that I would change and grow and evolve. I demanded perfection from myself, yet I was ready to meet my children wherever they were and to laugh with them and encourage them to make mistakes and be gentle with themselves. I was not gentle with myself. It was not just my classroom or my year; it was theirs, too.

Insisting that I be perfect, I had a long way to fall. On the first day of school, I plunged to the earth like the swollen fruit in *James and the Giant Peach.* The authentic and hefty fishing boat pulley that I had carried from Maine had almost become Steven's javelin within the first twenty minutes. Bryan's mom informed me that I might want to explain the bathroom routine the next day because Bryan had held it till the end of school, not knowing where to go. Everything I had planned for the day took much longer than I had anticipated. As a result, I had scrapped half of my plans; among them was the one thing I had really wanted to do, which was read *Miss Rumphius.* Looking for company in my misery, I asked one of the other teachers at my school, a veteran, how her first day of teaching had gone several years before. She proceeded to tell me about all of the limitations that she had faced on that day; yet she ended by whispering with fond remembrance: "It was wonderful." Great. I had all of these things going for me, and I still could not get it right. I was ready to quit. Make myself sick. Stick the thermometer under the lightbulb and wheeze and cough and sneeze. I was feeling far from perfect. Dragging my limp, balled-up-like-a-dirty-sock body through my front door, I wept at my boyfriend's knees. I resolutely declared that I would not go back. It was awful. I was miserable. I had probably scarred those kids for life, and would they not be better off if I jumped from the burning ship now?

Wallowing in the pain of one of the first "failures" of my life, I could not have even imagined that there was another imperfect soul on the other side of town, a child in my class, sobbing at the thought of returning to that horrid place called School. We resembled each other to the extent that, later in the year, she exclaimed: "I look like a little Abby!" Sarah and I were both in the throes of misery. It nearly broke me the next day when her mother came in and told me that Sarah had locked herself in the bathroom that morning and made herself vomit to avoid going to school. Some perfect teacher I was turning out to be. I could not maintain a class of twenty kids for two days! Forget inspiring a love of reading and writing or helping to develop a heightened consciousness. I took it personally. I took it hard. I did not understand the journey.

It is not wrong or bad to want to do your job well. It gets tricky, however, when you expect and demand that you be perfect. My relentless striving for perfection got me into trouble with the parents in my class, too. Wanting to be the ideal teacher, I was convinced that I needed to please everyone—not just my twenty different and diverse kids, but their forty-two parents as well. Literally and figuratively backed into a corner of the classroom at our Open House, I began my relationship with my children's parents. Answering rapid-fire questions about my "curriculum" and how exactly I was going to meet their child's individual needs, I did not dare acknowledge that I really did not know what I was doing but that my heart was in the right place. On that very first day, I placed myself at the parents' beck and call, establishing a dynamic that pleased them greatly, but left me with far less energy for my kids, never mind myself. No matter what I was doing, whether I was organizing a project to be done later that day or attempting to use the restroom before my window of opportunity closed for the next six and a half hours, I dropped whatever it was for a parent.

Many days, parents would arrive late to school and actually ask to speak with me while I was teaching! In the middle of our daily ritual of beginning the day with silence, they would approach me. One parent attempted to tailor the curriculum to her specific needs, ignoring the fact that they were not her child's needs, let alone the needs of our collective class. On the bright side, many of the parents, especially those who had experience in education, backed off and let me find my way. Yet some of the parents knew they could dictate to me because of my vulnerabilities and insecurities as a first-year teacher. They took advantage of my inexperience and lack of confidence. I did not tell them where to get off; I did not know how to. In some way, I cared too much about what they thought.

Late in the spring, something in me changed. I broke. I felt harassed and hunted down. Some days, I left school with the panicked look of a deer caught in headlights. It got to a point with one of the parents where it had to stop. I had taken more abuse from her than I had from anyone before in my life. I was intimidated. However, once I got mad enough, I pulled out my inner strength and drew the proverbial line in the sand. I had to get to the point where I could hold my head up and know I was doing a good job, the best job I could at the time, before I was able to stand confidently. I stopped letting her get to me. I focused on my kids and the successes that we were having instead of the constant deficiency that this parent saw in me. I grew. I realized that a lot of people believed in me—most importantly, my students— and that I had to believe in myself.

I acknowledged that I was imperfect and needed to own my mistakes, but I knew that I had also done lots of things well and that I should not allow one person's issues to cheat me out of those successes. When she wanted to speak to me about her child, I decided the time and length of our conference. I took control of what was legitimately mine to decide and demanded respect for my position as her child's teacher. After all, how is a child or anyone else supposed to respect someone who is so clearly undervalued by his or her main role model and parent? Ironically, that mother now hugs me whenever we see each other. Evidently, children are not the only ones who need clear boundaries.

> Just then there was a strong wind. It blew the list out of Toad's hand. The list blew high up into the air. "Help!" cried Toad. "My list is blowing away. What will I do without my list?" "Hurry!" said Frog. We will run and catch it." "No!" shouted Toad. "I cannot do that." "Why not?" asked Frog. "Because," wailed Toad, "running after my list is not one of the things that I wrote on my list of things to do!"
>
> (from *Frog and Toad Together*, Lobel, 1979)

During my first year of teaching, it seemed we had gale force winds in our room every day. No matter how hard I tried to stick to my carefully laid out plans, some hurricane in the form of Jordan or Jesse or Kinley would come along with an amazing idea and blow my list away. Like Toad, I would be back at the fork in the road, insisting that we could not take the imminent detour because it was not on the list, *my* list. These weather changes frightened me quite a bit at first. In the same way that I was overly concerned with the opinions of the parents, I also cared too much about my plans and agenda and just could not let them go. But learning and teaching do not happen on an empty road. There are hidden paths and open fields and wild grasses. In fact, that landscape is where the beauty and opportunity live. How boring my first year would have been had I never relaxed and let our class take the detours that redefined our journey together and became our main road. The Georgia O'Keefe Flower Quilt would never have bloomed, our Alexander Calder-inspired metal and desert glass mobile would be scattered in garbage piles throughout our city, and "Casa Abierta" ("Open House") would not have evolved into our class anthem and love song to each other. We all would have missed out on our discussion that began with AIDS, moved to the importance of things higher than money, included an analysis of Disney stereotypes, considered the attempts to silence activists like Gandhi and Martin Luther King Jr. through assassination, and ended with Keith's insistence that Gandhi and MLK were not the only ones who had died, "The King" had died too. "The King, Keith?" "Yes, Abby. You know, Elvis!" These were redefining detours not unlike Robert Frost's "road . . . that . . . made all the difference."

When I was in high school, one of the most formative moments of my life occurred. As I waited with deep crystal breaths on the side of a field hockey game for the whistle to hail me into play, I caught sight of a tree across the grass. The tree, still dressed in a sweater of leaves the color of pear skin, was caught by a sudden gasp of hard autumn wind to reveal the underside of its coat. Pulling off its cover of green, it wore a blanket of aluminum-foil silver. I gasped. I almost wept. At that moment, I touched the part of myself that holds all of my inspirations and passions, those things that make my life important and valuable to me. They pull me out of bed when I am without myself. As a first-year teacher, for far too long a time, I forgot my silver beacon, my need for solace and quiet, my love of reading, and the warm feeling that autumn delivers to me like a brown paper package in the mail. While encouraging my kids to search themselves and discover their interests, I sacrificed those things that make me who I am.

To be the perfect teacher, I devoted myself to my work. I did it all day. I never rested from it. I couldn't; my kids deserved the best, and their parents demanded it. I stopped reading for myself. I read one "pleasure" book in three months instead of one every week or two. The teacher of emergent writers, I stopped writing. I stopped calling my family and friends. I worried through my day and through my night. Grinding my teeth, I slept without gaining much rest.

Showing signs of wear like an eroded streambed, I did not understand my unhappiness. I thought that stress was causing my teeth to become as flat as popsicle sticks. Here I was persevering and succeeding through my first year of school with love for and from my children, much support from my colleagues, and respect and kindness from many of my parents. But I was miserable and empty. It was not until the day when Kinley was building a structure of egg cartons, toilet paper tubes, and marker caps, and he told me how he was going to design amusement parks when he "grew up," that I realized that I was "grown up" and had sacrificed many of my dreams for the fulfillment of one. In neglecting myself, I had grown unhappy, bored, and uninspired—an empty learner and teacher. As a teacher, I believe that the best thing that I can do for my kids is be an example of how to live openly, passionately, and compassionately. I had to leave something for myself. Don't we all?

Firsts are always special. More extreme, more impassioned, more intense, and more painful. The vulnerability that I allowed during my first year as a teacher will never be as strong, as open. I gave to my children pieces of myself that are no longer mine—like the ocean's necklace of beach glass that I collected many years ago, unaware of the value of those gifts of memory that I picked up one by one. The love that grew between my children and me in those nine magical months is as deep and painful as the romantic love that I have experienced in my life. I loved my children "with [my] hands wide open . . . with the doors banging on their hinges, / the cupboard unlocked, the wind / roaring and whimpering in the room / rustling the sheets and snapping the blinds / that thwack like rubber bands / in an open palm" (Piercy, 1991, pp. 43–44).

My first-year children showed me the love that I am capable of nurturing as well as the loss that I am able to overcome. They enabled me to find my thumbprint and use it to help create something that brought beauty to my fragile life and our small community. As I left my imprint, they also left their thumbprints on me; their marks continue to reveal themselves and their impact on my journey as a teacher and compassionate human being. Sometimes, I wonder who did the teaching and who did the learning. I guess we all did both, as it should be—a family of twenty-one learners and twenty-one teachers.

## References

Cooney, B. (1994). *Miss Rumphius.* New York: Puffin Books.

Dahl, R. (1988). *James and the giant peach.* New York: Puffin Books.

Lobel, A. (1979). *Frog and toad together.* New York: Harper Trophy.

MacLachlan, P. (1985). *Sarah, plain and tall.* New York: Harper & Row.

Piercy, M.(1991). To have without holding. In Sewell, M. (ed.) *Cries of the spirit: A celebration of women's spirituality* (pp. 43–44). Boston: Beacon Press.

## Bibliography

### Abigail Foss

*Professional resources that have been especially important to me include:*

Bigelow, B., et al., eds. *Rethinking our classrooms: Teaching for equity and justice.* (1994). Milwaukee, WI: Rethinking Schools.

Derman-Spears, L., & the ABC Task Force. (1989). *Anti-bias curriculum: tools for empowering children.* Washington, DC: National Association for the Education of Young Children.

Gardner, H. (1993). *Multiple intelligences.* New York: Basic Books.

Heard, G. (1989). *For the good of the earth and sun: Teaching poetry.* Portsmouth, NH: Heinemann.

Holt, J. C. (1976). *Instead of education: Ways to help people do things better.* New York: Dutton.

Nieto, S. (1992). *Affirming diversity.* New York: Longman.


*Children's books that I especially enjoy using with children include:*

Cisneros, S. (1991). "Eleven." In *Woman hollering creek and other stories* (pp. 6–9). New York, NY: Random House.

Cooney, B. (1982). *Miss Rumphius.* New York: Viking Press.

Cruz Martinez, A. (1991). *The woman who outshone the sun/La mujer que brillaba aun mas que el sol.* San Francisco, CA: Children's Book Press.

Grimes, N. (1994). *Meet Danitra Brown.* New York: Lothrop, Lee and Shepard.

Hamanaka, S. (1994). *All the colors of the earth.* New York: Wm. Morrow.

Nye, N. S. (1995). *The tree is older than you are.* New York: Simon & Schuster Books for Young Readers.

Polacco, P. (1988). *The keeping quilt.* New York: Simon & Schuster.

Rosen, M. J. (1994). *The greatest table.* San Diego, CA: Harcourt Brace.

Young, E. (1997). *Voices of the heart.* New York: Scholastic.

# 20 An Open Letter from a Principal to New Teachers

**Fredrick R. Burton**
Wickliffe Informal Alternative Elementary School,
Upper Arlington, Ohio

Dear New Teacher,

A few years ago, I was invited to the University of Maine to give a talk to a group of teachers interested in integrating the curriculum. As usual when I go off on these little trips, I was feeling a bit sad to leave my family in Columbus, Ohio. My four-year-old daughter, Sarah, had noticed my feelings earlier and informed me that she had left a special message for me in my suitcase. As soon as I arrived at my Maine accommodations, I opened my suitcase to find the following letter:

> Dear Dad,
> I miss you already.
> I love you. Come home soon.

I was misty-eyed and grateful for her sensitivity and caring. I then noticed she had written an additional line on the back of the paper. It said:

> P.S. You're a slug.

Oh well. I share this with you because, like my letter from Sarah, teaching isn't always what it appears to be on the surface. In fact, it is full of surprises. Some will delight you. Others will make you feel like, well . . . a slug. What follows are seven below-the-surface educational "surprises" that you might encounter, as well as some of my thoughts on how to negotiate them.

## Surprise #1

*My undergraduate training didn't fully prepare me for my new job.* Oh really? Did you expect your undergraduate training to completely prepare you for your life in the classroom? Forget it. It can't, and you shouldn't expect it to do so. It would be like me thinking that reading all of those parenting books and spending time with other people's children would actually prepare me for parenthood. Your undergraduate training provided you with a base of knowledge about teaching and learning. It helped to launch your career by providing you with experiences and time to reflect on those experiences. However, you will encounter many situations that are simply beyond the scope of your undergraduate training (see Surprises #2 through 7 below). I've heard it said that when a problem occurs, the Japanese look for solutions and the Americans look for blame. In short, you must take responsibility for yourself, for your actions, and most importantly, *keep learning.* In fact, I was the best parent in the world *before* I had children. Since then I have discovered a great source of power that will serve you well as a teacher . . . *humility.*

## Surprise #2

*I send in my resume, but school districts ignore me.* Yes, they do. But don't take it personally; they ignore everyone. Never assume that a principal is sitting excitedly, waiting for your resume. The last time I opened a letter to find a resume was the exact same moment that Jennifer, a sandy-haired second grader, was simultaneously holding her hand over her mouth while trying to tell me that she was about to throw up. Right after that, it was time to start our afternoon assembly. Then right after that, school was out, and I received a call from a parent who wanted me to get her neighbor's cat out of her tree. Principals and district personnel don't intentionally ignore you, but it does happen for reasons that have nothing at all to do with you personally. So call. Sub in the building. Drop by the school. Write again. Oh, by the way, when you write, never address the letter to "Dear Principal." When I see those resume cover letters, I immediately throw them away. If you do decide to address the letter to "Dear Principal," you might as well sign it "Yours sincerely, Applicant #106." Seriously, call the state department of education to obtain a directory that lists the names and addresses of every school in your state. Finally, if you can, make a "connection"—letters that say, "Dear Dr. Burton, I was reading *Teaching Language Arts* and one of the authors (use his or her name) suggested I write to you." A personal connection will make a principal pause every time. It may not get you a job, but it will get you noticed and perhaps get you an interview. The better you know your audience's needs and interests, the more likely school districts *will* no longer "ignore" you.

## Surprise #3

*I got the job, but when I looked in my classroom there were no materials.* As a teacher you would certainly be surprised by this. As a principal, I would certainly be embarrassed by this. It shouldn't happen, but occasionally it does. Sometimes hiring occurs late in the summer because districts don't know their staffing needs because several children move into the district at the last minute. Most schools have spent their budgets prior to June and simply have no money to begin ordering right away. At other times, it could happen that your room was empty the previous year, and staff members simply "borrowed" a bookshelf, a globe, or an extra chair and "forgot" to return the materials. Typically, after we (i.e., a teacher committee and I) hire a new teacher, I sit down with the person and ask, "What can I do to help make you successful, and what materials do you need?" I usually spend extra money to supply this person with what he or she needs, knowing that it's a great investment. If you've been hired, then immediately inform the principal that, although it's June, you want to get started right away (this will make him or her smile). Furthermore, tell the principal that you want to begin familiarizing yourself with existing classroom materials and ordering additional items that you consider essential for making children successful. This might not make the principal smile anymore, but how can anyone argue with such enthusiasm and professionalism? If the principal says there is no money, just say you can wait until the next fiscal year's budget kicks in (which is typically in July). The worst that can happen is that you still don't get money for all of that great children's literature you want to order, but I would bet that you'll get money and some respect for your efforts.

## Surprise #4

*The other first-grade teachers that I'm teaching with don't have any children's literature, and what's worse, they don't really care.* Uh-oh. This gets a bit sticky. It's sticky in part because you've been trained in whole language and you feel like the Goodmans, Donald Graves, and Lucy Calkins (as well as your university professors) would be personally disappointed if you didn't start writing conferences and a literature-based reading program right away. It's even more complicated when you realize that, despite your university training, almost all new teachers use methods identical to their first experienced-teacher teammate. Now that first experienced teacher acting as a mentor for you *may* know more about teaching than any of the experts mentioned above or may be using a turn-of-the-century, "skill and drill boot camp" approach to teaching. Even if you did explore this in your interview and found that your fellow first-grade teachers were well-grounded in current research and practices of literacy learning, you might get moved to third grade the following year and encounter a literacy teaching perspective completely different from your own. What to do? First of all, realize that this is not a "problem." Problems can be solved. Instead, this is a "predicament." Predicaments occur now and then, and you can only "hope to cope" with them. My advice is to be polite. Agree, and use your fellow teachers' advice whenever possible, listen respectfully, but *don't* sacrifice what you know about how children develop oral and written language, because if you do, children lose. And if you don't do what you believe is right, then you lose (some of your soul) as well. Again, do what's right with a great deal of humility, and you'll get through it.

## Surprise #5

*I work so hard for these kids, but not all of the parents appreciate me.* Most parents will appreciate you. But if you have twenty parent–teacher conferences, and nineteen parents think you walk on water and one implies that you could be doing a better job teaching math, guess which conference will keep you awake at night in bed? Remember, many parents are very anxious about two things: their money and their kids. Schools take both. And when parents find out that you are a *new* teacher with no "real" classroom teaching experience, then they will *really* be anxious. Have you ever wished to be extremely popular? Well, you will be. Parents will be talking about you at the pool all summer long. Whenever I hire a new teacher, I always have a few parents demanding that I promise them that everything will be all right and that their child will have no problems the entire year. My advice to you is to stay confident, smile a lot, and be your enthusiastic self. Believe it or not, most parents aren't discussing the merits of whole language in the evening over dinner. Instead, they are listening to their children talking about how much they liked hearing the new read-aloud book or how special they felt when being chosen to sit in Authors' Chair or how impressed they were that you talked to them about yourself as a writer, your college days, your wedding, your dog, your *genuine* self. If parents feel you really care about their child as a person, then their anxiety will quickly fade, and other parents will be demanding that the principal place their child in your classroom the following year.

## Surprise #6

*Not everyone is happy all of the time.* I frequently come across people who are surprised when they face difficult situations. Quite frankly, I'm surprised by this "life should be an amusement park" philosophy of life. However, conflict happens, and it is *normal* for it to happen. You and everyone else I know got into teaching to be with kids. Nothing throws a new or even an experienced teacher off more than dealing with adult anger (e.g., from parents or fellow staff members). Ask a group of people what they think and feel when they hear the word "conflict" and you get responses like: "I hate it." "My palms sweat." "My heart beats faster and I get scared." Yet, democratic school life requires us to examine and even seek out conflicting opinions. Sometimes this leads to anger. Though I don't have enough space in this letter to completely lay out an effective conflict management approach, here's my advice when you get "blindsided" by an angry parent or staff member. First, listen. Then listen some more. At this point, it may simply be appropriate to apologize rather than explain away their concern. Of course, this is counterintuitive. When being verbally attacked, people instinctively either "run" or "retaliate." Do neither of these. Instead, "step to their side," listen, and try to understand what they are saying. Often, this alone de-escalates the situation. Once the other person truly feels you understand him, ask questions and engage him in solving the problem. For example, if a parent catches you after school and angrily accuses you of not teaching phonics and ruining her child's ability to learn to read, it's not the time (yet) to prove how you *do* teach phonics in context. Instead, you might say, "We both want your child to learn to read [this shows you have a common interest] and I'd really like to hear more about how you feel your child's not learning to read in my class." By doing this, you're not saying the child isn't learning to read in your class. You're just disarming the person by wanting to listen to her perspective and letting her know that you truly want to learn from her. Believe it or not, it helps to anticipate this type of situation and have a stock phrase to use in case you panic. For example, if I get an angry phone call, I might say, "Mrs. S., you've really given this a lot of thought and I'd like to do the same. When will it be convenient this evening for me to call you to discuss ideas to solve this dilemma?" You hang up, breathe, and then get thinking creatively about the problem. For some reason, we often think life in classrooms should be easy. We love pleasure; we hate pain. Fortunately, life is made up of both. And so is teaching.

**Surprise #7**

*More often than not, you will know more about children's literacy learning than the principal.* I've attended NCTE national conferences for about twenty years, and I have never walked out of a single one. Recently, I attended a two-day administrator's conference and lasted about two hours. There just weren't the number of sessions on children's learning that I had hoped to attend. I am ashamed to say that many principals know little about teaching literacy learning. It's usually not because they're bad people or don't want to know more; it's because they're overwhelmed. It's also because teachers don't often expect them to know much about teaching and learning. Now that statement may sound a little strange, but few teachers lose sleep at night over the fact that their principal hasn't read up on psycholinguistics. However, they do lose sleep over the cafeteria lines not running smoothly, or the recess duty schedule being messed up, or the building not having been cleaned properly by the custodians. I think we need to expect more from principals. If we do, they will often rise to the occasion. Here's how, as a new teacher, you can help. First, send kids to the office to brag about their reading and writing. Principals love it when kids come to the office beaming about their work. Kids love it too. And it's not bad public relations for you either. Second, invite the principal to your classroom. The principal should model reading to kids and share some of his or her own writing. By putting the principal in touch with your kids, you will be helping to preserve his or her sanity. Third, your principal should expect there to be noise in your room. I worry about quiet classrooms. I worry about too much control. You should not only invite your principal into your classroom to hear the creative conversational buzz of a productive reading–writing workshop time, but you should then follow this visit with one of your own to his or her office after school to further discuss the good things that were happening. Finally, give the principal informational articles on literacy learning and make an appointment to discuss the articles. At that time, talk about how your classroom is built on a solid foundation of language theory and research. Show work samples that highlight the results you are getting. Principals and parents like tangible results and "stories" of children's learning. You should too.

---

Despite all of the little "surprises" that I have described, I am incredibly optimistic. Every staff needs new teachers. New teachers can bring new ideas to a staff that is continually learning. New teachers ask wonderfully naive questions that can jolt a staff that is a community of learners into rethinking what they are doing. My hope for you is that you expect surprises. And, as my tai chi instructor says, "move with their energy" and "breathe!"

## Bibliography

**Fredrick R. Burton**

*Professional resources that have been especially important to me include:*

Barth, R. (1990). *Improving schools from within.* San Francisco: Jossey Bass.

Butler, A., & Turbill, J. (1984). *Towards a reading-writing classroom.* Rozelle, N.S.W., Australia: Primary English Teaching Association.

Fried, R. L. (1995). *The passionate teacher.* Boston: Beacon Press.

Meier, D. (1995). *The power of their ideas: Lessons for America from a small school in Harlem.* Boston: Beacon Press.

Wood, G. (1992). *Schools that work.* New York: Dutton.

*Children's books that I especially enjoy using with children include:*

Babbitt, N. (1975). *Tuck everlasting.* New York: Farrar, Straus & Giroux.

Hunter, M. (1975). *A stranger came ashore.* New York: Harper & Row.

Paterson, K. (1978). *The great Gilly Hopkins.* New York: Crowell.

Paton Walsh, J. (1986). *The green book.* New York: Farrar, Straus & Giroux.

Sleator, W. (1979). *Into the dream.* New York: Dutton.

Wilner, I. (1977). *The poetry troupe.* New York: Scribner.

# Appendix A Themes

*Theme: Group Discussion*

Hoffman/Sharp
Silvers
Espinosa/Fournier
Seifert
Glover
Whitin
Kitagawa
Pierce
King
Krogness
Bachman/Fournier
Strieb
Bigelow
Foss

*Theme: Writing*

Hoffman/Sharp
McLure/Rief
Seifert
King
Five
Krogness

*Theme: Literature*

Paley
Silvers
Gallas
Espinosa/Fournier
Pierce
King
Five
Krogness

*Theme: Reading/Writing Connections*

Paley
Hoffman/Sharp
McLure/Rief
Silvers
Siefert
Krogness

*Theme: Art Expression*

Paley
McLure/Rief
Silvers
Seifert
Glover
Whitin
King

*Theme: Language Across
the Curriculum*

Hoffman/Sharp
McLure/Rief
Seifert
Glover
Whitin
Kitagawa
Pierce
King
Krogness
Strieb
Bigelow

*Theme: Teacher Talk/Listening*

Kitagawa
Pierce
Krogness
Taylor

*Theme: Group Problem-Solving*

Silvers
Kitagawa
Pierce
King
Krogness
Bachman/Fournier
Bigelow

*Theme: Time*

Hoffman/Sharp
McLure/Rief
Five
Krogness

*Theme: K–3*

Paley
Hoffman/Sharp
McLure/Rief
Gallas
Espinosa/Fournier
Seifert
Glover
Whitin
Pierce
King
Bachman/Fournier
Strieb
Foss

*Theme: 4–8*

McLure/Rief
Silvers
Espinosa/Fournier
Whitin
Kitagawa
Five
Krogness
Bachman/Fournier
Bigelow

*Theme: Multiage*

Hoffman/Sharp
Espinosa/Fournier
Pierce
King
Bachman/Fournier

*Theme: Assessment*

Hoffman/Sharp
McLure/Rief
Seifert
Pierce
King
Five

*Theme: Diversity*

Paley
Gallas
Espinosa/Fournier
Five
Krogness
Taylor
Strieb
Bigelow

*Theme: Social Issues*

Silvers
Gallas
Espinosa/Fournier
Pierce
Five
Krogness
Bachman/Fournier
Bigelow

*Theme: Critical Literacy*

Silvers
Espinosa/Fournier
Krogness
Bigelow

*Theme: Building Community*

Paley
Espinosa/Fournier
Whitin
Kitagawa
Pierce
King
Five
Krogness
Bachman/Fournier
Strieb

*Theme: Home–School Connections*

Hoffman/Sharp
Espinosa/Fournier
Seifert
King
Taylor
Strieb
Foss
Burton

# Appendix B Activities: Some Ideas to Get Your Thinking Started

## Keeping Journals and Notebooks

## Expressing Through Art

## Building Community

## Languaging Across the Curriculum

## Interacting with Those beyond the Classroom

# Index

# Editors

**Judith Wells Lindfors** teaches courses in child language acquisition and in language arts at The University of Texas at Austin. Her major publications include *Children's Language and Learning* (1980, 1987) and *Children's Inquiry: Using Language to Make Sense of the World* (1999). She is active in NCTE, having served as a Research Trustee and currently serving as Director of the Commission on Language.

**Jane S. Townsend** teaches in the School of Teaching and Learning at the University of Florida. Her teaching interests center on language use in education, K–12, and she teaches courses in early childhood language acquisition, elementary language arts, secondary writing, and language and inquiry. Her research includes work on classroom discourse and language diversity, and she has published articles on these topics in *Language Arts, English Journal, English Education,* and others.

# Contributors

**Renée Bachman** has been teaching in the public schools for thirteen years. She received her undergraduate degree in elementary/special education from Kearney State College, Kearney, Nebraska, and in December 1995 she received her master's degree in elementary education with an emphasis on multicultural/bilingual education from Arizona State University.

In 1986 Renée began teaching special education at Frank Elementary School in Guadalupe, Arizona. She taught there for three years and then spent a year teaching primary and special education in Guatemala, Central America. While teaching in Guatemala, Renée worked on her fluency in her second language, Spanish, and developed a deep love and respect for the language and culture.

Renée is presently teaching an intermediate, multiage bilingual class at Machan Elementary School in central Phoenix. There Renée continues to study and deepen her understanding of emancipatory pedagogy as she works to build a child-centered democratic environment for her students.

**Bill Bigelow** <bbpdx@aol.com> teaches at Franklin High School in Portland, Oregon. He has written or co-written several curricula, including *Strangers in Their Own Country* (Africa World Press) on South Africa, and *The Power in Our Hands* (Monthly Review Press) on U.S. labor history. He co-edited *Rethinking Columbus* and *Rethinking Our Classrooms: Teaching for Equity and Justice* and is an editor of the journal *Rethinking Schools*. He has led workshops throughout the United States and Canada on critical, multicultural teaching.

**Fredrick R. Burton** is principal of Wickliffe Informal Alternative Elementary School in Upper Arlington, Ohio. Wickliffe is a public alternative school choice program that is based on the progressive education philosophy of John Dewey. Dr. Burton has published over thirty articles, done extensive consulting work, and has been a Visiting Professor at the University of Northern Michigan. He has also taught courses at the University of Maine and the Ohio State University. Dr. Burton received his B.S., M.A., and Ph.D. degrees from the Ohio State University. Most recently, he was one of four principals selected in Ohio to attend the Reggio Emelia Institute in Reggio Emelia, Italy. He maintains that, despite the obsession with testing and the pressures teachers face in the United States, the progressive education tradition will continue to survive and grow.

**Cecilia Espinosa** was born in Quito, Ecuador, South America. Cecilia's native language is Spanish. She learned English as a second language throughout her elementary and high school years in Ecuador. She developed her bilingualism further when she came to the United States to study education. Since Cecilia became a bilingual teacher, she has committed herself to bringing to the children with whom she works the beauty and wonders of the Spanish language and of the Hispanic/Latino culture. One of Cecilia's interests is discovering, talking, and learning about children's literature in Spanish. She has spent many hours researching, interviewing, reading, sharing, and documenting ways to bring the best of this literature to the classroom. Through this process Cecilia has learned the immense value of also making space for oral tradition to flourish in the classroom, helping the children and families feel more connected with school, and deepening their roots in their traditions.

**Cora Lee Five** is a fifth-grade teacher who is also a mentor for new teachers in her school district. She is the author of *Special Voices* (Heinemann, 1992), which describes her case studies of students with special needs in a regular classroom, and she is co-author of *Bridging the Gap: Integrating Curriculum in Upper Elementary and Middle School* (Heinemann, 1996). She has written chapters for many books, and her articles have appeared in *The Harvard Educational Review, Language Arts,* and *The New Advocate.* She has made presentations at numerous conferences and has been a member of various committees in the International Reading Association and National Council of Teachers of English. In 1990 she was given a Professional Best Leadership Award by *Learning Magazine.* She is a current member of the National Council of Teachers of English Executive Committee and serves as Assistant Chair for the Elementary Section Steering Committee. She is co-editor of the NCTE publication *School Talk.* She serves on the Middle Childhood/English Language Arts Standards Committee for the National Board for Professional Teaching Standards.

**Abigail Foss** was raised in a small coastal town just north of Portland, Maine, and spent summers with her grandparents in a gingerbread cottage on Martha's Vineyard. After receiving her B.A. in English from Wesleyan University in Middletown, Connecticut, she moved to the southwest in 1994. Abigail taught kindergarten/first grade for three years at Awakening Seed School in Tempe, Arizona, before completing her master of arts degree in language, reading, and culture at the University of Arizona in May 1999. Her masters paper, "Mapping the Word and the World: Pedagogical Approaches to Multicultural Literature," focused on using multicultural literature to facilitate development of the Freirian notion of "critical literacies." A frequent traveler between Maine and Arizona, Abigail plans to return to the classroom, teaching middle school language arts, in the fall of 1999; concurrently, she will begin coursework toward her Ph.D. at the University of Arizona. She lives in Tucson with her husband and their puppy.

**Julia Fournier** has been teaching for nineteen years. She has been at Machan Elementary School in Phoenix, Arizona, for the past thirteen. She received her undergraduate degree in special education from Arizona State University, and in December 1995 she received her master's degree in elementary education with an emphasis in literacy and biliteracy.

In 1985, while working as a special education teacher in Guadalupe, Arizona (a Yaqui Native American community), Julia "discovered" whole language. Since that time, she has worked to develop her understanding and practice of child-centered, language-based education. In 1989 she participated in learning the Descriptive Review process in seminars with Patricia Carini. This life-changing work broadened and deepened her view of children's work and of her role as an educator.

Julia is an active writer and presenter. She is presently co-teaching in a bilingual, primary, multiage setting. She considers her classroom language-centered with a strong emphasis on democratic pedagogy.

**Karen Gallas** is an elementary teacher in Brookline, Massachusetts, and is also a member of the Brookline Teacher Research Seminar. She has taught children in the public schools of Massachusetts since 1972, with the exception of four years when she was a member of the faculty of the University of Maine. She received her doctorate in education from Boston University in 1982. Her work as a teacher-researcher has focused on the role of the arts in teaching and learning, on children's language in the classroom, on the dynamics of gender and power in the classroom, and on the process of teacher research. She has published three books: *The Languages of Learning: How Children Talk, Write, Dance, Draw, and Sing Their Understanding of the World; Talking Their Way into Science: Hearing Children's Questions and Theories, Responding with Curricula;* and *"Sometimes I Can Be Anything": Power, Gender, and Identity in a Primary Classroom,* all by Teachers College Press.

**Mary Kenner Glover** has lived and worked in Arizona since the early 1970s. Seeking an alternative educational setting for her two young daughters, Mary co-founded Awakening Seed School in Tempe, Arizona, in 1977, where she is currently the director and second-grade teacher. She completed her Master of Arts degree in Elementary Education at Arizona State University in 1988. Mary has authored *A Garden of Poets, Making School by Hand, Charlie's Ticket to Literacy,* and *Two Years: A Teacher's Memoir.* In addition to her work as a teacher and educational consultant, Mary is a poet and an artist. She lives in Tempe, Arizona, with her family.

**Cyndy Hoffman** teaches at Forest Trail Elementary School in Austin, Texas. Cyndy was one of the founders of the multiage program in the district and teaches in a K/1 combination class. She began her teaching career in secondary speech and drama with an undergraduate degree in secondary education, but shifted almost immediately to teaching in early childhood settings. She completed her certification program at The University of Texas at Austin, and has been teaching for twelve years. She is an avid reader and collector of children's literature.

**Rebecca King** is currently a public school teacher in a multiage kindergarten/first-grade/second-grade classroom at Travis Heights Elementary School in Austin, Texas. She received a Bachelor of Arts degree in psychology at The University of Texas at Austin in 1978. She later became certified in early childhood education. She recently received her Masters of Education in Curriculum and Instruction from The University of Texas at Austin. Becky has been teaching primary classes at Travis Heights for nine years and is a very big advocate of developmental, experiential, multiage classroom environments.

**Mary M. Kitagawa** is a fifth- and sixth-grade teacher at Mark's Meadow School in Amherst, Massachusetts. A teacher since 1957, she has also taught in Michigan and Arizona, primarily in the upper elementary grades. Influences that she counts as most significant have been participation in the Southern Arizona Writing Project, course work in the Language, Reading, and Culture Program at the University of Arizona, participation in the National Council of Teachers of English and the Whole Language Umbrella, as well as local Teachers Applying Whole Language (TAWL) groups in Arizona and Massachusetts. Her publications include *Making Connections with Writing,* co-authored with her husband (Heinemann, 1987), and a number of articles and chapters related to writing and literature study.

Being a classroom teacher of students K–8, both urban and suburban, who represent a grand cultural, racial, and socioeconomic mix of young people, is the oxygen—maybe helium—that has kept **Mary Krogness** in the classroom for thirty years. Krogness has written *Just Teach Me, Mrs. K: Talking, Reading, and Writing with Resistant Adolescent Learners* (Heinemann) and a sixth-grade English/language arts textbook (Houghton Mifflin). *Tyger, Tyger, Burning Bright* is an award-winning creative writing series Krogness wrote and produced for the Public Broadcasting Service. She has authored numerous articles for *Education Week, English Journal, Voices from the Middle, Language Arts,* and *Youth Theatre Journal.* Krogness is the writer and editor of "Middle Ground," a column in *English Journal,* and "Changing Voices," a column in *Ohio Reading Teacher.* Krogness is the recipient of the Kate and Paul Farmer Writing Award (1988, 1992). She has written chapters for *Stories to Grow On* (Heinemann), *Workshop 6: Teachers as Writers* (Heinemann), *All That Matters* (Heinemann), *Oops: What We Learn When Our Teaching Fails* (Stenhouse), and *Meeting the Challenges in Today's Classrooms* (Heinemann). Krogness is an active member of NCTE and has served on numerous boards, commissions, and committees.

**Patricia McLure** teaches a multiage first- and second-grade class at Mast Way Elementary School in Lee, New Hampshire. An elementary teacher for thirty years, she has given presentations at NCTE meetings and has taught inservice courses through the New Hampshire Writing Program. Her classroom has served as a collaborative research site for many published projects, including those by Donald Graves, Jane Hansen, Ruth Hubbard, and Brenda Power. *Listening In: Children Talk about Books (And Other Things)* was published following a research project with Thomas Newkirk.

**Vivian Gussin Paley** writes and teaches about the world of young children. Her most recent books are *The Boy Who Would Be a Helicopter, You Can't Say You Can't Play, Kwanzaa and Me, The Girl with the Brown Crayon,* and *The Kindness of Children,* all published by Harvard University Press.

**Kathryn Mitchell Pierce** is a multiage primary classroom teacher in the School District of Clayton, Missouri, where she also serves as facilitator of the district's Multiage Study Group and as a member of the Action Research Collaborative. Kathryn's research interests include talking and learning in small groups, particularly literature discussion groups and mathematical problem-solving groups. Kathryn serves as co-editor (with Carol Gilles) of the "Talking About Books" department in *Language Arts* and as editor of *Adventuring with Books,* both published by NCTE. Previous publications include *Talking about Books* (1990, edited with Kathy G. Short) and *Cycles of Meaning* (1993, edited with Carol Gilles), both published by Heinemann. She presently serves on the editorial review boards for *The New Advocate, Research in the Teaching of English,* and *Journal of Children's Literature.*

**Linda Rief** is a full-time language arts teacher at Oyster River Middle School in Durham, New Hampshire. She is also an instructor in the University of New Hampshire's Summer Reading and Writing Program. She is the author of *Seeking Diversity: Language Arts with Adolescents* (1992) and *Vision and Voice: Extending the Literacy Spectrum* (1999), published by Heinemann Educational Books, book chapters, and numerous articles that have appeared in *Language Arts, Learning, Educational Leadership,* and other professional journals. She is co-editor with Maureen Barbieri of *All That Matters: What Is It We Value In School and Beyond?* (Heinemann, 1994). She is also co-editor with Barbieri of *Voices from the Middle,* a journal for middle school teachers, published by the National Council of Teachers of English.

Linda chaired the Early Adolescence English/Language Arts Standards Committee of the National Board for Professional Teaching Standards. In 1988 Linda was the recipient of one of two Kennedy Center Fellowships for Teachers of the Arts. She spent the month of July at the Kennedy Center in Washington, D.C., authoring prose and poetry based on the Vietnam Veterans Memorial. She read her writing in performance at the Kennedy Center, later broadcast on National Public Radio.

**Patti Seifert** has been a teacher of young children for over thirty-five years. She has been a kindergarten teacher in the Aspen elementary schools for the past twenty-seven years. She received a B.A. from the University of Colorado and an M.A. in Early Childhood Education from Lesley College in Cambridge, Massachusetts. While at Lesley College, she worked with Don Holdaway at the Literacy Center. She has continued her studies at Teachers College Writing Project under the direction of Lucy McCormick Calkins and Shelley Harwayne. In 1987 she received the Outstanding Teacher Award from the Colorado State

Board of Education. She was a Teacher on Special Assignment in the Aspen School District, working with teachers in their classrooms on process writing. She has conducted a study group on reading–writing connections for teachers grades K–12 for the past several years. She has spoken at numerous inservices and conferences on writing in the kindergarten, inquiry, and staff development. She has published an article in *Instructor Magazine* on poetry in the kindergarten, and a nonfiction book entitled *Exploring Tree Habitats* (Mondo Publishing Company).

**Carol E. Sharp** currently teaches in the Eanes Independent School District, Austin, Texas, where she is developing a second- and third-grade multiage program. She received her M.Ed. (1986) and Ph.D. (1993) in Language and Literacy from The University of Texas at Austin. As Assistant Instructor at The University of Texas, Carol taught courses in reading methods in the elementary school and supervised student teachers. She received certifications as a Reading Specialist, an Educational Diagnostician, and in Special Education and was employed as an Educational Diagnostician with Services in Education in Austin, Texas. Her research interests include literacy development of special needs students and multiage education.

**Penny Silvers** is a language and literacy coordinator in a school district in Buffalo Grove, Illinois. She is also a literacy consultant and adjunct professor in the Reading, Language, and Literacy Department at National-Louis University, where she has recently completed her doctorate in Instructional Leadership.

Penny has given many presentations at local, national, and international conferences, including the International Reading Association (IRA), the National Council of Teachers of English (NCTE), and the Association for Supervision and Curriculum Development (ASCD). She has published articles in professional journals and contributed chapters to several books. She has also co-authored and produced a series of audiotapes for parents about beginning reading and how they can support their child's emerging literacy at home. Penny has appeared on an NCTE national teleconference with some of her fourth-grade students, exploring "What Matters" as her students engaged in literature discussions and reflected on their learning in the process of exploring the national language arts standards developed by NCTE.

Committed to teacher action research, Penny is currently researching ways in which reflection about reading socially relevant books can lead to deeper understanding and exploration of personal beliefs and biases.

**Lynne Yermanock Strieb** has taught kindergarten through second grade in Philadelphia public schools for thirty years. She is currently at the Greenfield School. She is a founding member of the Philadelphia Teachers' Learning Cooperative, which has been meeting weekly since 1978, and has been associated with the Prospect Center in North Bennington, Vermont, since 1973. She is currently on Prospect's Board of Directors. She has led many workshops, most recently for the

Philadelphia Writing Project and the Prospect Center's Summer Institute on Descriptive Process. She has written *A Philadelphia Teacher's Journal* and "Community and Collegiality" in *Speaking Out: Teachers on Teaching,* edited by Cecelia Traugh (both published in 1985 by the University of North Dakota); "When a Teacher's Values Clash with School Values" in *Exploring Values and Standards: Implications for Assessment* (published by NCREST, Teachers College Press, 1992); and "Visiting and Revisiting the Trees" and "Journals for Collaboration, Curriculum and Assessment" (with Deborah Jumpp) in *Inside/Outside: Teacher Research and Knowledge* by Marilyn Cochran Smith and Susan Lytle (published by Teachers College Press, 1993). Her "Trees: Entries from a Teacher's Journal," formerly published in *Outlook* in 1983, has been translated into German and Dutch.

**Dorothy M. Taylor** teaches English as a second language (ESL) in Fairfax County, Virginia. She has taught ESL to children and adults for the past twenty years and is interested in all aspects of language acquisition and development. She has collaborated with Katharine Davies Samway on a project investigating the connections between reading and writing in children, for which they received an NCTE grant. She has had the good fortune to listen to and learn from a number of students and colleagues through her various teaching positions in Washington, D.C., Buffalo and Rochester, New York, and Brookline, Massachusetts.

**Phyllis Whitin** says it is the element of surprise that nourishes her love of teaching. Her teaching experience spans preschool through middle school. She has recently taken a position as assistant professor of early childhood and elementary education at Queens College in Flushing, New York. Phyllis believes in the importance of connecting theory to practice by listening closely to children, reflecting upon classroom events, and engaging in professional collaboration. She is interested in teacher research, literacy, and integrated learning. She has published two books, *Sketching Stories, Stretching Minds: Responding Visually to Literature* (Heinemann, 1996), and *Inquiry at the Window: Pursuing the Wonders of Learners* (Heinemann, 1997, co-authored with David Whitin).

*This book was typeset in Palatino and Optima by*
*Precision Graphics of Champaign, Illinois.*
*Typefaces used on the cover and spine were Officina and Adobe Garamond.*
*The book was printed on White 60-lb. Offset by Versa Press, Inc.*